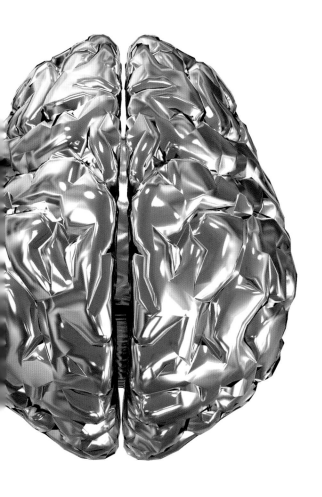

DESIGNFORWARD

CREATIVE STRATEGIES FOR **SUSTAINABLE CHANGE**

HARTMUT ESSLINGER FOUNDER OF FROG DESIGN

ARNOLDSCHE ART PUBLISHERS

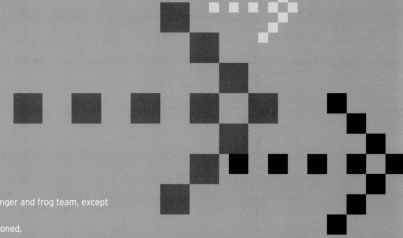

Library of Congress Cataloging-in-Publication Data available.
ISBN: 978-3-89790-381-4

Printed in China

Designed by Gregory Hom, fishbowl design and
Cathi Marsh, Marsh Design

Cover image by Peter Kossev

10 9 8 7 6 5 4 3 2 1

Arnoldsche Art Publishers
Liststrasse 9
D-70180 Stuttgart
www.arnoldsche.com

CONTENTS

COAUTHORS AND MASTER CLASS TEACHERS IN VIENNA

MARTINA FINEDER is a designer, researcher and curator, currently working for the Austrian Museum of Applied Arts/Contemporary Art in Vienna (MAK), and doing her doctoral thesis at the Academy of Fine Arts Vienna. She has been researching the life and work of Victor Papanek in collaboration with Thomas Geisler at the University of Applied Arts Vienna, and is coeditor of the German re-edition of Papanek's *Design for the Real World* (Springer Vienna/New York, 2009). Their joint work led to the establishment of the Victor J. Papanek Foundation in 2011. She has published widely on the history and material culture of socially and ecologically responsive design in academic, professional and popular publications. She also was a founding partner of D+ Studio for Design. At the University of Applied Arts, Martina worked as a teaching assistant of Hartmut Esslinger.

THOMAS GEISLER is design curator at the MAK in Vienna. He cofounded *Vienna Design Week* and curated the festival's program until the 2010 edition. A trained and practicing designer, he shifted his interests to design history and material culture studies, teaching and researching at various design schools, including the University of Applied Arts Vienna, Vienna Technical University and University of Applied Science in Graz. Publications include *Career Ladders: (No) Instructions for Design Work!* (Vienna, 2007) and *Victor Papanek: Design for the Real World* (annotated German re-edition, Vienna/New York, 2009). He also curated the 2012 exhibition *MADE4YOU—Design for Change* together with Hartmut Esslinger at the MAK.

NIKOLAS HEEP grew up in Ghana, Sudan, England, India and Austria. He studied architecture from 1996 to 2001 at the Technical University, Berlin and at the Architectural Association, London. In 2000 he co-taught the architecture and design summer academy at the Boston Architectural Center. From 2002 to 2005 he worked at Eichinger oder Knechtl Architects. In 2005, he founded KIM+HEEP—Office for Design and Architecture, with his wife and partner Mia Kim, and now is co-CEO. His work has been featured in exhibitions at the Museum of Applied Arts in Vienna, among others. Since 2005 he has taught at the University of Applied Arts Vienna. In this position he has worked with both Ross Lovegrove and Hartmut Esslinger.

PETER KNOBLOCH studied electronics and telecommunications from 1982 to 1987 at the TGM Vienna and industrial design from 1991 to 1998 at the University of Applied Arts Vienna. From 1987 until 1991 he worked as a maintenance engineer for air traffic control equipment at the Vienna International Airport. Since 1991 he has worked as a freelancing developer on a variety of projects including interactive media installations for clients like Arts Electronica Center Linz, Mozarthaus Vienna, the Salzburg Museum and the Vienna Parliament Visitor Centre. In 1996 he started teaching at the University of Applied Arts Vienna in the computer studio, and since 2007 he also works as a teaching assistant with an emphasis on user interface design.

MARKUS KRETSCHMER studied industrial design between 1991 and 1996 at the Berlin University of the Arts and at the University of Art and Design in Helsinki. From 1996 to 2002 he worked at the R&D department at Daimler AG. From 2002 to 2006 he was a professor of product design at the Free University of Bolzano, and since 2008 he has been a professor of product design and design management at the University of Applied Sciences Upper Austria. Since then he has also provided strategic design consulting. From 2008 to 2011 he did his Ph.D. under the advisory of Hartmut Esslinger in the field of strategic design at the University of Applied Arts Vienna.

MATTHIAS PFEFFER studied mining and mechanical engineering from 1980 to 1984 in Leoben and Vienna, then product design at the University of Applied Arts Vienna. In 1985 he started his own studio for design engineering. Matthias has taught since 1990, and since 2000 he has been a professor of industrial design at the University of Applied Arts Vienna, where he worked with Hartmut Esslinger in technology, model making and prototyping. In his free time Matthias restores classic race cars.

JOHANNA SCHOENBERGER started to study architecture in 2001 at the Accademia di architettura in Mendrisio, Switzerland, and after one year changed to industrial design at the University of Applied Arts Vienna, where she graduated in 2007 with an emphasis on solar energy. From 2007 to 2011 she did her Ph.D. under the advisory of Hartmut Esslinger in the field of strategic design. She worked for frog design in New York and Deutsche Telekom in Bonn, Germany, and has been a research associate for the FWF-sponsored project Strategic Design at the University of Applied Arts Vienna. Currently she works at BMW in Munich, Germany, in the field of design strategy and advanced design. In 2011 she published her doctoral thesis *Strategisches Design, Verankerung von Kreativität und Innovation in Unternehmen*, at Gabler Verlag, Springer Fachmedien Wiesbaden GmbH.

STEFAN ZINELL (*1963/A) studied industrial design at the University of Applied Arts Vienna. Since 1987 he has worked professionally in the fields of industrial design, interior design, exhibition design and design consulting, and since 1995, in educational and scientific work at the University of Applied Arts Vienna. He has also taught and lectured widely at the Tongji University in Shanghai, IADE Lisbon, the Royal College of Arts in London, Istituto Universitario di Architettura di Venezia and the University of Applied Arts in Sarajevo, among others.

INTRODUCTION

After a long career with frog – the design agency I founded in 1969 – and as a creative consultant for some of the world's best and most successful entrepreneurs, executives, and companies, I wrote my first book, *a fine line – how design strategies are shaping the future of business.*[1] In that book, I focused on the corporate side of the business-design alliance and outlined why Strategic Design is most successful when it is an integral part of a company's innovation and business strategy. Due to both the business focus and the limited space, *a fine line* wasn't as complete as many would have wished, and I fielded many questions about organization and process in the field of design and in the working relationship between business and design. Because *a fine line* was published in German, Chinese, Japanese, and Korean, the feedback was – and still is – global in nature. I used the questions, comments, and criticism that I received about my first book as my motivation for writing *Design Forward* as well as for structuring the information I offer within it.

In general, the input I received fell within three categories. I used those categories to structure the contents of *Design Forward* in three parts:

- **Part I: Creating a New Culture of Design.** In this part, I offer an overview of the design profession, its historic development, current challenges, and future opportunities. The chapters in this part explore what we mean when we talk about creativity, the role of creativity in business, and how my earliest creative experiences helped to form my own design practice and approach the process of "right brain-left brain" collaboration. This part also offers specific ideas that can help any company make the best use of design in its strategic plan and operation.

- **Part 2: Shaping the Design Revolution.** Here, we explore the educational opportunities and challenges of training students – of both design and business – in the professional competencies necessary for effective cross-disciplinary teamwork and collaboration. To illustrate the outcomes of the educational approach I outline here, this part includes a portfolio of the work of my own design students.

- **Part 3: Leading By Design.** In this part, we examine the role of design in business today and how that role must evolve if we are to create a more productive, sustainable future. I offer my perspectives on the growing urgency for a more integrated, strategic role for design in business, along with a careful review of the power of business-design collaboration in driving the evolution of material and social cultures around the world. I provide advice for finding and choosing the right designer – and the right design clients – and examine the potential benefits of business leadership with a deeper understanding and appreciation for creativity and its processes.

History is inextricably linked to the future. In this book, I offer my personal views about the road that has brought design and business to their current states, and the best ways we can move forward along a new path by building competitive, globally networked industries fueled by Strategic Design. Much of what you are about to read is my opinion, and many may disagree with my views. But, I have been blessed with great success, and I have learned much from my failures, so my views, ideas, and proposals are, at least, worth considering. The only constant in life is change, and with that truth before me, I have kept the focus of this book trained on the burning challenges we face in transforming our current business relationships and models – issues such as outdated forms of corporate structure, overproduction of goods, financial and ecological waste, and unjust social imbalance. There will be many solutions to these problems, but they all will require new ways of thinking and working, not only between different professions – Strategic Design being well positioned as a holistic catalyst – but also across different countries, cultures, and mentalities. No matter what specific form these transformations take, we must move from a "money culture" to a "human culture." That power shift has already begun, but we need to accelerate the change.

The urgency I feel for this goal sparked my second professional passion, that of educating a new generation of designers. Although education has assumed a larger role in my life during the past few years, I am not new to the profession. My first official assignment as an educator began in 1989 when I accepted a call to be one of ten founding professors for the Hochschule fuer Gestaltung (HfG; College of Design) Karlsruhe in Germany, where I pioneered the first convergent design class in Germany – which we called Digital Bauhaus – combining work in both physical and virtual products. I was given a substantial boost in my work with that class by the ZKM (Center for Art and Media) in Karlsruhe, the world's first "digital museum." That first teaching experience taught me that educating students in design wasn't the same as mentoring designers at frog; open education has different objectives. Accepting that students have different talents, and that all of those talents have to be encouraged, was a major step for me. A quote by Galileo Galilei became my great inspiration: "We cannot teach people anything; we can only help them discover it within themselves."

From 2005 to 2011, I taught at the University of Applied Arts in Vienna, Austria, where I took over the Master's class ID2, which became a great success. My students won many national and global design awards, the class was ranked highly by Bloomberg Business Week, and my graduates landed good jobs around the world. Together with assistants Stefan Zinell, Nikolas Heep, Matthias Pfeffer, Martina Fineder, and Peter Knobloch, the students and I invented new methods and processes with a clear focus on *convergent*, *social*, and *sustainable*.

Some of my student's best work appears in this publication. In addition to a portfolio of student designs, this book includes chapters by some of my doctoral students, including Johanna Schoenberger's research into creative business leadership, and Markus Kretschmer's examination of creative sciences. In addition, you will read about two research projects my students conducted on the economic effects of design and its legacy, and the important recovery of the estate of the great Austrian-American designer Victor Papanek, whose work is described and analyzed in this book by Martina Fineder and Thomas Geisler.

I think it fair to say that the past six years of teaching and researching have opened up for me some new perspectives about the professional education of designers and about creative education in general. I am convinced that in order to meet our global challenges, we need radical changes and improvements in creative education. We also must understand that young people have the perspective of an entire life ahead of them, and we cannot afford to limit the potential of creative children by pushing them through a school system that basically stifles their talent. Students shouldn't have to wait until they've graduated from high school to enjoy, explore, and expand their creativity.

Finally, I also take time in this book to look ahead toward new opportunities, as I propose some practical ideas for positive change. To expand upon these ideas, I describe my decision to accept the invitation by the DeTao Masters Academy, Beijing, to set up the new Master Class for Strategic Design at the Shanghai Institute of Visual Arts (SIVA) within Fudan University, Shanghai. Why China? As you will learn in this book, I have agreed to help build a Strategic Design program in China because that's where most consumer-tech products – and, soon, most automobiles – are being produced. As I argue in the final chapters of this book, because most of these products are designed in the United States or Europe, the motivation behind them is "make it cheap" rather than "make it sustainable," and the processes involved are fragmented. I believe that we have to educate a new creative elite in China, which will be able to collaborate on a global scale and create great products following Lao Tzu's dictum that "Less is more." If we want to drive an environmentally responsible, sustainable form of manufacturing, we have to end disjointed and often wasteful manufacturing processes, and China is a good place to start that work.

Right now we have a very emotional and sometimes irrational discussion about the relationship between the United States and China, which actually has emerged as a kind of codependency. There is a lot talk about cheap products made in China, trade deficits, and currency politics. The Chinese view on these issues is often overshadowed by China's reputation for exploiting its people and natural resources in order to produce zillions of products, most of which have been badly designed in the West. Naturally, there are many books written on this subject by investment bankers chasing money or wannabees like Donald Trump as well as too many naïve speeches by politicians who only want to get re-elected. In my view, none of this helps solve the very real problems we face in global production. What we need is a new and creative way to solve the challenges – ideas that extend beyond the United States and China – and we need to begin by designing the right stuff. Only then, can we convert the challenges before us into great opportunity. We may not all agree on the "how" behind this movement, but we all should be able to agree on the "why" that drives it. The bottom line I propose in this book is simple: We need dramatic change by new thinking and bold action, and the watchwords for this change are *convergent*, *social*, and *sustainable*.

Design creates physical and visual results, and we have tried to encapsulate both forms in *Design Forward*. The design of this book supports its role as an object both for reading and for viewing. Gregory Hom – frog's longtime creative director – created a visual code that elevates the book's storytelling function into a visual experience. I hope you will enjoy that experience and remember the thread of fundamental design principle that runs throughout these pages: Form follows emotion.

1 Hartmut Esslinger, *a fine line: how design strategies are shaping the future of business*, San Francisco: Jossey-Bass, an imprint of John Wiley & Sons, Inc., 2009.

⌃ WEGA TELEVISION 3020+, 1970-1978, NEUE SAMMLUNG, MUNICH. PHOTO: DIETMAR HENNEKA

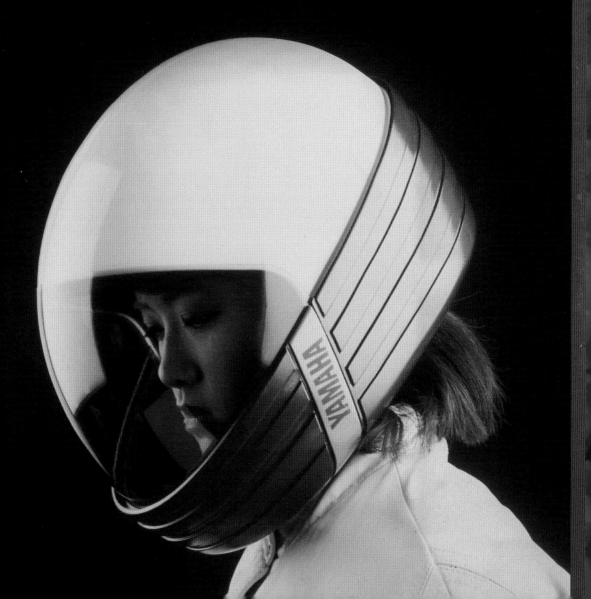

CREATING A NEW CULTURE OF DESIGN

1 A CREATIVE POWER SHIFT

"If you haven't found it yet, keep looking. Don't settle." STEVE JOBS

Creative people change the world, but they rarely command it. The eighteenth-century American pioneers got the glory, but the settlers gained wealth. Designers inspire corporate success, but executives reap the monetary rewards. Visionary entrepreneurs build magical companies and brands, but their conservative heirs dilute or even destroy them. My personal mission is to change this destructive pattern. As you will learn in this chapter, I'm not alone in working toward that change. The first shock waves of the cultural design revolution are already being felt in businesses and economies around the world. But we have a long way to go before we can declare victory.

The electronic high-tech industry offers a good example of the gap that still separates the pursuit of profit from the designs and designers who create it. According to John Markoff, a senior writer for *The New York Times* in 1997, Michael Dell – who by himself built Dell into the world's number three personal computer company after Hewlett-Packard (HP) and Lenovo – was asked at a technology conference shortly after Mr. Jobs returned to Apple what might be done to fix Apple, then deeply troubled financially. "What would I do?" Mr. Dell said to an audience of several thousand information-technology managers, "I'd shut it down and give the money back to the shareholders."[1] HP, a company that ships more personal computers (PCs) than any other in the world, certainly supports design as an idea, but doesn't always seem to embrace design as a strategic element of its operation. HP touts instead the technical superiority of its products and its reduced use of hazardous materials – both great accomplishments on their own. These efforts seem targeted at controlling the symptoms of bad design, however, rather than providing its cure. And, certainly, design isn't the first thing that comes to the mind of anyone looking at HP's personal computers.

AT&T DIGITAL ANSWERING MACHINE, 1991. PHOTO: DIETMAR HENNEKA

And then there is Apple, with its near-constant strategic focus on design, thanks to the visionary leadership of Steve Jobs. Long being belittled as a niche company, Apple today gives us good reason to rethink the link between brilliant design and dazzling profits. Let's take a look at the recent quarterly reports of HP, Apple, and Dell, from March of 2012:[2]

	Revenue	Net Profit	Cash Flow	Market Valuation
DELL	$16.0 B	$0,765 B	(~$6 B) in debt	$31 B
1 year change	+ 2%	- 18%		
100,300 employees				
HP	$30.0 B	$1.5 B	(~$24 B) in debt	$50 B
1 year change	- 7%	- 44%		
320,000 employees				
APPLE	$46.3 B	$13.0 B	~$97.6 B in cash	~ $500 B
1 year change	+ 73%	+ 110%		
46,000 employees				

Do these results encourage the "money people" to believe in design? You would think so, but the systemic nature of business can still cloud the vision of a hard-headed old-school CEO trying to see the benefits of putting well-designed products and customer satisfaction at the center of organizational strategy. Traditional business models can be deeply entrenched; consider, for example, that most large businesses still operate within corporate structures much like those of the Roman Empire. Yes, we have different names for the players in these systems – chief executive officers replaced Caesar, vice presidents replaced the Consuls, and union leaders replaced the Tribunes of the Plebeians – but the systems in which they operate remain much the same.

Overturning this system is a major challenge because the autocratic imperial model is more powerful than most of its democratic economic alternatives. Cooperatives, for example, unite small business owners in non-industrial enterprises such as agriculture and microbanking, but they can prove very difficult to manage and maintain. Taking all of the legal, financial, and systemic complexities into account, it is no surprise that rational left-brainers have an edge when it comes to the benefits of command and control, while creative right-brainers typically are left with the crumbs that fall from the table. And so, the world of business remains largely unchanged. The creative people create, the administrators rule.

Who is guilty for this sad state of affairs? As I outline in this chapter, I believe that both groups share the blame. If the creative people in our society want to take their place among leaders in the business world, it is up to them to master the game by acquiring the skills and competencies of leadership. At the same time, the administrators – the business people – must learn to collaborate more closely with top creative talent and to embrace creativity and design as central elements of their business mission and strategy.

As a designer, I am mostly interested and experienced in working with corporations and companies who "make stuff." In the firms I partner with, excellence in creating new objects or experiences is a matter of elite training, visionary thinking, and ethical leadership. The magical formula for these organizations is to offer the products, experiences, and content that consumers would dream of, if they could. Accomplishing that goal requires these companies to draw from top creative talent and cross-disciplinary collaboration throughout the process, from strategy to design, and on through engineering, manufacturing, marketing, sales, and support.

But no organization can succeed in producing great, creative offerings without qualified, courageous management and lots of money invested the right way. The right-brainers and left-brainers, therefore, must work together as partners to achieve the greatest success – or even to survive – in today's design-driven economy. Those changes are all part of the cultural design revolution that I see unfolding around the world. Now, let me outline for you some of the most important aspects of that revolution, and how changing social, economic, educational, and business systems are driving us toward more creative, design-focused strategies. As you will see, we all can take part in this revolution and benefit from the economic, cultural, and social advancements it offers.

The End of Left Brain Versus Right Brain

Anatomically, our brain is symmetrical in appearance but not in function. As a result of evolution and the advancement of our ability to use tools, the two sides have taken on different roles. In terms of cognitive definitions, the left side processes rational information, such as numbers, words, and abstract knowledge, and the right side processes more complex information, such as images, icons, and emotional context. These are facts.

Another fact is that we tend to separate people into two groups: the arty, emotionally inspired right-brainers and the pragmatic, less creative left-brainers. But it is very dangerous to adopt these definitions as part of our identity and destiny, particularly when it comes to the way we work. One-sided thinking can't produce sustainable success in today's world economies. Designers, for example, who want to take their professional place in an age of rapidly advancing digital tools, must develop both sides of their brains (I talk more about this need in "Chapter 4: Creating with Hands and Mind"). But business leaders can't fall back on one-sided thinking, either.

The ongoing global financial crisis is an excellent example of the result of one-sided thinking – a left-brain strategy based on the premise that what makes money today will make money forever. In fact, many left-brain strategies are similar to "snowball schemes" that demand a never-ending supply of a finite resource and are therefore unsustainable. After all, there are only so many victims to go around. Once you have cheated them of all their money, they can provide no further profit for an unscrupulous mortgage company or hedge fund. Still, Wall Street keeps trying; in fact, as I write this, the market for mortgage-backed securities continues to thrive, some four years after that same behavior triggered a worldwide economic collapse.

The same one-sided thinking has resulted in hyper-effective business strategies based on wringing value from a practice or product through cost-cutting without any new investment in the product's ongoing development or brand value. At some point, there will be no corners left to cut, no further savings to be gained. Since the product has no remaining brand value, customers flock to the next lower-cost offering. Then, as crisis strikes, the rational power-people whose demands for ever-greater profits from ever-lower investments caused the problem call for creative solutions – not understanding that this also means to accept creative and often vague proposals. Unfortunately, many of the people with the talent and ability to solve this kind of crisis have grown tired of being suppressed and have moved on to other organizations. Those who remain have stopped trying.

Now, do all of these rational business leaders accept that they need creative people as equal partners? Do creative people accept that they need to come out of their comfort zone, stop playing victim and fight for equal power by developing the professional competencies necessary to wield such influence? No! With one-sided thinking, the power people – and some so-called creativity consultants – try another twist, such as promoting the idea that "everybody can be creative," an idea with special appeal for non-creative people. In my opinion, that idea is a myth. The environment we are born into and grow up with obviously plays a major role in our creative development. Our family, teachers, friends, community, and country shape our appreciation for and approach to the creative process. As Craig Venter, who decoded the human genome, said, "We simply do not have enough genes for this idea of biological determinism to be right. The wonderful diversity of the human species is not hard-wired in our genetic code. Our environments are critical!"

It is true, however, that everybody with creative talent can learn to be more creative, and that everybody who is more rational can learn to respect and better understand creative people. Both sides need to focus on ending the "right brain versus left brain" war by learning to collaborate and to share and execute power. And this change has to take place in institutions, companies, and communities. Apple's stellar success through a design-driven strategy has offered irrefutable proof of the power of design and creativity. Saying "we want to be the Apple of our industry," however, isn't enough to muster that power. Creativity is about competence, leadership, and ethics. These are virtues in short supply – and this we have to change. We also have to ensure that everybody who can be creative has the tools and opportunity to develop their abilities, beginning at a very young age.

Unfortunately, environments that nurture creativity can seem in short supply. The solely rational – and, therefore, measurable – focus of traditional business education and practice has created huge obstacles in the development of creative talent. That same focus has stifled most attempts to foster professional competence and humanistic ability throughout many organizations. Creativity also suffers at the hands of political correctness, especially in the United States. Driven from the Left by excessive liberalism and on the Right by hypocritical, religious zeal, this movement has made many young children the victims of a political agenda.

People on both extremes of the political spectrum do their worst to block the development of extremely talented children. The ultra-liberals kill talent and creative thinking by insisting on equality; the ultra-conservatives kill talent and creative thinking by enforcing medieval topics such as creationism in our education system while demanding funding cuts that eliminate arts programs. Starting in school, too many of our talented children are either blocked or indoctrinated. By the time they are old enough to enter a liberal arts college or design program where they might actually be able to develop their creative talent, most children have had their ideas about creativity preset to unfortunately low levels.

Ending the "left brain versus right brain" war requires that we change our attitude and approach to creativity, but it also demands that we understand the true differences in the ways highly creative and highly rational people think. Dr. Aljoscha C. Neubauer, department head and professor of differential psychology at the University of Graz in Austria, and his colleague Andreas Fink researched human brainwaves during creative tests that involved simple tasks, such as asking subjects what they could do with a brick. The results, as illustrated in the figure below, show that highly creative people rely more heavily on the right hemisphere of their brain to solve creative challenges than people who are extremely uncreative.[3]

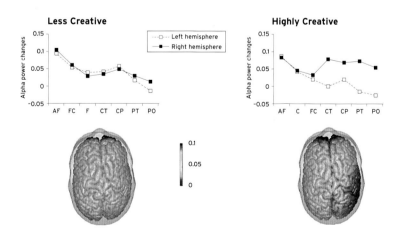

Highly creative people rely more on the right hemisphere of their brain when faced with creative challenges than those with lower levels of creativity.[4]

Another physical effect of "creativity at work" is the brain's production of dopamine, which enhances cognitive performance, the ability to form conceptual associations, linguistic skills, and positive emotions. Neubauer's tests revealed that the right hemisphere produces alpha waves as a sign of inner concentration, which is based on a positive attitude, high motivation, interest, knowledge, experience, and high intelligence. These tests support the idea that creativity thrives in a positive, secure environment. I think it is important to also remember that creative work isn't a random act; it can be trained – like playing music. And, as in all training, practice makes perfect.

These differences in brain use might explain why some people with low creativity exhibit little respect or even aggressive dislike for those who are highly creative, either because they want to assert their control ("I have the money and the power") or because of simple idea envy. In order to create a good relationship and a productive collaboration with colleagues, people of every level of creativity must be aware of and understand the right brain-left brain mechanism. Strong collaboration also requires personal translational skills that enable all collaborators to make a new idea or a process understood, including its creative benefits, rational relevance, and potential effects.

Understanding these physical/neurological differences is a start in the process of nurturing creativity within people and organizations. Many businesses and educational programs also are setting up positive environments that really do promote creative thinking and action. But there is much more we can do to nurture creative potential, beginning with adjusting the dismissive and negative attitude toward creativity that has permeated so much of our business and economic environment. When we are open for new experiences and ideas and accept complex challenges as something positive, our creative mind accelerates. We also must see risk as something positive and reject the notion of failure as something bad – actually, we all should embrace the fact that we can learn much more from failure than from success. Creativity also blossoms when we can enjoy the adventure of exploring unknown territory and receive the personal recognition and rewards of opening up whole new areas of ideas and understanding.

For all of the physical and environmental factors that impact our levels of creativity, we also need to understand that creative capability isn't forged in iron and incapable of changing. As briefly outlined above, creativity can be developed through training – like playing music. What does this mean for businesses seeking to build their creative potential? After having located creative talent, who will almost always be the minority in a corporate environment, leadership's most important task is to mentor and empower the leadership capabilities of those creative people. Organizations get the biggest creative boost when they build up creative talent into creative leaders and collaborators, who then are able to bring value to the organization on an almost universal scale. At the same time, we creative people – strategists, entrepreneurs, designers, and educators – must earn the power necessary to help shape the system.

TEAMWORK AND THE NON-CONFORMIST

Creative thinking needs to feel comfortable with ambiguity and unconventionality, since creativity and conformity rarely go hand in hand. In fact, we should expect creative people to be non-conformists – or maybe even a bit crazy. Finally, we must understand that the only effective amplifier of creative thinking is collaborative teamwork. This combination of non-conformity and teamwork may sound like a contradiction, but I have seen the truth of it in my experiences with colleagues at frog and with my students. Aljoscha Neubauer also proved the truth of this "illogical" phenomenon in a series of tests with discrete test groups.

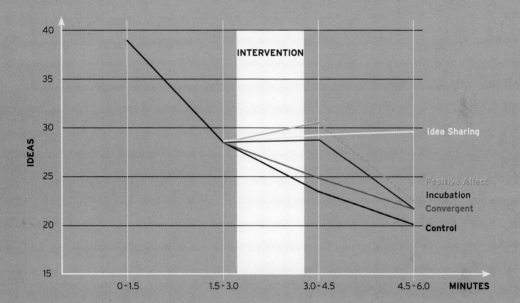

The creation of new ideas tapers off very fast for any individual or group. The effect of most interventions, including incubation, on this decline is limited. Neubauer's tests revealed that idea sharing was the only form of intervention that sustained or increased the quality and quantity of ideas generated by test subjects.[5]

Our objective in ending the "left brain versus right brain" paradigm is quite simple: We need to convert short-minded money-capitalism into sustainable creative-capitalism, which means we advance our societies from "wanting to buy" to "wanting to use – and enjoying the experience." Our big challenge is to drive enough change throughout our culture to inspire creative talent, to motivate those people to accept the professional challenge of leadership, and to sustain them as they draw upon the iron will that it takes to get to the top, where decisions can be made the creative way. That challenge forms the roots and fruit of the creative revolution.

How do we get to a more creative paradigm in business, and thus, in the world economy? Even now, after a very successful and rewarding personal career partnering with successful businesses, I remain a realist when it comes to the subject of advancing creativity in a corporate environment. I think that we cannot expect fundamental change from the current people in power who, like frogs slowly lulled to their deaths in water that builds to a boil, will float along in their increasingly dysfunctional environments until they or their organizations perish. And the same goes for many established creative people who are neither able nor willing to jump into the role of leadership. Therefore, I propose that we join a creative revolution–a revolution that starts in education (Markus Kretschmer explains this well in "Chapter 2: Establishing the Creative Sciences") and continues on to include every aspect of industry and the economy. We must scout, educate, mentor, and promote a new generation of creative talent and leaders in design, business, and politics, make them fit and competent so they can focus on the skills necessary to humanize industry and business and to master the many challenges we are facing as humans. Now, let's explore how shoots of this creative revolution are already underway, and how we can help promote its growth to impact creators, policy makers, and influencers in every aspect of our society.

Sparking a Professional Revolution

We humans are the creators, the makers, and the users – and way too often also the wasters – of our material culture. Creation is the start of the industrial process, but a strategic designer must also have some understanding of the remaining elements of the process. Creation begins with thinking, strategizing, and dreaming. Whatever designers plan and do, they first have to project and even simulate what the results and effects along the product life cycle will be. Strategic designers are advocates of the user experience for any product or process they create. To make the decisions necessary to ensure the most satisfying and effective user experience, designers must have fantastic imagination coupled with broad professional competence.

In his book *A Whole New Mind*, Dan Pink states: "The future belongs to a different kind of person, creative and empathetic right-brain thinkers whose abilities mark the fault line between who gets ahead and who doesn't."[6] Pink goes on to list six elements for creative success, which may sound a bit too much like gung-ho "American can-do," but I like the list: design, story, symphony, empathy, play, and meaning. For me, empathy is the most important of these

SUN MICROSYSTEMS SPARC LINE, 1987. PHOTO: DIETMAR HENNEKA

elements – which, I think we should note, does not include money at all. Pink's argument falls a bit short for me, however, in his assumption that everybody can be creative if they only follow his advice – I explained my resistance to this concept earlier in the chapter. You could say, for example, that everybody can cook, but that doesn't mean that everyone can cook something we would care to eat. Not everybody can design well, either. To make matters even more selective, nobody can design alone. Designers are involved in a very complex ecosystem with many professional influencers. This system offers limitations, but it also provides a great opportunity. Using the power of teamwork and asserting creative leadership enables the strategic designer to lead the revolution.

In my book *a fine line* I described different kinds of designers – classic designers, such as Dieter Rams, Kenji Ekuan, Mario Bellini, and Ettore Sottsass, whose work is known for both beauty and high performance; artistic designers, such as Philippe Starck, Karim Rashid, and Ross Lovegrove, who are known most for the visual appeal of their designs; and the vast army of unrecognized corporate designers, whose low-profile work fuels the output of companies and agencies around the world. Today, I would like to add a fourth group to this mix, that of the Strategic designers—the designers whose work truly commands worldwide influence. Some, such as Apple's Jonathan Ive, Volkswagen's Walter DaSilva, or former Philips' and now Electrolux's Stefano Marzano, hold high-level executive positions within their corporations. Others are influential and avant-garde leaders in outstanding design agencies such as Porsche Design, GK Design, or frog, where they define strategies and serve as consultants to global industry leaders.

Each of these groups has made its contribution to our visual and material culture. Classic designers have helped to extend the influence of design beyond beautification, and their work has redefined consumer electronics, appliances, and other industries. Artistic designers have taken low-tech lifestyle products such as furniture, lighting, and luxury products to whole new levels of style and beauty. But because these designers are defined by style and personal brand rather than by the paradigm-shifting power of their designs, their sphere of influence is typically limited to niche companies and lifestyle publications. They rarely have the tools or desire to use their work strategically – in order to dramatically alter the user experience, for example, or to revolutionize production, conserve natural resources, or change the way the world thinks.

In my view, the classic and strategic designers are those who will lead the cultural design revolution. Training designers to join these groups and educating business leaders in the most effective ways to use and reward them has become the focus of my efforts. There are already way too many designers churning out new styles of T-shirts and travel mugs – the fashion victims of the profession. My goal is to build the ranks of highly trained and professionally competent designers who can earn and use the type of influence necessary to bring the many contributions of their work to the world.

Shifting the Balance of Power

For designers, compromise is a bad word and being submissive is a near fatal mistake. When I started my business in 1969, most business people treated me like some kind of idiot or economic slave because they were used to working with designers who accepted such abuse. I was offered lousy pay, or no pay, for projects that were neither strategically sound nor promising in any substantial way. I wasn't willing to compromise or submit. Convinced that design was supposed to have a tremendous economic impact on a company – opening up new markets and providing innovative products and solutions that appealed both to the mind and the heart – I kept looking for the few clients out there whose need and vision made them want to go somewhere new. Driven by a positive spirit, lots of stubborn resilience, and also by "refusing to see reality" (as my wife and partner Patricia calls it), Lady Luck started to smile on me.

My first life-changing client was Dieter Motte of Wega – at the time, a $3 million family-owned German consumer electronics company – who drove me to create a new dimension for his business. Even our frequent disagreements didn't make me doubt my inner voice. Dieter was a great mentor. His ambition regarding design was without limits, and he stuck with me through my numerous beginner's mistakes and clashes with his engineering and marketing teams. Our collaboration was successful on multiple levels. Wega gained international recognition and their revenue grew tenfold over a four-year period that culminated in the company's sale to Sony in 1974.

That successful collaboration set the trend for my future career and list of clients: Kaltenbach & Voigt became a global leader in dental systems (today owned by the American Danaher Corporation); Hansgrohe, a specialty maker of shower heads, grew from roots in my father's small hometown of Schiltach in the Black Forest into a global player in bathroom design (today owned by the American Delta Faucet Company); Louis Vuitton evolved from a small specialty luggage maker, with two shops in Paris and Nice that made about $14 million revenue, into a global luxury empire. In addition to the successes I achieved with these organizations, I was privileged to help Sony convert its technological acumen into a global success. The culmination of my first professional phase came in 1982, when I was hired by Steve Jobs and joined Apple.

The important characteristic of all these successful relationships was that I worked directly with top management. With the interest and backing of the entrepreneurs, owners, and CEOs that ran the companies I worked with, I was able to gain the cooperation and support of their engineering, manufacturing, and marketing groups. The driving passion on both sides of these collaborations sprang from a simple conviction: The success of any business and any brand is based upon its products and the experience they create, which must be better than anything their competitor would dare to dream off.

All of my early clients understood that creativity and design are the best strategic tools available for them and that a culture of innovation cannot be achieved by counting pennies and treating people like numbers. They also understood that design isn't a matter

PACKARD BELL BRANDING AND COMPUTER, 1992. PHOTO: DIETMAR HENNEKA

of democracy, and that you have to work with the very best people to achieve the best results. These visionary leaders didn't fall into the trap of believing that economic success is the sole foundation of personal and corporate power. They didn't use their position to dictate what creative people should be allowed to do, or to exploit them through abusive treatment and pay. Because I have had the good fortune to work in such exciting, rewarding collaborations, I have seen firsthand the benefits they can bring to designers, the organizations they work with, and the industries and marketplaces shaped by their output. That's why I have focused so intently on promoting the cultural design revolution that will make these kinds of relationships the norm within my profession.

Winning Through Design-Centric Strategies

Today, the power shift is a reality. The rational administrators still hold onto the power, but the end of their reign is in sight. Businesses everywhere have learned that competing on money, price, and overproduction results in shrinking profits and eventual losses. While cost efficiency is still the most prominent economic strategy, it is one doomed to economic and ecological collapse. As management expert Gary Hamel has said: "Efficiency-focused strategies are like trying to squeeze water out of a rock." In 2010, Apple's iPhone was 8% of the global volume in phones, about 32% in global revenue and about 46% in global profits. Those who still talk of design as an added expense just don't get it – and the seeds of this ignorance continue to emerge from business schools, take root in venture capital firms, and fully blossom in far too many executive suites and boardrooms.

Today, the most successful new companies aren't created around new physical products but on new ideas and interactive participation of people – think, for example, of Google, originally a search engine with a business model for personalized advertising; Facebook, a social-media platform, which invites people to share personal experiences and content; and Tumblr, the micro-blogging platform. Even established virtual companies such as Microsoft, Oracle, and SAP are faced with the challenges of changing strategic demands. When young companies such as Salesforce.com dismantled the closed and exclusive enterprise software model by distributing smart applications via the Internet, Oracle and SAP were forced to spend billions to acquire companies with cloud competence, because they didn't have the internal creative talent to compete in that emerging market.

The late Steve Jobs made Apple the most valuable American company by inviting and accepting creative people as key players in his leadership model, and business leaders everywhere are beginning to learn from his example. Automotive companies like BMW or Audi know that the majority of their customers buy their cars for their superior design and brand image, and so they invest hundreds of millions in design. The leaders of these and many other industries understand that investments in design have a 100:1 return ratio, a ratio no other rational influencer for product success – such as quality, technology, or performance – can achieve.[7] By embracing design as a central element of their business strategy, these companies are winning big in the market. And, ironically, they also are learning that by applying design the right way, they can lower process costs, streamline development, improve product life-cycle management, build brand value, transform customers into followers, and maximize profits.

Numbers talk, and nearly every business leader I talk to today wants his or her organization to be like Apple. As more left-brain executives and venture capitalists grasp the economic power of creativity and design, more companies are adopting the kind of design-centric strategies that mark Apple's success. (Johanna Schoenberger describes this new way of conceiving and leading business strategy in "Chapter 9: Creative Business Leadership.") As more designers develop the professional competencies, courage, and discipline necessary to assume leadership roles within organizations, more organizations are leveraging the power of design-based strategies to grow and shape their marketplaces. As I said earlier, from creative education to professional practice, it takes a better and more realistic understanding of the competencies required on both sides of the battle lines to replace internal left brain-right brain discord with cross-disciplinary and collaborative partnerships. This revolution isn't about false promises and power-grabs; it is about the reality of vision, jobs, and shaping people's lives – today, and for generations to come.

Changing the System, from the Ground Up

Our material world is converging with virtual experiences, with social and ecological issues becoming ever more vital for human life, but creative education is in dire straits. Even though we have brilliant and motivated teachers and talented students everywhere, the current systemic neglect of life's realities requires a revolution of creative education – in all disciplines from design to life sciences, business, technology, and social-cultural professions. Our world is too complex to leave this revolution to the specialists with the money. We need creative humans with both a mind and a heart – and we need the means and the tools for leveraging creativity. The following chart illustrates the structure of a system that generates and supports that kind of creativity.

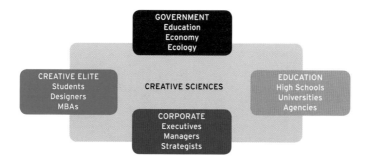

CHART: DETAO MASTER CLASS OF STRATEGIC DESIGN AT SIVA/FUDAN UNIVERSITY, SHANGHAI

Strategic sciences aren't limited to the corporate world but influence and advance creative thinking and processes across all areas of social and political life.

As you can see, a new model for creative education lies at the center of this system. It is fundamentally wrong that many creative children are neglected or even terrorized in school, and that most designers are educated in art departments, detached from social, ecological, and economic realities. It also is naïve to believe that superficial new management models, such as "design thinking," can enable left-brainers to become more creative. Like playing music, the design process is defined by doing and not by talking. The only way to achieve the ambitious goal of transforming the role of design within an economic model is to create new cross-disciplinary institutes from high schools to universities and then to use them as crystallization zones for creative and innovative design communities that can provide a creative home for the pioneers who will open new frontiers of sustainable development.

These new design education hubs would not only improve students' collaborative and leadership skills, they would also help nurture individual creativity by enabling students to live out their creative potential. In the traditional, rationally minded school system, creative disciplines like visual arts, music, and poetry are considered inferior or even mere distractions from the real business of education. The non-linear, visceral, or even chaotic thinking of creative students often earns them a reputation for being a disruption within schools whose main goals are to deliver the highest possible standardized test scores. These students soon learn to operate within a cynical, creative-survival mode that can encourage them to forever see themselves as outsiders and pivot their focus inward, on their own egos. The kind of revamped educational system you will see described within this book can put an end to this unproductive pattern and prepare creative students to take their place in every aspect of society where they can drive the cultural changes that will help advance us all.

Making it All Worthwhile: The Color of Money

Reframing social attitudes, business environments, and the educational system is a critical step in launching a cultural design revolution. But turning the ideas that sparked the revolution into a long-term reality will require that we also reframe our ideas of what constitutes a fair price for the contributions of strategic designers. If designers are to assume the responsibilities of leadership and help form the heart of organizational strategies, they must be compensated for those contributions. Without adequate compensation, the very talent we most need will look elsewhere when choosing a career. To understand the current economic realities for designers, let's take a look at some cold, hard figures.

Here are the 2009 average annual gross incomes, before taxation and social insurance, for Austria, Germany, and the UK. For comparison, the annual salaries paid in all fourteen frog studios in the United States, the Netherlands, Germany, Italy, South Africa, Ukraine, India, and China in 2009 averaged €68.000.

• Austria = ~ €16.000 [8]
• Germany = ~ €28.000 [9]
• UK = ~ €32.000 [10]

The income disparities revealed within these groups are even greater than they appear at first glance. Around 80% of all German designers have an annual income of between €18.000 and €36.000. At the lower end of this scale, designers are earning close to the German poverty level. The official German design associations seem resigned to this catastrophic situation. Commonly heard opinions such as "One cannot get rich as a designer" or "You have to choose between design and money" demonstrate that designers have a long way to go in order to be accepted as an equal to other academic professionals.

In Austria the situation is even worse. In 2010, my then doctoral student Johanna Schoenberger and I conducted some extensive research into the financial situation of designers in Austria, with special focus on the alumni from my former workplace, the University of Applied Arts in Vienna. Thirty-seven of the designers within our study group had an annual income in 2008 of €10.068, which is under the poverty line of €11.400 for single households in Austria. Another 25% earned just €20.000. The alumni of the University of Applied Arts worked, on average, 52 hours a week, and 80% of them had to work in a second job. In fact, 65% described their financial situation as "very bad and stressful." [11] The majority also states that they aren't happy and cannot even think of starting a family.

I want to be clear on this point: Money isn't the primary goal of a creative career, but it is an indicator about how employers, and society as a whole, view creative people. Even more disturbing, it may also be an indicator of the obviously catastrophic lack of competence and professional abilities most designers have to offer after studying for four to five years.

Brief conclusion of the research project I conducted together with Johanna Schoenberger for the Austrian Science Fund (FWF):

Questions

• How did the competence spectrum of design change internationally during the last years, and how does the Austrian practice and teaching stand up or lag regarding international ranking?

• And what has to change in order to achieve a level playing field for Austrian designers – and, as a direct result, also for the Austrian enterprises and economy at large?

In order to answer these questions, this research project has been structured according to the qualitative method of "grounded theory" (by Glaser & Strauss, 1998).

Results

1 The quality and relevance of the work by designers in regard to economic, ecological, and social sustainability are very different on an international scale. The design industry in the United States, for example, has created new processes and working methods that have resulted in giving designers more influence and better results in strategic planning and implementation. Called Strategic Design, this new practice is defined by applying creative methods and processes to innovation and business challenges (for example, physical-virtual products, services, experiences, business models, and all kind of human interactions). The goal is to help enterprises and organizations become global leaders by unleashing their dormant creative and strategic potential and therefore creating responsible and sustainable success. In contrast, the "Austrian way of design" still is defined by mostly esthetic aspects and artistic self-reflection and to this day refuses to live up to internationally relevant – and already proven – concepts.

2 With very few exceptions, the practice of teaching design in Austria is a major cause of this. There still is a strong focus on "Author Design," which requires some artistic talent but is based on traditional and low-tech arts and crafts, such as working in wood, fabrics, ceramics, and glass, and is applied mostly to furniture, visual arts, fashion, and objects for the home. The pioneering function of the Strategic Design model, as defined and applied in the United States, has resulted in technological innovation, anthropological advances, and a new mix of economic, social, and ecological sustainability. So far, these advances are a minuscule component in Austrian design education. Therefore, the Austrian design industry and its practicing designers are not relevant in the international context, conceptually or economically. The conclusion is as follows:

a Austrian designers must accept the new responsibilities of risk and leadership and skip the cheap excuse of being a "misunderstood artist" and acquire the competencies necessary for resolving the vital tasks in our economy, society, and environment.

b The technophobic arts and crafts-oriented design education are not acceptable anymore when we look at the new global challenges and opportunities. Design schools must change their antiquated methods to more holistic ones, and therefore the selection process of professors and teachers must be based upon adequate professional qualifications and work ethics on an international scale.

The governments and citizens of Germany and Austria invest about €200.000 in the five-year-long arts and crafts-focused education of designers, most of whom, as you have seen, have no positive career or life prospects, let alone the competence necessary to design a sustainable, industrial future. The statistics indicate, that only about 10% of all design students will succeed with an acceptable career, and only a tiny portion of that group will make it into positions that give them an opportunity to make any kind of meaningful impact on corporate strategies or economic success. We can do better than this.

The stigma that labels designers as perennial losers labels us all, and I can illustrate this point throughout my own personal experience. Whenever I revisit my old roots in Germany's Black Forest, it is a must to have dinner at Gino's osteria in Nagold, the best Italian restaurant north of Sicily (www.dagino-nagold.de). Gino's doesn't take reservations, and once, after having met some executives at a major German company in Stuttgart, I was able to catch the last free chair at a table of six. I got into a nice conversation with a gentleman across the table, and naturally, the conversation eventually turned to "What do you do for living?" He told me that he had been a successful executive and corporate consultant after his retirement. When I said, "I am a designer," he sighed and asked, "But how do you earn a living?"

Nobody wants to be a loser or to encourage their family members to pursue a thankless career. If we want to attract top talent to take on the challenges of becoming a designer, we are all obliged to push for a positive change in the economic realities of the profession. And, change is already in the air. Students leaving my class ID2 at the University of Applied Arts in Vienna have been taken on by good companies and agencies around the world, and (to my knowledge) their annual starting incomes were around €38.000. Of course, when I left my class in Vienna, the "Empire" struck back. The advancements we had made didn't motivate the university to continue down the path we had forged, and school administrators chose an artist-designer as my successor because "it was time for the arts again."

For all of these reasons, I have been working to change the professional paradigm for designers by working for better creative education, professionalism, and educational institutions. I try to inspire and mentor students by lecturing around the globe, I have spent years as a founding professor at the HfG Karlsruhe in Germany, and from 2005 to 2011 I taught at the University of Applied Arts in Vienna, Austria. Since October 2011, I have been organizing a Master's class for Strategic Design at DeTao Masters Academy, Beijing, and at SIVA, at Fudan University in Shanghai. I am happy to report that "new" countries, such as China, are embracing new initiatives and programs, which will provide positive change in the position and compensation-levels for emerging strategic designers. But none of these changes on their own will be enough. Change comes about through people—smart people, creative people. We need less mediocrity and more excellence, and fair salaries and engaging, meaningful careers are essential drivers for that shift.

The Time is Now

Creativity is in. Urban studies theorist Richard Florida even thinks we can see creativity's mark on our planet. Working with the night images of metropolitan centers around the world, Florida put for the theory that, where there is a lot of artificial light, there is a center or a corridor of a "rising creative class." Florida argues that higher concentrations of technology professionals, artists, musicians, lesbians, and gay men—and a newly defined demographic group called "high bohemians"—indicate a better economic status for that area. Florida's theory isn't all wrong, but neither is it all true. Cutting-edge economic development isn't just defined by urban lifestyles but also by entrepreneurial eco-spaces, such as Silicon Valley, smart and modern factories, the geopolitical ambitions of governments, and, of course, by history. Just look at the corridor that runs from Italy through Germany and Holland to England, and all of the great universities it contains. This corridor, which fostered the Renaissance and the Industrial Revolution, is the footprint of the Roman Empire, which continues to have a huge influence on Europe.

The geographic areas that were the focus of Richard Florida's study—such as the American East and West Coasts, Tokyo Bay, and the Chinese East Coast—are still centers of exploitation and abuse, where left-brainers in power rule over creative people. But the revolution has begun. As you will learn through studies, accounts, and stories throughout this book, we creative people are in the process of winning and are positioned to achieve superior professional success, a more vibrant creative culture, and, ultimately, a happier world. The creative power shift has started. Now, we must turn it into a movement.

1   John Markoff, "Michael Dell should eat his words, Apple chief suggests," in: *The New York Times*, January 16, 2006. Available online at: www.nytimes.com/2006/01/16/technology/16apple.html

2   Sources: www.brightsideofnews.com; Silicon Alley Insider 2/2011.

3   A. Fink et al., "The Creative Brain: Investigation of Brain Activity during Creative Problem Solving by Means of EEG and FMRI," in: *Human Brain Mapping*, Mar;30 (3), 2009, pp. 734-748.

4   A. Neubauer and A. Fink, *Human Brain Mapping*, University Graz, 2009.

5   Ibid.

6   Daniel Pink, *A Whole New Mind: Moving from the Information Age to the Conceptual Age*, New York: Riverhead Hardcover, 2005.

7   A former BMW executive, speaking on condition of anonymity, told me that of its total new product investments, BMW invests about 0.8% in design while about 78% of customers buy a BMW car based upon its design.

8   Austrian Report on Creative Industries, 2009.

9   German BDG; VDID Report, 2010.

10 Design Council UK, 2009.

11 Source: University of Applied Arts; *Der Standard*, newspaper, Vienna, August 2009.

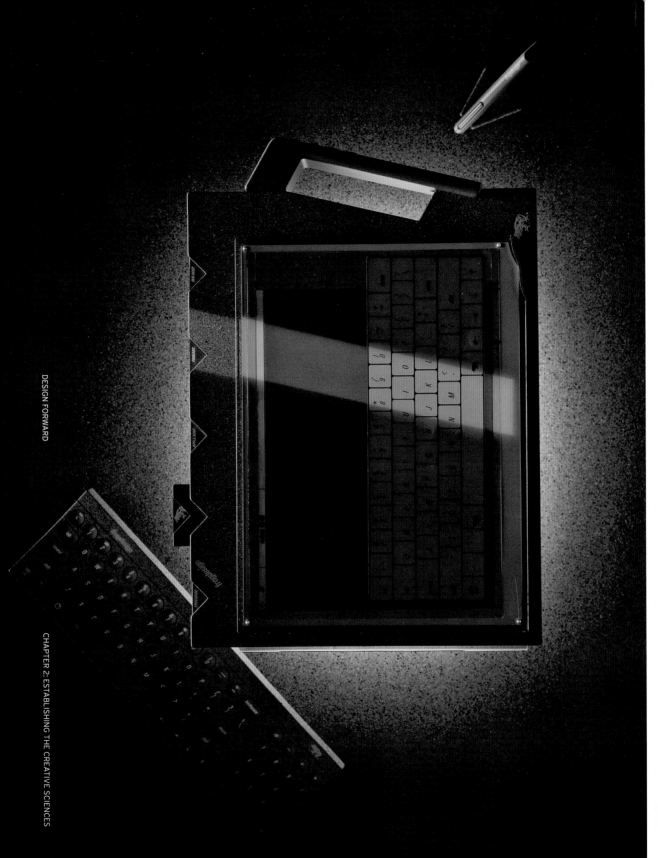

2 ESTABLISHING THE CREATIVE SCIENCES

BY MARCUS KRETSCHMER

To build a new culture of design, we have to begin working from the ground up. As I mentioned earlier in this book, I have focused much of my career on design education. Through my work at the University of Applied Arts in Vienna, I have had the great fortune to work with some of design's most promising young talent. In this chapter, I want to share with you the work of one of my doctoral students, Markus Kretschmer. Taken from his dissertation, the ideas and information here provide us with a broad and deep perspective on the way we address creativity in our educational systems, including a brief history of how we arrived at our current educational model and a well-conceived vision of the course we can take toward a more creative approach to designing a sustainable culture. H.E.

"The world that we have created is the result of an obsolete mindset. The problems that have resulted cannot be solved with the same mindset that caused them." ALBERT EINSTEIN

We take it for granted that our current world, environment, and lifestyle will never change, even as we watch the global community become increasingly helpless in the face of ever more complex problems. We think, "And so it will always be," even though reality tells us "This must change." Only a revolution in the way we conceive, produce, and interact with our material culture can awaken us to this reality, and that kind of revolution demands a new educational approach for the designers who are responsible for creating that culture. We need a new model for creative education and especially for education in design, a model I call the Creative Sciences. Education in its present form constitutes only limited preparation for the complex tasks and creative competence required to cope with our challenges and find sustainable and human-driven solutions for our problems.

TABLET MEDIATOR STUDY, 1986. PHOTO: DIETMAR HENNEKA

Climate change is probably the most urgent and most complex problem that faces us. Most respected scientists agree that, within no more than eight generations, we will have succeeded in heating up the earth considerably – and of those eight generations, six will already have become history. Climate change goes hand in hand with the vast and long-standing crisis of our product culture. We have products that are highly perfected technically, esthetically, and economically, but we have neither the time nor the inclination to actually utilize them sensibly. We throw away devices – and consequently extremely valuable raw materials – merely because one button doesn't work. And, at the same time, we often don't know why we even needed the features controlled by that button.

The enormous crisis of our wasteful product culture makes it urgently necessary for designers to think about necessary alternatives to "And so it will always be." The way we have approached product development within the past century cannot be allowed to continue without serious negative consequences for all of mankind. Just as every specialized discipline must undertake a critical dialogue about its own role in the problems we face, the professional and academic world of Design must begin thinking immediately about its own contributions to these problems – and their solutions.

For designers, this perhaps means "the end of the world as we know it," but we have every reason to look forward to a new and better world. The creative opportunities for designers could hardly be greater than they are today; in fact, they are as numerous as the opportunities that existed more than a century ago, when there was a need to give industrial modernism a permanent face. Design did that brilliantly – and there is no reason to assume that it would be unable to give the era of sustainability that has just begun a much more convincing and charming face. In fact, after decades of widespread lethargy and aimlessness in the profession of design, designers today have the huge opportunity to actually influence product culture and fundamentally improve it. A positive climate change by Design is vital for our survival, and we cannot leave that change to chance but must actively shape it. Design must finally assert its influence.

Designing a Culture of Sustainability

As a discipline, Design is linked inseparably with industrial modernism. Industrial production processes, entrepreneurial dealings, and individual consumption are the fertile fields on which Design has been able to develop successfully. By continuously influencing consumer preferences, Design shapes and drives industrial modernism. As a result of this influence, Design has contributed to the massive global problems facing us at the beginning of the twenty-first century, but it should also be able to provide important impetus for a sustainable and more humanistic economic system.

Unfortunately, most current design output, with its basically esthetic, artisan nature, is increasingly helpless in the face of complex global problems. This failure stems, in part, from a failure in the way we educate designers, most of whom are inadequately qualified and lacking in the motivation necessary to initiate the kind of cultural revolution necessary to affect *positive* change. The discipline of Design must, therefore, undergo a rapid and dramatic evolution in content and concept in order to respond to the massive global changes before us. The Creative Sciences educational approach can help drive that evolution and put designers back in the cultural forefront where they belong. Before I describe that educational approach in more detail, let's examine some of the most important new roles and challenges it must take on.

Confronting the Three Dilemmas of Design

Any attempt to rethink Design's role in the current cultural and economic model demands that we designers examine the very nature of our professional image and self-understanding. That examination reveals three fundamental dilemmas Design must confront if it is to shape an era of sustainability. And, the first of these dilemmas is quite basic: Can designers be both promoters of consumption and moralists?

Most educational programs today do a better job of teaching creative, artistic students – always too few in number – how to worsen the problems of our time rather than solve them. Such a waste of creative resources is unconscionable in view of the massive economic and environmental problems these students and their children will face in decades to come. In order to ease the crisis of our industrial product culture and to exert a far-reaching influence on the paradigm of consumption as a cultural norm, young creative talent must be encouraged and educated within an ethical, human, and culturally sustainable understanding of Design. And this encouragement should begin in early education. Design as a discipline has long profited from over-consumption. As gratifying as this relationship may have been in the early days of industrial modernism, it is no longer sustainable. A shift of the paradigm of consumerism, of consumption as a cultural norm, will have to be part of any sustainable development.[1]

This is an apparently unsolvable dilemma for designers: On the one hand, most Western economies have directly assigned to Design the task of driving ever-higher levels of consumption by creating more and more new products. On the other hand, most of the world – including most designers – now understand that this practice is morally suspect and environmentally and economically unsustainable.[2] Many designers seem impotent in the face of this dilemma.[3] To intervene in a truly effective and far-reaching manner, designers must question their own business model and help to create far fewer, more sustainable products. Accomplishing those goals will require a new approach to educating and training designers in the way they think about the *business* of design.

That brings us to Design's second dilemma: Are designers agents for change or are they cultural beautifiers? This second great dilemma is more complex than it might first appear. Design is fully integrated into – even dependent upon – the complex structures of globalized production, but due to its traditional role as an "estheticizing problem solver," it has little, if any, influence on those structures. If Design is to create real added value in our culture, it must expand its focus beyond product development and consumerism and develop the skills necessary for creating truly sustainable products and supply networks. This reorientation is essential on a purely economic basis because the esthetic skill of design is becoming increasingly valueless. In fact, the world has an oversupply of designers educated solely as beautifiers.

Businesses around the world are increasingly looking for designers with talent in problem solving, a capacity for collaborative thinking, and an ability to find holistic design solutions that go beyond esthetics. These design skills, applied to the important problem areas of our time, offer long-range added value for society and companies, open up future prospects for design itself, and permit the motivation of a positive climate change by design. To help resolve this dilemma, we must change the creative educational curriculum to include work in problem solving, collaboration, and leadership.

Are designers to function as strategists, or opportunists? This third dilemma facing designers and the discipline of Design today also poses a challenge to the world of business.

At the beginning of the twenty-first century, entrepreneurs and designers still do not adequately recognize the potential that a strong strategic alliance between them has for shaping a sustainable future. And too many managers still massively misunderstand the cultural, intangible potential hidden in purposefully applied creativity.

Logically, a highly skilled designer would have to appear as a strong partner for entrepreneurs and managers engaged in the monumental task of building an era of sustainable material culture. Unfortunately, however, many companies do not recognize the full cultural, creative potential of design. As a result, most approaches toward a sustainable future revolve primarily around questions of technical efficiency and effectiveness, without making the concept of sustainability come alive.

In order to resolve this third dilemma, entrepreneurs and designers must reach a stronger and more comprehensive understanding of each other's roles, responsibilities, and potential. If Design is to bring value to its partnerships, it must acquire much more skill in collaborating within economic, entrepreneurial relationships.[4] At the same time, solving this dilemma demands that we make a shift of focus in the ways we educate creative entrepreneurs and managers as well as designers.

In order to be able to help in shaping a truly sustainable product culture, Design obviously must first find ways out of its three dilemmas by strategically reorienting itself. By expanding its esthetic, artisan orientation, it can position itself as a humanistic catalyst of technology, economy, ecology, and social sustainability. And if we are to leverage Design to find convincing answers to complex global issues, we need more and better creative talent in design, in

BREAKAWAY VOCALIZER, 1987. PHOTO: DIETMAR HENNEKA

business, and in society. Education must prepare designers to have a substantial influence on the quality of our global living environment—a change that will require forging totally new educational pathways. We need a pervasive creative structure in education, beginning in school at age ten and continuing through college education toward universal design understanding. This Creative Sciences approach will enable Design to react rapidly and effectively to the dramatic changes and challenges we face today.

Integrating the Three Levels of Design into One Fundamental Discipline

Most of us have fond memories of our first bicycle. While many of those memories revolve around the feelings of freedom our bikes gave us, in retrospect we can see that it was *that feeling*—the thrill of a first bike, the places we cycled to, the people and events we encountered—not just the bicycle itself that made that important phase of our childhood most memorable. In the same way, any product is an essential element of a holistic user experience, but the whole of that experience is more than just the sum of individual parts. This phenomenon, also referred to in Gestalt psychology as supra-summativity, describes why the whole arises only from the orderly relationships and structures between the individual parts. It is only by a definite system of interplay of design elements that the whole is formed.

None of mankind's products function in a vacuum; instead, products are functional parts of complete systems. As designers, therefore, we are involved with multiple design levels: The level of the product involves the design elements, and the level of the system involves the whole structure. But, the whole exists only if we can perceive it as a whole. How we perceive the whole, and how we classify and ultimately appraise it, depends on the quality of the information we use to communicate about the structure. The third level of design is, therefore, the level of perception within the system.

The success of the Apple design, for example, is founded on all three of these levels of design. First, there was the product. In designing Apple's products, Hartmut Esslinger and later Jonathan Ive combined some of Dieter Rams's "functional" abstractions from his Braun designs of the 1950s and 1960s with Mario Bellini's and Ettore Sottsass's interpretations of high-tech design, as demonstrated in their avant-garde work for Olivetti. On the level of system, Apple has long followed the end-to-end system idea. The concept of the Apple iPod is successful not simply because all of its individual elements work optimally together as a product but because all elements of the overall systems were designed for music listeners. In creating the iPod, Apple optimized the product for playing back music (iPod), its interplay with other products (Mac and PC platforms), the process of buying music (iTunes store), and the process for using music (iTunes). As the success of the iPod shows, this interaction not only creates a holistic user experience but also high added value from the viewpoint of the user.

Apple also excelled in addressing the third level of design, perception. Apple's consistently communicated concept of the digital lifestyle has become the company's DNA. The success of Apple design cannot be limited exclusively to the esthetic, semantic aspects of conventional product design but must be seen as the optimized interaction of three levels of design with consciously designed user experience. As Lucius Burckhardt once noted, "A design of tomorrow is able consciously to consider the invisible complete systems."[5]

As Apple's success illustrates, in order to help shape the era of sustainability successfully, design must adopt an expanded, systematic understanding of innovation and abandon the old notion that progress is primarily something technical and, in most cases, associated with new products. A much more holistic understanding of innovation is urgently necessary here, one that moves beyond the product level to have an impact on a cultural level. And this certainly means Design must learn to focus on human needs and how to satisfy and even transform them.

This shift of focus revolves around innovation—of societal systems, organizations, usage trends, and more. Of course, product innovations also can represent the best solution to a problem, and certainly this idea should remain central to any design work. In fact, that idea offers our only realistic chance of reducing resource consumption. As Dieter Rams says with reference to improving a sprawling and increasingly haphazard goods environment: "Less, but better!"[6] But we all must learn to understand that innovation means more than just a never-ending stream of new products.

An expanded concept of innovation necessarily goes hand in hand with new creative tasks of design. Against the background that an ever-increasing proportion of the world's population lives in densely populated areas and megacities, this means for Design, for example, a much deeper examination of urban infrastructures and a renewed appreciation of the urban environment as an important design field. Urban gardening, inner-city transportation infrastructures, or functioning product service systems (PSS) are but a few examples of urban fields where Design plays a critical role. The design of product service systems and of products commonly used in urban environments confronts us with numerous questions, not least of which is how we can better use existing infrastructures and products. Postindustrial Design must, therefore, address its role in redesigning and reassembling existing products as innovative product service systems. In this way, a future-oriented design paradigm takes its place in actively shaping the basic infrastructures and systems that will make up a more sustainable, more humanistic industrial model.

Driving Cultural Innovations from Sources to End Users

If Design is to see itself as a driver of sustainable, cultural innovation, then it must influence the origins of products much more than in the past. Not until our products are sustainable according to the history of their origins as well as to other purported objective criteria will they truly play a significant role in a culture of sustainability. Accordingly, designers must regard the hidden history of products as an important part of the design task.

Using the guiding model of sustainability, design must orient the quality of whatever invisible properties (with regard to genesis and cultural values) are innate to products, since these properties carry the products' cultural moral values. Good examples of such cultural origins are the factories in Dresden and Leipzig in Germany that produce the glass Volkswagen and Porsche use in their high-end cars. In those factories, leadership and staff celebrate the production process as an important part of the customer experience, in order to imbue their product with cultural significance based on the local culture (Dresden, for example, is a cultural metropolis) and its values (such as the tradition-rich Saxon china and clock manufacturers). This is just one example of how important the visibility of the origins of the product, the association with cultural values, and the design of a holistic hidden history has become for mainstream products.

Given that so much merchandise today includes products and processes that are interchangeable technically, functionally, and esthetically, this hidden history will become increasingly important as a driver of competitive advantage. As the Pulitzer Prize-winning author Thomas Friedman has noted, "Today it is necessary to rise above the competition by the manner and style in which the business is operated, or in other words, by the how."[7]

Accordingly, the customer's trust in the system, not just in the product itself, is gaining ever more weight in the competitive arena. Typically, those who use or buy a product have no say whatsoever in defining and producing it. A change to a sustainable product culture, however, will demand a shift in that norm. As Klaus Krippendorff, professor of communication at the University of Pennsylvania's Annenberg School for Communication, has noted, "No artifact can survive within a culture without being meaningful to those that can move it through its defining process."[8] If we want to create a sustainable product culture, therefore, we must include the people much more intensively in the origin of the product. When people play a more engaged role in the design and creation of goods, they will be more inclined to treat those goods with greater care and preserve them for long-term use, rather than tossing them away at the first excuse to buy a replacement. In other words, Design must help to establish an alternative plan to industrial mass production.

New innovations in collaboration and communication with consumers via Web 2.0 technologies and crowd-sourced funding make these kinds of designer-user engagements possible. To manage these relationships, Designers must be prepared to cooperate closely with users and to manage complex processes of product creation in the sense of a sustainable product culture. This means forging cooperative relationships with the most sustainable suppliers and producers, maintaining knowledge of their capabilities, and managing the processes. Ultimately, Design must be capable of coordinating extremely sustainable "virtual design factories," which integrate customers and suppliers as equal stakeholders. Designers must be prepared for such a factory-related design approach, and Design education has to embrace this economic focus.

Another central aspect of the hidden history of products is the supply chains "global value-creation chains, a form of horizontal cooperation between suppliers, dealers, and customers, in which the useful value and thus the monetary value of goods is increased in successive steps." [9] Currently, companies consider supply-chain management primarily as a means of improving efficiency. Companies devote great attention to optimizing their supply chains, and so the efficiency of supply chains — in particular, the optimization of transportation logistics — is gaining more and more importance. These same companies, however, frequently disregard the history of product origins, which is an increasingly important focus for consumers. At the same time, we are experiencing a shift to product bundling, which has far-reaching consequences for our focus on the supply chain. It means that the economic value of *symbol* production (in the sense of creating cultural significance and importance) is clearly increasing.[10] In short, authenticity, credibility, and transparency of product origins are becoming increasingly important factors for consumers. As a result, processes concerned with product genesis are becoming important competitive differentiators, with great design potential. To once again quote Thomas Friedman: "To make something is simple. To develop a value-creation chain — that is really difficult." [11] For many reasons, therefore, a future-compliant design must exert much more influence than ever before on product origins and supply chains.

SUSTAINABLE CULTURE DESIGN (SCD)

Design must help to shape and even initiate our culture's vision of the future. Its decades-long history with the culture of mass production, however, complicates Design's ability to assume this role. That's one reason the design discipline must change itself – and many indices suggest that it must evolve to become a universal, culture-changing force, so that it can make a relevant contribution to a sustainable, postindustrial era and a culture of sustainability. If Design can make this transition to become a driver of cultural innovations, a new professional image for designers will emerge. We can think of this new approach as sustainable culture design.

The basic assumption that Design has both the opportunities and the responsibility to change culture clearly differentiates the role of the designer from that within the traditional model of industrial design. With its focus on innovation, SCD pursues the transformation of culture to one made up of sustainable living environments; in the process, it encompasses the entire bandwidth of innovation to include product, process, and organizational innovations. This approach combines a global understanding of culture and design with the goal of acknowledging and integrating local circumstances and culture. SCD proactively fulfills the important mediator function between all stakeholder groups and positions itself as a humanistic catalyst of technology, economics, ecology, and social sustainability. In this way, it exerts a proactive influence on industrial and economic processes. Preparing designers to participate fully in the tasks of SCD will require an appropriately established, holistic approach to creative education that includes a pervasive creative curriculum and structure beginning in grade school and continuing into college. Only through that kind of holistic structure can educators communicate to students a universal, culture-changing understanding of design.

Designing Creative Sciences: Creativity for a New Era

At the beginning of the twenty-first century, we are faced primarily with a cultural and intellectual challenge in solving global problems. If we want to change the root causes for the crisis of our industrial product culture, we must look beyond the mindset of industrial modernism and work to overturn our culture's collective lack of creativity. We can transform our technology and consumer-centered culture with its basis in the massive consumption of raw materials into a culture of sustainability, but this challenge requires all of our intellectual abilities. We must turn our attention, therefore, to educating the young people who will be charged with shaping that sustainable future.

This kind of transformation has occurred before. In the mid-eighteenth century, society became aware that industrialization in Germany was creating the need for a new breed of experts with radically new qualifications. As a result, colleges of technology began to emerge within Europe. Today, we find ourselves in a similar situation. As the need for an era of sustainability becomes more apparent, educational and business leaders are beginning to understand that we must qualify many people, quickly and effectively, to address our many looming global problems.

We also find that where our educational training is most lacking isn't in the area of technical and scientific skills but in cultural understanding, creative skills, and problem solving. Typically, we approach problem solving in a piecemeal fashion, focusing on higher material efficiency, lower energy consumption, better cars, more economical aircraft, and so on. But sustainable development doesn't evolve from partial solutions; it demands that we shape complete systems that function holistically. Our current narrow and short-sighted vision impedes not only our understanding of sustainable development, but also makes comparatively inefficient use of our ability to find solutions.

The great advantage of design education has long been in its role in imparting a holistic mindset and encouraging creative, artistic skills. Today's design education imparts three decisive skills that are critical to the process of promoting a sustainable culture: [12]

- Mastering strategies for solving complex problems, which is essential for overcoming barriers in the process of transitioning to a sustainable culture.

- Encoding and decoding the symbols of a product culture, which we must do in order to build awareness about products and their global effects as well as for creating completely new artifacts of an era of sustainability.

- Developing skills in visual thinking and acting, skills that are indispensable in the effort to make the abstract concept of sustainability clearly comprehensible and positively tangible.

NIKE-BAUER BIONIC SKATE. PHOTO: DIETMAR HENNEKA

Thus far, we haven't developed the educational processes and approach that would prepare designers to lead this kind of sustainability revolution. To provide this kind of radical new direction in design education, I propose that we develop the Creative Sciences, with the specific goal of educating a generation of professional designers capable of providing the creative impetus for a sustainable future.

Structuring the Role of Creative Sciences in Education

Mihaly Csikszentmihalyi describes creativity as the ability "to create something new that is so valuable that it is added to the culture."[13] In this context, the aspect of cultural change is of decisive importance. Creativity changes culture and its component domains only when it is introduced by experts within those domains.[14] In order for designers to use creativity to change our present non-sustainable product culture into a sustainable one, they must understand the specifics of the domains that define that culture and be able to communicate about creativity with experts within those domains.

Cultural transformation for sustainability demands design intervention in ecology, economy, and social affairs — three dimensions or domains of sustainability that typically play no role in design education. In order for design to drive cultural change, we need designers who have advanced powers of imagination and the creativity necessary to design products, processes, business models, and complete systems according to the guiding principle of sustainability. In developing educational programs within the Creative Sciences, therefore, we must first understand these three domains in terms of their peculiarities and relationships, so that we can apply creativity purposely within them. This means removing manual, artistic design as the center of all creative interventions of Design. Here is my proposal for how the Creative Sciences model would be structured and implemented.

Education in the Creative Sciences would tread a different educational path, treating the understanding of ecological, economic, and social relationships as essential for any purposeful creativity. Rather than focusing on the drafting board, Creative Sciences must emphasize a profound understanding of fundamental cultural relationships, in the middle of which mankind is positioned. Through the understanding of complete systems, we can drive progress within the subsystems that we must sustainably change through design. The education model of the Creative Sciences approach must make logical allowance for a clearly changing professional image of design (which I described in an earlier sidebar as sustainable culture design) and new task areas. The focus of education in the six-semester bachelor's study, for example, would be on developing a profound understanding of ecological, economic, and social relationships as the basis of any creative intervention.

This education model is built around transdisciplinary projects, each extending over one semester and managed in coached groups. In accordance with the professional image of sustainable culture design, the themes can – and should – cover a broad bandwidth. Thus they can concern both concrete product-related projects from research institutes or companies and problems without explicit product focus, such as cities, infrastructures, or certain user groups – all with a central focus on sustainable development and the high societal relevance of the task. These projects include the three dimensions of sustainability in the form of integrated, compulsory sustainability courses, which ideally would be matched in content to the respective project. Here are some examples:

• Economic Sciences: Elements of political and business economic theory, business ethics, supply chain management, business law, and so on.

• Ecologic Sciences: Elements of climatology, marine science, meteorology, geography, ecology, and so on.

• Social Sciences: Elements of anthropology, communication, fine arts, sociology, political science, and so on.

The goal of the transdisciplinary project work is not to educate experts for every compulsory sustainability course. The goal is rather to consciously thematize cross-relationships and dependencies in the process of problem solving, to make them comprehensible, and to impart a fundamental understanding for the complexity of those design tasks oriented toward sustainable development. The compulsory sustainability courses would be taught with support from experts in the respective disciplines. In addition to the semester projects, three compulsory design courses extending across all six semesters would continually impart the fundamental skills of design. These courses would include:

• Design Changing: Teaching fundamental methods of design and innovation development and strengthening problem-solving skills.

• Design Shaping: Focusing on elementary analog and digital representation techniques, such as drawing, plastic molding, and software-based representation methods.

• Design Theory: Covering reflective skills in design, such as esthetics, design history, and new research, as well as projections, simulations, and impact.

These compulsory design courses would educate students in the necessary universal design skills and impart the absolutely necessary artisan skill-set the discipline requires. They also serve as the basis for more profound involvement in design tasks in the subsequent master's study curriculum. An additional compulsory course, Cross Cultural Competence, must be a fixed part of the curriculum. With its elements of ethics/religion, performing and graphics arts, culture and history, this course would prepare students for the reality of an increasingly intercultural working life.

In conjunction with the compulsory sustainability courses, the Creative Sciences model aims to promote a more profound understanding of culture – especially from abroad. Additional elective courses could be chosen according to each student's interests. Depending on the main themes of the project, further courses (even technical and scientific, of course) may be additionally necessary. The project of the last semester would be designed and worked on at the student's own initiative. It would have to be passed without exception in a foreign cultural environment and represent the student's final thesis. In this semester, teaching in the compulsory courses takes place exclusively via online learning platforms.

In the developmental four-semester master's curriculum of Creative Sciences, three specializations need to be offered, corresponding to the long-range purpose of sustainable culture design:

- Creative Teacher is the pedagogical branch specialization. Its purpose is primarily the education of qualified teaching personnel for imparting Creative Sciences in schools and in continuing adult education. Graduates of this specialization serve as multipliers for creativity, sustainability, and holistic thinking in the educational institutes.

- Creative Entrepreneur is an area of specialization focused on the education of artistic, creative entrepreneurs capable of changing culture in the sense of sustainable development.

- Creative Designer is that more profound specialization that prepares the graduates for an increasingly complex design reality and makes them capable of providing design impetus for a sustainable future.

Building on the bachelor's study, the master's curriculum provides deeper understanding of these specializations, with the focus on the three compulsory courses of the bachelor-level study: Design Changing, Shaping, and Theory. At the same time, the master's curriculum allocates more space to imparting artisan, manual skills. Technological Sciences is the corresponding compulsory course, which would cover applied aspects from the areas of renewable energies, mechanical engineering, electrical engineering, and mechatronics.

Transdisciplinary project work – in the best case, initiated by the student – is once again at the center of the four semesters of the master's study. Since the design colleges offering Creative Sciences would need to work closely together, tasks within the projects would be performed in teams composed of students from different college centers.

Once again, the curriculum includes compulsory courses in addition to the project work. Here are some examples:

• Creative Projects: Short-term projects with, for example, external designers, politicians, performing and graphics artists, and scientists.

• Creative Project Management: Preparation for transdisciplinary management of design projects inside and outside companies.

• Creative Research: Joint work in research projects without the applied focus present in the semester projects.

The master's thesis in the Creative Design Scientist specialization would consist of demonstrating skill in initiating cultural changes toward sustainable living environments and in being able to provide design impetus for a sustainable future. The most important appraisal criteria are potential, scope, and sustainability of the cultural transformation capability. After completion of their study, the creative design scientists will not only have developed a common value basis but will also have created a far-reaching network and acquired extensive skills, enabling them to initiate changes of the product culture.

In the best case, the curricula of the Creative Sciences model will produce many truly creative and talented designers. Furthermore, they will promote purposeful cooperation of these talents in innovative networks. Networking among colleges and a lack of visibility has been a problem that plagues traditional design education. That is one reason why educational institutes offering Creative Sciences must be interconnected in both real and virtual networks. Internet-based crowd funding platforms have already outlined an important component of this network structure by serving as an open marketplace for the development of sustainable living environments, product service systems, and product concepts. Besides the interlinking of schools, design colleges, and other design institutions, these platforms also serve the public discourse about design proposals. Through the outlined network structure, the Creative Sciences will get the visibility they need to establish a public dialogue about future living and product environments and to introduce solution proposals into society.

Creative Sciences for Schoolchildren

The Creative Sciences must be rooted in the overall educational goals of school education. From grade school onward, education must be directed consistently toward the cross-linking of skills necessary for this purpose and not as in the traditional models that focus primarily on education for individual specialized and isolated areas. After all, we must educate our children for a reality in which the importance of specialization and knowledge is rapidly being overtaken by an emphasis

LOGITECH KIDZ MOUSE, 1993. PHOTO: DIETMAR HENNEKA

on the ability to manage complexity, to cooperate, and to network. The creative education model therefore begins from human perceptual capabilities and places people at the center of the analysis. It promotes a differentiated perception in students as well as their creativity and imaginative power – an approach that also appears in alternative teaching models, such as in the pedagogy of Maria Montessori. Thus the goal of the Creative Sciences in school education is not simply to overcome "sector-bound people" – Gropius and Moholy-Nagy already pursued that goal at the Bauhaus. Instead, the goal is the education of creative people who act holistically and with awareness of responsibility.

The Creative Sciences educational model assumes a secondary-school time of nine years, divided into lower, middle, and high school, with students aged from approximately ten to eighteen years. The lower-level classes focus on the human senses – seeing, hearing, smelling, tasting, and touching, supplemented by the "sixth sense" of perception. Over the academic years, groups examine all perception with equal intensity, some curriculum contents being permanent requirements while others are elective, depending on the amount of interest. Consider acoustic perception as an example. This study could involve music-making, physical phenomena of acoustics, the meaning of language, the loudness of animals, the noise of the sea, the human ear, the history of violin-making, loss of hearing, or the children's choir. Or, consider taste: In the lower-level years this study might focus on the structure of the tongue, the chemical structure of flavor enhancers, the mysteries of Indian cuisine, or the sensations of eating. The advantage of this approach consists not only in sharpening students' senses but even more importantly on developing knowledge of context. Each of these possible themes would be worked on in groups, supported by holistically educated pedagogues.

Subject-specific contents would be imparted competently and professionally by experts in the respective disciplines, and the program would promote independent research. In parallel, with the focuses on perception, the Creative Sciences school coursework at the lower level would purposefully encourage creative, artistic capabilities, for example, by making choir, theater, and gardening compulsory. And, of course, the general educational subjects covered in our current standard secondary schools would also be part of the curriculum.

In middle school, the focus would move on to building students' conceptual capabilities. As in the concept phase of an operative design process, this area of teaching would involve the recognition and shaping of diversity and the linking of individual elements to unmistakable complete solutions. Conceptualization therefore means both comprehending the individual parts and searching for possible solutions in principle by combining them, so as to form variants of the interplay. The guiding idea of the middle-school study of Creative Sciences, therefore, would be the principle of convergence, and the program would make available respective semester-spanning guide themes.

In the middle-school phase of this model, education retains its group character. Each semester, depending on their leanings and capabilities, the students could choose among guide themes. Fixed components of these project-like guide themes are the subjects Discovery and Modeling. Discovery subsumes the technical and scientific subjects plus engineering, whereas the subjects of art, music, design, crafts, gardening, and theater are combined in Modeling. Intercultural Skill, Language, and Circus (emphasizing the interrelationship, collaboration, and coordination of all subject areas and disciplines) represent the compulsory subjects outside the guide theme. Intercultural Skill subsumes the subjects of ethics/religion, social science, history, economics, and politics. The traditional sports instruction is consistently provided according to the template of a circus school.

In the high-school phase of Creative Sciences, the focus would be on expanding the semester-spanning themes and implementing the superstructure. Students will already have learned to perceive with all their senses and to think and act in highly conceptual and cross-linked patterns. They also will have well-founded knowledge in all general educational subjects. In high school, they would be required to apply all of this knowledge and the learned capabilities in concrete design exercises. During high school, therefore, coursework will devote more time to the subject of Modeling.

In the Creative Sciences model, high-school students would assist students in the lower grades in the form of a mentor model – since inhomogeneous teams are clearly creativity-promoting. Starting from the basic idea of the design of the complete system, the final examination within the Creative Sciences scholastic program would not consist of successfully passing examinations in isolated individual subjects, as is the model in most high schools today. Instead, the final examination would consist of testing students' abilities to successfully awaken joint creative, artistic work supplemented by individual aspects of knowledge. The final examination would, therefore, be a community project. As an example, it may be the presentation of a joint play, with all the elements necessary for the purpose: designing stage scenery and costumes (Modeling), writing the screenplay and newsletter (Language), and content and organization (Intercultural Skill) as well as the many other tasks and aspects of such a joint production aimed at the awakening of learned capabilities.

Extending Design's Educational and Cultural Borders
As you can see, the perspective of the Creative Sciences consists not only in encouraging designers to cooperate with one another but also in building up a network of people and organizations, creating public acceptance for sustainable design concepts, and, thereby, contributing step-by-step to sustainable cultural innovations. Moreover, the college as a center for research and imparting knowledge will then become reestablished as what it must be: a "free space for discovery and discussion of ideas, new as well as old." [15]

3 THINK GREEN AND SOCIAL: VICTOR PAPANEK

BY MARTINA FINEDER & THOMAS GEISLER

"This chapter is the work of my former assistant Martina Fineder and my colleague Thomas Geisler, who were instrumental in uncovering the archives of Victor Papanek and bringing them to Vienna – the place of his birth. These intrepid scholars republished Papanek's seminal *Design for the Real World*, and here they tell us about the relevance of their findings in regard to Papanek's thesis and its call to designers to look forward. I hope that this chapter inspires us all to read – and reread – Victor Papanek's writings and to reexamine his once radical proposals, which I believe are more relevant today than ever before. H.E.

These two quotes could have come from one of the current books about new strategies in design, such as *design thinking*, *inclusive design*, *design interaction* or *open design*. But they do not. Instead, they come from Victor Papanek's *Design for the Real World: Human Ecology and Social Change*, originally published in 1971, revised in 1984, and considered today to be one of the most thought-provoking design books of its time. Against the background of an awakening environmental movement, which characterized the break from the principles of the prevailing industrial culture, Papanek developed a model for a holistic design practice. In addition to massive criticism of the design and consumer cultures of his time, Papanek offered guidelines and examples for socially and ecologically responsive design. His book, which has sparked controversy since its publication, is one of the most widely read design books in the world. And now it is enjoying a renaissance. This renewed popularity may even transform the image of the author, Victor Papanek, from defiant polemicist to international pioneer of social and ecological design. Both author and book have achieved cult status.[1] Why is this so? What makes Papanek's ideas astonishingly relevant for the modern design scene and why are he and his book more than just a historical reference?

Some answers to these questions are obvious. The current sustainability debate in economics and politics fueled by the media has ushered in a revival of the notion of responsible design reminiscent of that of Papanek and his critical contemporaries. For example, the current push for sustainable development to avoid the problems caused by mankind for "Spaceship Earth."[2] Efforts to reduce environmental pollution and the depletion of natural resources, the search for alternative energies and decentralized production methods, the call for more self and joint determination – these are just some of the ways society is pursuing sustainability. Papanek's theses, which society once considered radical, are enjoying increasing topicality as we search for socially relevant design fields that offer alternatives to our prevailing culture of incompatible design.

"In an age when we seem to be mastering aspects of form, a return to content is already long overdue." VICTOR PAPANEK, 1971

Numerous mission statements of design institutions or forewords in exhibition catalogs are convincing evidence of the search for a positive change.[3] This search takes on new urgency in the first decades of a millennium shaken by crises. The horrifying events of September 11, 2001, are just as much a part of today's design discourse as are the seemingly permanent economic crises and political/social upheavals that rock the globe. In his revised edition of 1984, Papanek drew a parallel between crises and opportunities in design:

"Maybe we learn best from disasters. Detroit is floundering in high unemployment, and, with three oil crises, four unusually cold winters, two major droughts leading to water shortages, extensive floods, a global energy shortage, and major recession behind us, this book has been slowly accepted even in the United States over the last thirteen years."[4]

Against this background, we have written this summary of *Design for the Real World* to address current questions. But, we must say in advance that we are asking these questions as design researchers with specific interests in the history and material culture of design as they relate to the environment. As such, we are concerned with value shifts and cultural upheavals that have a substantial influence on the development of design and consumer culture. Elsewhere in this book you can see the works of the Master Class ID2 at the University for Applied Art in Vienna, where we simultaneously taught and conducted research. In the context of this work, our interests became focused on the significance of Papanek's legacy for the future generation and practice in design.

Papanek's role in the current expert debate about design was a primary driver of our investigations – a legacy that today's critics must view in connection with his biography, which was published amid some turmoil but receives little attention today. To provide that biographical background, we have included here an overview of the important stages of Papanek's life. Taken together, a fuller understanding of the book and its author gives us a closer perspective on his model for a holistic development toward "human ecology and social change." We expanded our investigation with a brief review of influences of societal and political changes that took place before Papanek published *Design for the Real World*. And, because Papanek's book focuses on "industrial design," we also examined his notion of technology. Was he a friend or foe of progress? How can Papanek's fundamental criticism of design, with its roots in the counterculture of the 1960s and 1970s, be forward looking? At best, we can approach these questions by placing Papanek's statements in context with other "rediscovered" pioneering works of that time, such as E. F. Schumacher's *Small is Beautiful: Economics as if People Matter* (1973) and Stewart Brand's *Whole Earth Catalog*. Our investigation and examination of these issues and questions resulted in the chapter you are about to read.

During our research into Papanek's writings, we followed the trail of the deceased author in the United States, where we discovered his previously unnoticed estate, consisting of personal documents, artifacts, and archives. Just one short year later, at our initiative and with the enthusiastic support of Hartmut Esslinger and others, we were able to secure funds from the Austrian Federal Ministry for Science and Research to purchase Papanek's estate for our home university and secure it for future research. A design school, especially in the city of Papanek's birth, seemed to us to be an ideal site to make his archives accessible for research and education. The estate, which besides personal documents and artifacts includes a working library and the archive of the designer, is now administered by the Victor J. Papanek Foundation, established in 2010 at the University for Applied Art in Vienna. There, the diverse material legacy and the intellectual work of Papanek will become part of a living study program.

"As we see the divisions that the last few generations have painstakingly erected out of the quicksand of their statistician's minds crumbling away, we find no need for more such distinct areas but for unity. Not the specialist, but the synthesist is required. VICTOR PAPANEK, 1984

Papanek's interests were as broad and meaningful as his contributions. The bibliography of the first edition of *Design for the Real World* alone included approximately 500 titles. In the second edition, which he expanded by another 200 titles or so, Papanek writes: "Since I was writing a book about design as a multidisciplinary approach, I also

tried to compile a multidisciplinary bibliography." In the appendix to the expanded edition, he
added these words:

"From the linear thinking of the Renaissance (that great setting of the sun, which man mistook for
the dawn), when men still thought all their knowledge classifiable, we have inherited our graphs,
divisions, classifications, and lists. Typically when we wish to classify areas of knowledge too vast to
be so comprehended, we make the crowning mistake: we educate specialists." [5]

We believe that both the life and work of Victor Papanek offer ideas
that can inspire everyone – not just the specialists. We hope that our work can help readers of every
interest and discipline find the kind of inspiration that Papanek offered through his writings, his
teaching, and his designs."

A Book for Everyone, about Design for Everyone
Papanek's best seller, originally published in 1971 in an English edition by Pantheon Books, New
York,[6] dealt with moral responsibility in design. In it, Papanek presented a new type of designer,
one who functioned as a "generalist" and as a "mediator"[7] of a design team working with a
multidisciplinary and process-oriented purpose. By offering exemplary products and services for
what was known at that time as the "Third World," the book questioned the consumer culture of the
Western industrial nations and proposed a future of more important work for designers, aimed at
solving the needs of a growing society in harmony with nature.

Papanek saw the global redistribution of resources as being central
to this examination, along with the strengthening of the new environmental movement, and
others, that were gaining importance in social, cultural, and political life. To illustrate the
disconnect between these movements and the design of the era, Papanek pointed to gadgets
such as electrically heated Queen Anne style footstools being produced and sold for US$16.95
in one part of the world and to stoves made from used license plates, which were selling in other
parts of the world for eight cents and being used as a household's sole means of cooking.[8] In
this way, Papanek challenged the prevailing design attitude and the corresponding industrial
manufacturing and marketing culture. "Why the Things You Buy Are Expensive, Badly Designed,
Unsafe, and Usually Don't Work" he exclaimed boldly on the cover of the 1973 Bantam edition
of his book.

The volleys began early in *Design for the Real World*, beginning
with attacks in the book's preface on Papanek's professional colleagues in design and related
fields such as advertising and continuing with the merciless but often humorous criticisms of
consumer culture in the book's first section, "Like It Is." The book's second part, "How It Could
Be," provides concrete ideas for socially responsible and ecologically aware design. Papanek

summed up the new obligations for designers and their professional discipline in the chapter "Design Responsibility: Five Myths and Six Directions." This chapter also contains fields of activity for designers in developing countries with which Papanek had become acquainted as early as the 1960s while working for UNESCO in the International Technical Expert Program, among other activities. He placed simply constructed, easy-to-repair appliances at the center of the discussion, along with communication and transportation devices that can be operated without fuel or electricity in remote regions.[9] Papanek also pointed out design and consumerism-related difficulties in the United States, such as the self-created crisis in the automobile industry, which continues to present challenges to leaders in politics, economics, science, and design. Detroit offered one of Papanek's worst-case scenarios. The monocultural and therefore extremely inflexible structure of any such massive industry is problematic not only economically but also socially and ecologically because it cannot react swiftly to problems and changes. Such industries, as Papanek would point out, are focused on the objects to be produced and not on a holistic system.

Design for the Real World also scrutinizes the restrictive handling of copyright protection and patent rights. Ultimately, Papanek linked this issue to the question of social responsibility in industry when he stated, for example, that no one should profit from the needs of others. Papanek also based his call for democratization of information and production on this interpretation, which leads to the development of his models for a participatory and "open-source" design practice (which we will revisit in more detail further on).

The Life of "Design's Gadfly"

In *Design for the Real World*, we find numerous anecdotes from Papanek's own life woven together with his radical ideas for mankind and the environment, illustrating the dynamic relationship between his life and work. This forward-thinking, idealistic, critical commentator was ahead of his time. The evolution of his demands for eliminating the divisions between the disciplines can be seen clearly in his journey through life, which was marked by experiencing and exceeding limits. To explore Papanek's personal history, we turned to the German reissue of his book *Design for the Real World. Guidelines for Human Ecology and Social Change* of 2009.[10]

Victor Papanek was born on 22 November 1923 as the only child of Helene and Richard Papanek in Vienna. The Papaneks ran a food business in the inner city and occupied a sophisticated apartment on the Ring, the eclectic, stately nineteenth-century boulevard that encircles Vienna's medieval city center. As the son of merchants, Papanek's education reflected his family's standing. But the worldwide economic collapse of 1929 altered the Papaneks' lifestyle. Their financial situation became increasingly precarious with the premature death of the father in the 1930s and the political and societal radicalization of Austrofascism, which lead to Austria's annexation by Nazi-Germany's Third Reich. The final turning point for the Papaneks was the Nazi's confiscation of the family business. With the assistance of relatives, Victor and his Jewish mother fled to the USA in 1939 and were thus rescued from further reprisals of the Nazi regime and certain deportation to a concentration camp.

The fifteen-year-old Victor and his mother arrived penniless in New York. It is difficult to reconstruct the family's early years in exile, although it appears that they found menial work adequate for their financial needs. In *Design for the Real World*, Papanek hints at some of the jobs he held during this period, including work in sweatshops, as a storeroom laborer in the Museum of Modern Art (MoMA), New York, and as stand-up comedian in Greenwich Village. The most verifiable part of his early life in the States is his service in the US army, which for Victor Papanek, as for many young immigrant men, offered a substantial opportunity for accelerating citizenship. After his discharge from military service, Papanek accepted the invitation of a comrade to visit the San Ildefonso Indian Reservation in southwestern USA. This withdrawal from the demands of modern life, as his last wife Harlanne writes, was "emotionally healing" for him. It also pointed the way for his further journey through life.

Back in New York, Victor Papanek studied at evening classes at Cooper Union college in 1946 and 1947. Even now, we don't have evidence of what convinced him to take up art and architecture. It may have been the promise of financial prosperity, status, or the opportunities to become a designer in the booming industry of the postwar years, joining American design idols such as Raymond Loewy or Henry Dreyfuss. Even while he was studying, Papanek ran a studio for interior and product design with the distinctive name DESIGN CLINIC, which looked for everyday solutions to problems. In his memoirs of those years, Papanek tells of first encountering Frank Lloyd Wright's buildings and of his growing enthusiasm for Wright's work following his visit to the Rose Pauson House in Phoenix, Arizona. While taking unauthorized photographs on the grounds of Wright's studio in Spring Green, Wisconsin, Papanek had a personal encounter with Wright, which resulted in his acceptance into the internship program in Taliesin and Taliesin West.

Wright subsequently became one of the most influential personalities for the young designer. Papanek's esthetic sensitivity was shaped by the preferences of his mentor, such as hexagons, the color combination of black-white-red, and interest in the material culture and philosophy of the Far East. Ultimately, Papanek's understanding of modernism and its relationship to nature and the environment developed in the discourse with Wright. Stylistically, Papanek in his barely documented early design work was oriented toward American postwar modernism. The interplay with organic forms, new materials, and elements of indigenous cultures was reminiscent of contemporaries such as Charles and Ray Eames, Isamu Noguchi, and George Nelson. In those years Papanek was seeking an independent language of form, which could amalgamate the societal and technological changes of the postwar era in a more contemporary manner.

In the mid-1950s, Papanek took courses in Creative Engineering and Product Design at the Massachusetts Institute of Technology (MIT), where Richard Buckminster

JENAGLAS RECYCLED BOROSILICATE WARE, 1993. PHOTO: DIETMAR HENNEKA

Fuller was teaching. It is uncertain whether the two had already met at that time, but Fuller joined Wright as another important guiding figure for Papanek's growing holistic, system-encompassing, and questioning approach to design. Other key works from that time, such as Henry Dreyfuss's *Designing for People*, which Papanek praised in *Design for the Real World*, helped to form his notions of a new type of designer as a "human engineer." His critical attitude toward superficially designed goods, which served nothing more than consumer pleasure and short-lived satisfaction of needs, grew stronger in reaction to the shallow, media-driven glorification of the "American way of life." This nation's cultural orientation toward cheap, mass-produced goods had a substantial influence on Papanek's critical teaching.

Papanek became a new father at this time, and family economic obligations may explain his acceptance of a financially secure position at the Ontario College of Art and Design, Toronto, Canada. There, as a pedagogical novice, Papanek had the opportunity to develop a new degree course in Industrial Design. Further appointments at the Rhode Island School of Design and at the State University of New York in Buffalo followed. During this time, Papanek also created and presented several television programs with the title Design Dimensions for WNED-TV. Provocatively, he combined the discussion of design with that of consumer culture and questions of taste, thereby expanding these topics beyond the realm of elite discourse and into everyday life. In order to make design a part of daily life accessible to the broadest possible public, the "design commentator" as he called himself, returned many times to the mass media of radio and television.

In the early 1960s, Papanek moved to North Carolina State University, College of Design and began producing design studies commissioned by UNESCO. Among these works is the tin-can radio Papanek designed for use in developing countries. Beginning in 1964, Purdue University in West Lafayette, Indiana, became his new center of activity, where he led the new Department of Art and Design. Papanek's pedagogical work at Purdue with future engineers and designers as well as students of other specialties in interdisciplinary teams makes up a good part of the teaching examples in *Design for the Real World*.

While at Purdue, Papanek collaborated with the graphic designer Al Gowan to produce the experimental film Biographics, which they later presented at the renowned Design Conference in Aspen, Colorado.[11] Thereafter Papanek and his new pedagogical methods and approaches in design gained influence beyond the borders of the USA. His pedagogical model was also shaped by his frequent trips to Scandinavia. In the 1960s, the Pan-Scandinavian Student Design Association invited Papanek to conduct lectures and workshops, which brought him back to Europe for the first time since World War II. While in Sweden, he wrote some chapters of *Design for the Real World*; in fact, the book was first published under the Swedish title *The Environment and the Millions*.

In the early 1970s, Papanek's growing international recognition led to his appointment at the newly established California Institute of the Arts in Valencia, Santa Clarita, east of Los Angeles. Around the same time, *Design for the Real World* was published in English in the USA, splitting the professional world into vehement critics from the design establishment and fervent disciples from the alternative design scene. Whereas the Industrial Designers Society of America (IDSA) excluded Papanek from membership because of his critical attitude toward the profession and industry, his opinion was highly esteemed elsewhere. Numerous invitations to lecture followed from all over the world. Guest professorships and research grants from institutions such as the School of Architecture at the Royal Danish Academy of Fine Arts and Schumacher College in Devon, England, brought Papanek and his young family to Europe for prolonged stays. This was an opportunity for the critic, who had even been reviled as "design's gadfly,"[12] to escape from the strong headwind in the USA for some time.

In the mid-1970s, the family returned to the United States, where Papanek had been offered a position as chair of the Design Department in the Kansas City Art Institute. It is noteworthy that from then on Papanek undertook an enormous number of research trips to West Africa, Southeast Asia, and South America. He collected artifacts, recorded his observations, and compiled an extensive photographic record of the places he visited – over his lifetime, this photo archive grew to over 20,000 slides. Papanek's extensive library reveals his cross-disciplinary interests and familiarity with methods of cultural anthropology and ethnology, which contributed to his universalistic perspective in design.

In the early 1980s, an offer to become the J. L. Constant distinguished professor brought Papanek to the University of Kansas School of Architecture and Urban Design. There he worked on, among other topics, *Design for Human Scale*, which was published in 1983. *The Green Imperative*, Papanek's last published book, appeared in 1995, when Papanek had already retired. Besides many international research and teaching stays, his practical design activity, such as for Volvo in Sweden, for Darlington Industries Ltd. in England, and for Planet products in Bellingen, Australia, remains largely unrecognized and vastly under appreciated.

Victor Papanek died in Lawrence, Kansas, on 10 January 1998 from the effects of long years of lung disease – during his life he had been a heavy smoker. For his work the designer, critic, and teacher had already been distinguished during his life with countless awards, including the United Nations (UNESCO) Award for Outstanding Design for Developing Nations (1983), the IKEA Foundation International Award in Amsterdam (1989), and the Lewis Mumford Award for the Environment (1995). Between 1982 and 1992, Papanek was nominated several times for the Alternative Nobel Prize.

ROSENTHAL, SERIES AVENUE DECOR NEW YORK, 1991. PHOTO: DIETMAR HENNEKA

Papanek, the Counterculture, and Progressive Thinking

The revolutionary stance Papanek advocates in *Design for the Real World* can be best understood when viewed against the background of two extremely contrary perspectives that prevailed at the time of its publication. On one side was the newly formed environmental movement, which, as Tim O'Riordan describes in his book Environmentalism, became an "institution pervading and determining everyday life and affecting judgment, moral attitude, the value system, and daily routine."[13] On the other side was the euphoria that began with the economic miracle of the 1950s, whereby industrial mass production geared toward profit maximization was seen as a successful and prosperity-favoring economic model. That view relied on a technique-based belief in progress, motivated by the proven achievements of industrialization, such as work streamlining and standardization as well as on new trailblazing successes in space research and telecommunication. The era was closely related to the history of development of industrial design with its Western influence and its functional-esthetic dogmas.

In this context, more holistic views began to expand the image of the designer as a "human engineer," who placed special importance on design work at the human-machine interface. This appreciation for design was based on the idea that modern technologies and engineering principles offered suitable answers to the challenges of humanity and – paradoxically – could also solve emerging side effects, such as environmental problems. This purely technocratic model began to totter with the first signs of global crisis in the 1960s.[14] The growing development of alternative movements led to a reassessment of needs and focuses in design, which in 1976 were discussed from extremely opposite viewpoints at the prominently attended conference Design for Need: The Social Contribution of Design.[15] The design historian Pauline Madge describes the opposing positions as being made up of those – including Papanek – who saw in the ethical use of technology and design an opportunity for change in society and the environment versus those who on the other hand wanted to have technical progress (and its spread) determined purely by society.[16]

Thus, the debate began to revolve around a central question: Is adaptation of the environment to mankind really the right path? On this point, alignments among the various alternative movements shifted and/or drifted apart. While some alternative movements began to coalesce around the backward-oriented view of nature as the primary cultural driver and were thus completely opposed to powerful new technologies, a circle of sorts also developed around Stewart Brand, who established his reputation through a revolution in the distribution of (technical) production equipment. The objective of Brand's *Whole Earth Catalog* is the reinforcement of a decentralized production culture, in which the users have easier access to information and tools. Therefore, the *Whole Earth Catalog* is part shopping source, part manual, which shares with kindred spirits the building instructions for computers, solar systems, and even toilets.[17]

Papanek's global view and access to technology is close to the *Whole Earth Catalog* community, even though he promoted few technical developments in this sense. Most of Papanek's designs have an extremely low-tech basis or are concentrated on furniture and living environments. Papanek himself was not a specialized technologist. He rejected technology for technology's sake but advocated "smart" technology in the sense of simple and accessible solutions, such as those he described in *Design for the Real World*. Papanek also focused on repairability of products, work which required technical understanding but not a "diploma." Certainly his knowledge of new technologies was more theoretical but also holistic in nature – entirely in the sense of the "synthesist."

Papanek's "low-tech" motivations may explain his closeness to E. F. Schumacher and the Appropriate Technology Movement. Schumacher's *Small is Beautiful* is programmatically supplemented by Papanek's book in many areas. In the preface to the second edition of *Design for the Real World*, Papanek noted the agreement between him and Schumacher that "nothing big works."[18] He also related this idea to Arthur Köstler, whose ideas were important to Papanek and whom he quotes in the same preface: "A changed environment requires flexible action and reversing the trend toward its technization."[19] In *Design for the Real World*, Papanek condemns technization as narrow-mindedness, unilaterally conducive to a purely capitalistically oriented world view, which also aims at generating artificial consumer desires that eventually lead to a dead end.

Papanek himself links *Design for the Real World* with *Future Shock* (1972), Alvin Toffler's apocalyptic opus that was published at almost the same time. The common denominator of these publications is their preoccupation with a society constantly in flux and the effects of the advancing technization on mankind. Papanek's understanding of these issues is also marked by the mobile principles of human ecology revealed to us by the subtitle of *Design for the Real World*. The strengthening of this discipline, which has its roots in the 1920s, may well have something to do with one of the most important changes in modernism – the idea that nature and mankind are not antagonists but linked parts of a larger system. This development toward a systematic understanding of the world describes one of the most important paradigm shifts in modern Western thought. Thus Stewart Brand's *Whole Earth Catalog* is no more a chance occurrence than Papanek's *Design for the Real World*. Both spring from a counterculture that is not averse to progressive thinking, which partly explains why, more than forty years later, they continue to provide stimulus for forward-looking change.

Design by the People, for the People

As a reaction to the cultural, political, and economic crises of 1970, numerous new social movements, including the environmental and antinuclear movements as well as thousands of small citizens' initiatives, became increasingly stronger in Europe and the USA. As diverse as the alignments of the individual groups who formed these movements were, all shared certain common priorities and interests. Among these were an increasing concern about the destruction of nature, the rising demand for joint and self-determination, and the desire for a new harmony between work and life. In turn, these concerns triggered an intensive examination of issues such as the production and consumption of goods.

The young critical generation of the 1970s was propagating a new passion for do-it-yourself (as opposed to professional) design, which corresponded to its lifestyle. Victor Papanek played a central role in this international development. Together with Jim Hennessey he published the manuals *Nomadic Furniture: How to build and where to buy lightweight furniture that folds, inflates, knocks down, stacks, or is disposable and can be recycled I* and *II* (1973/1974). Both editions combined a collection of hand-drawn DIY building instructions and a selection of qualitative and inexpensive furniture items and play equipment. Unlike he *Whole Earth Catalog*, these publications lacked building instructions for energy-generating equipment or other supply systems or communication devices.

All of these manuals make a point of describing and listing the prices of products of other designers that the editors believe are worthy of recommendation. In the alternative design of these years, the price of objects and their component parts was a serious consumer consideration, and, in many cases, listing these prices was a direct reaction to the doctrine of "Good design," which many perceived as being elitist and expensive. Manuals such as the *Whole Earth Catalog* and the *Nomadic Furniture* volumes basically cast doubt on practices such as copyright and exclusive distribution rights. In this regard, Papanek writes in *Design for the Real World*: "Patents do not serve the social well-being." Papanek criticizes patents as a means for shutting out a large part of the world's population by denying them the opportunity to share in important developments. Papanek believed that patents and other legal barriers to shared design create or sustain imbalances between poor and rich in the system.[20]

Papanek accompanied this view with a denial of top-down design processes by rejecting design authorship. Papanek's conviction that professionals and laymen should be included equally in shaping the environment and that every human action should be considered as a creative effort can be understood as the guiding theme for his work. This perspective recognizes all people as designers – or, at least, as being capable of participating in a design process. Papanek explored this view by delving into working practices of professionals with laymen or other experts, as illustrated in *Design for the Real World* and elsewhere.

The twenty-first century finds us still in the grip of societal, political, and ecological challenges, and we continue to look to design as a powerful tool for solving those problems. The search for other viewpoints and historic parallels that might help us in this work has launched a reawakening of the movements for social and ecological responsibility that first took hold in the 1960s and 1970s. But, it is not sufficient merely to occupy the "old" positions or to shift responsibilities for change to others; instead, we must accept the challenge of expanding and evolving the priorities of these movements and develop collaborative approaches to forward-looking solutions. Even industry has long known that "human ecology and social change" represent market opportunities and that a critical attitude toward design is marketable. From this aspect numerous designers, researchers, and trustees are now suggesting, under contemporary auspices, that a new perspective be directed toward Papanek et al. in order to develop adequate design services for the here and now, and for the future.[21] Today, as in the past, Victor Papanek's ideas are not only current but also ahead of their time. As Hartmut Esslinger would say, they offer the world a fast forward to a better future.

1 We have commented on this phenomenon in several academic articles and conference papers. See in particular "Design for the Real World-Human Ecology and Social Change: Design Criticism and Critical Design in the writings of Victor Papanek (1923-1998)," in: *Journal of Design History*, 23/1, 2010, pp. 99-106.

2 Among other origins, this expression goes back to Richard Buckminster Fuller's *Operating Manual for Spaceship Earth*, Carbondale: Southern Illinois University Press, 1969. Fuller also wrote the introduction for the original English edition of *Design for the Real World. Human Ecology and Social Change*, New York: Pantheon, 1971.

3 In this regard see our paper "'Design Clinic'-Can design heal the world? Scrutinising Victor Papanek's impact on today's design agenda," presented in September 2011 at the Design History Society annual conference "Design Activism and Social Change" in Barcelona.

4 Victor Papanek, *Design for the Real World. Human Ecology and Social Change*, London: Thames and Hudson, 1984, p. xvi.

5 Ibid., p. 351.

6 In the past forty years, Papanek's best seller, which was initially published in 1970 under the title *Miljön och Miljonerna* [The Environment and the Millions] by Albert Bonniers Förlag in Stockholm and at first was declined by American publishers, has been translated into more than twenty languages. *Design for the Real World* has been periodically revised and reissued by the author, including by Thames and Hudson in 1984. This version is also the basis for the German edition, reissued in 2009 with annotations.

7 Papanek 1984 (see note 14), p. 315.

8 Ibid., p. 58.

9 In those years UNIDO also supported a program in which designers and architects from Europe and America were integrated. They included, for example, the Austrian designer and architect Carl Auböck. In his role as a design professor at the University for Applied Arts in Vienna, Auböck was also the person who repeatedly invited Papanek to Vienna. He was also one of the predecessors of Hartmut Esslinger's professorship for the Master Class ID2.

10 We therefore will not list the numerous archive and interview sources from which the biography is composed. See: Victor Papanek, *Design for the Real World. Guidelines for Human Ecology and Social Change*, Martina Fineder et al., (eds.), Vienna/New York: Springer Verlag and edition Angewandte, 2009, pp. 413-422.

11 The six-minute experimental and teaching film documented Papanek's examination of bionics in design and in 1968 was awarded the Art Directors Club of America Medal.

12 Al Gowan, "Design's Gadfly", in: *PRINT*, May/June 1998, p.33.

13 Tim O'Riordan, *Environmentalism*, 1976, cited in: Pauline Madge, "Design, Ecology, Technology: A Historiographical Review," in: *Journal of Design History*, Vol. 6, No. 3, 1993, p. 153.

14 To be extremely brief, these signs were the stagnating economic growth, the rising unemployment, the Vietnam War, the conflict between generations, and naturally the environmental crisis beginning in the 1970s.

15 From the International Council of Societies of Industrial Design (ICSID), organized at the Royal College of Art in London, little agreement was seen among the contributors, as the titles and contents of the lectures show: "The Role of Designers in Disaster Relief" (John Murlis), "Social Forces Determine the Shape of Technology" (Thomas Kuby), "Precariousness and Ambiguity – Industrial Design in Dependent Countries" (Gui Bonsiepe), or "Twelve Methodologies for Design – Because People Count" (Victor Papanek).

16 Madge 1993 (see note 23), p. 158.

17 Stewart Brand (ed.), *Whole Earth Catalog*, from 1968 on.

18 Papanek 1984 (see note 14).

19 Ibid.

20 Ibid., p. 237.

21 See for instance Nicola Morelli, "Social Innovation And Industrial Contexts," in: *Design Issues*, No. 23, 2007; Tim Brown, *Change by Design. How Design Thinking Transforms Organizations and Inspires Innovation*, 2009; Roel Klaasen and Maria Neicu, "CTRL-Alt-Design," paper presented in 2011 at the Design History Society annual conference "Design Activism and Social Change." Online at: www.historiadeldisseny.org/congres/pdf/.

PART 2

SHAPING THE
DESIGN
REVOLUTION

4 CREATING WITH HANDS AND MIND

"In design man becomes what he is. Animals have language and perception as well, but they do not design." OTL AICHER

The process of designing is both simple and complex. Simple, because we designers want to give physical shape to what we imagine so it can be experienced by others; complex, because nobody else can see and feel what we imagine. We need tools to convey our ideas; pencils, paper, rulers, templates, files, saws, drills, hand-tools, and machines, all serve this purpose. And for the past couple of decades, we also have had the use of digital tools with applications for computer aided design (CAD), three-dimensional digital printing, graphic artwork, and animation.

All of these tools have an influence on the process of designing. Sketching with a good pencil, for example, leaves a lot of freedom for fantasy; drawing with ink requires that we know what we want to draw and shaping a soft material like Styrofoam is a quick, rough method for understanding the object in its real proportions. The more sure we are about our progress, the more precise our materials and shaping tools become, the more steps we apply to their use, and the better the results we achieve. Nobody can go from a hand sketch to a final model and pretend that any step along the way is the best design possible.

Openness in the early stage of design has great value, but I didn't always realize this truth. At the beginning of my design studies, I was rather proud of my rendering skills, which I honed in automotive design competitions by the German magazine *Hobby*, as well as my technical drawing skills, which I acquired at the Technical University in Stuttgart. When my professor there, Karl Dittert, saw how I labored over each of my drawings, he told me, "Stop doing this American bullshit! It limits your ideation process. Sketches in design must be original, not nice. Always make a quick sketch model – or better yet, a couple – and leave the technical drawing for the very end." I followed his advice and learned very quickly that fluid tools enable fluid thinking.

With today's digital tools, Karl Dittert's advice is even more relevant. In addition to offering the visual gratification of a high-resolution color display, digital tools allow us designers to very quickly convert our ideas into attractive looking images, which are, however, far from being a great solution and the ultimate design. Beyond the theoretical and intellectual aspects of design lies the sometimes intense, challenging task of giving form to ideas. Design takes shape through consideration, experimentation, transformation – a process similar to the way discussion can help clarify and refine thoughts. In other words, designing "stuff" is a process, not an event.

In this chapter, I want to talk a bit about that process and all it entails. Designers are always seeking newer and better tools, but we must also master the tools we have available to us. Here, I will describe my own experiences in learning to use the tools of design, but I also want to examine the way we designers are shaped by the capabilities our digital and analog tools extend to us. Design is a creative process that enables us to give expression to our unique vision, but it also demands that we anchor that vision within the practical framework of our profession. The more mastery we hold over the tools of that profession, the more successful our ideas will be when they make the journey from our mind, through our hands, and into the public forum.

Learning to Give Shape to Ideas

From as early as I can remember, I wanted to create and make things. Even as a young child, I could recognize any car, motorcycle, or truck (true, there weren't that many models on German roads in 1948), and I also could draw them well and make models from bark and wood. After vacationing with my relatives at the River Rhine and the North Sea, I also began modeling boats and ships. I had the great luck to grow up in a tiny village where my parents had rented an apartment in a farmhouse. Our landlord, Georg Gauss, was both a farmer and the village carpenter, which meant that there was a wonderful workshop in a building next to the farmhouse. It became my paradise – and I became Mr. Gauss's nightmare until he gave up and assigned to me a small table and some tools.

On the other side of the house was the school – one class for all eight grades – and I began attending class there when I was four. It was a cool place. I realize now that our teacher, Mr. Hahn – who had escaped the Nazis into our pious little enclave – was way overqualified. But he was our lucky break; of the nine students entering his class during my four "official" years at the school, six qualified for high school, and two of us – Klaus Henning, who became a great painter and sculptor, and myself – went on to college. Now, why did Klaus and I make it through school as creative children, when all German educational models were then, as they still are today, rational systems that reward logical traits rather than visceral ones? Well, Mr. Hahn offered his students a deal: "When your grades are great, you have the freedom to do what you like." So we kids learned like mad – and we got the rewards. My payoffs were to build a scaled-down fire truck and to decorate the classroom for Easter, Thanksgiving, and Christmas. Klaus sculpted animals and, for Christmas, the Holy Family. We had wood, bark, paper, clay, and color to work with. And, thanks to Mr. Gauss's carpenter shop next door, we progressed well. My parents had started a small fashion business, and so I believed that my world was perfect. But life had some surprises for me.

When I was ten years old, my parents bought a live-in business in the next little town, Altensteig. There, I passed the entry test for the high school, which again was just across the street from our house. I also found two carpenter shops nearby, but they didn't want me hanging around, and so I started my own shop under the roof of our house. The shop would be a thorny issue with my parents until I left home for army service.

In Altensteig, life became more complex in many ways. My teachers didn't care for creativity, and even though I was an honor-roll student, they scolded me for all the "senseless stuff" I did, such as filling notebooks with sketches of cars, bikes, ships, and airplanes. I started to build model airplanes – around the corner there was a shop owner who was a true model-building fanatic and also allowed me to buy on credit – and to play American jazz and blues music. My parents became concerned. For them, I was clearly on the path "down into the gutter." It didn't help that my parents' work brought them into contact with various fashion designers, most of whom amplified their worst fears about creative types. As a result, my parents were determined to make me into an "orderly German."

My mom's idea of this process was to burn my sketchbooks, but my Dad took a more positive approach and funneled my energy into toy trains. I had a large table in my room where, in addition to the trains and rails, I built an entire landscape with a village from paper, plaster, matches, and small things I found in the junk buckets at a nearby hardware store. At fourteen, I decided to start a rock 'n' roll band, causing my parents to deeply regret giving me an electric guitar for Christmas. Due to lack of money, I had to build some of the band's instruments, such as drums and a skiffle guitar, from wooden barrels and cigar boxes. My sketching, making things, and interest in exotic music ramped up to a higher level, positioning me squarely for a culture clash with my parents and my teachers. It didn't help that I turned my cash flow negative by building a set of power amps from Fender kits I found in secondhand shops. But despite numerous oppressive circumstances, including my torment at the hands of a misguided art teacher, I was happy outside of school. And I even loved one of my classes.

That class was music, and its wonderful teacher, Arthur Kusterer, was a retired composer who had been a great pianist, playing in concerts at the Berlin Philharmonic with Herbert von Karajan. Mr. Kusterer explained to me – in musical terms – that creativity is rooted in believing and doing, and it leaves us with no other choice but to create. He let me play the blues but also requested that I learn at least the basics of Mozart and Beethoven. Mr. Kusterer didn't respect fixed times for class periods and always insisted that our weekly class, which was strictly voluntary, would make us better students and better people (the German word *Mensch* cannot be accurately translated here). He also instilled self-confidence in us by saying that if we do what we love and feel right about, we will do well.

Years later, after my detours of army service and studying engineering, I told Mr. Kusterer that I had finally found my ideal profession. He didn't know what design meant, but he liked it when I explained it that it involved thinking, creating, making models, experimenting, having fun, and being proud. He smiled and said: "You know, I live in sounds, and now you live in shapes. Be a hero, my 'Siegfried,' but be aware of the Hagens." (Here, he was referencing the Nibelungen Saga in which the hero gets murdered by being stabbed from behind.) Mr. Kusterer saw creative life as a heroic journey – and when he died in 1967, the fulfillment of his life overshadowed the sadness of his passing.[1]

As a design student, all that had been wrong in my life became right. It was a bit like being in the political opposition for twenty-three years and suddenly being given the responsibility of governing. I realized that 90% of my education at school had been a waste, and that the good things it had given me were an understanding of the relationships between events and ideas and the ability to learn. And, it also taught me to interact with non-creative people, which is the one major challenge most designers can't overcome (a failure marked by comments such as, "My client doesn't understand").

When I came to the College of Design in Schwaebisch Gmuend, my first trip was to the model shop, which became my "living room." I quickly learned that I had a *lot* to learn. Design is not like building model airplanes because it demands that conceptual thinking and practical shaping go hand in hand (or tool in hand) and the verdict is often: "Oh my God, how ugly." As my much-revered professor and composer Arthur Kusterer had said, "Notes written on paper only become music by an orchestra playing them" – words that later became the mantra of frog studio.

When I put together my own design garage, my first investment was in the same cool machinery that I had worked with in the workshop at my college. I also learned from the techniques of master modelmakers I worked with on the outside, such as Paul Hildinger of the former HfG Ulm. I often look back with nostalgia at my experience with Apple's Snow White project, and the hundreds of models we created for it. But, to understand how I developed my modelmaking processes, I think it may be even more revealing to look at frog's first breakthrough success, the Wega System 3000, which we launched at the annual German electronics trade show, the IFA Berlin in 1970.

Due to lack of time, Wega took my last design model for its advertising campaign and brochure – they took it in such a rush that there were even traces of sanding marks still visible on the surface. This was my fifth model of the TV, which I handcrafted from twenty-year old wood, plaster, and lots of Bondo. From the first idea to the IFA industrial exhibition, the design took eight months – and its success changed everything. Its popularity helped Wega grow by 500%

DISNEY CRUISE LINE, MAGIC AND WONDER, 1995. BOTTOM PHOTO: DISNEY

until its acquisition by Sony in 1974, and it established me as a designer committed to the idea that "form follows emotion" – another mantra that would guide frog in its work.

After my success with the Wega design, I hired Andreas Haug and Georg Spreng as my designer peers – they would become partners from 1977 to 1982 – and Thomas Gingele, and Walter Funk, one of the best master modelmakers I ever had the privilege to work with. It was a good mix of talent; we designers designed and made quick models and Walter added the magical touch to produce the final model masterpieces. Together, we all "designed by shaping" in our shop, working for clients such as Wega, Vuitton, Sony, and Apple, just to name a few.

I always believed in using great tools. In 1984, frog took the pioneering step into CAD, paying $1.4 million for four VAX and Intergraph stations. But I saw CAD as a creative tool, not as a seducer. Today, with digital tools affordable even for students and processing power increasing, many young designers have turned into digital rendering junkies – they even believe what they see on their screens! But, in fact, they're really just looking at the notes, not the music.

Understanding the Potential – and Limitations – of Technology

Digital tools are both pervasive and fascinating aspects of the design profession, but I think many people misunderstand what these tools can and cannot do. Digital design tools are based upon artificial intelligence technology, and they can connect to analog machines such as 3D printers or computer-controlled milling machines. Even for designs produced by these techniques, however, the modelmaker's analog interaction, both visual and manual, remain an important part of the process, enabling feedback, further experimentation, and improvements. In fact, the all-too-common practice of leaving the visual and physical execution of the design process solely in the digital domain has resulted in legions of dull and repetitive products, which have minimal functionality and are primary contributors to our escalating visual and physical pollution.

Of course, technology continually advances, and so we know that digital design tools will become better and more sophisticated over time. Author, scientist, and inventor Ray Kurzweil – who also gave us the voice synthesizer – coined the term "Singularity," which describes a point in time in which technology will be able to develop itself, without the need for human intervention. In his essay "The Law of Accelerating Returns," Kurzweil points out that technological change is progressing at an exponentially faster pace, so that in the twenty-first century, 100 years of progress will actually feel more like 20,000 years of progress. He writes, "Within a few decades, machine intelligence will surpass human intelligence, leading to The Singularity – technological change so rapid and profound it represents a rupture in the fabric of human history. [...] The implications include the merger of biological and non-biological intelligence, immortal software-based humans, and ultra-high levels of intelligence that expand outward in the universe at the speed of light." Kurzweil projects this (for me) nightmarish scenario to happen in the year 2045.[2] But, we aren't there yet.

The point for designers is that technical advances are providing all of us with extremely sophisticated tools that allow us within compressed time frames to simulate user scenarios, design multiple options, and ultimately produce highly creative products. However – and this is the big issue – with such radical technological advancements also come temptations and danger. The biggest temptation is to think and work with design templates, which means to start with something that you already have on file and just modify it. This method already has been established by large business consultancies such as McKinsey, where it is called a "process template:" just change the client name in the white paper and apply some minor modifications to a client's specific challenges. And we also see this method applied in the product world; many Original Design Manufacturers (ODMs) in Taiwan and China produce laptop computers and mobile devices for many brands, who then sell the products under their own label. The exterior designs of these products may vary microscopically from brand name to brand name, but all of them have the same interior components and feature sets. Pebbles on a beach have more individuality.

I fear that, without adequate education, competence, and ethics, more and more designers will rely on digital tools at the expense of their individual personalities, emotions, and creative instincts. Their imagination may become lost in the nearly limitless capabilities before them, and their physical interactions with their designs may be reduced to eyes on a screen and fingertips on a keyboard. If Ray Kurzweil's vision becomes reality, in a foreseeable future we should be able to display our thoughts directly on a screen and then use that data to create a three-dimensional print we can hold in our hands. This process may sound fascinating and attractive at first, but take a deep breath and think about it: Anything we think could turn into a physical manifestation? Most of it would be conceptual and visual trash – or worse. I remember a short animated film of a man who had a display on his head, which always illustrated his thoughts; that story progressed pretty quickly from a funny gag into shocking horror.

I would say that only through a productive and challenging meeting of critical intellects do valuable new thoughts become relevant. While digital tools might supplement these discussions, designers' intellect and collaborative skills are the most important tools they can bring to this process. At their best, digital design tools still are just tools, but with tremendous power and the capability of bringing the interaction between designer and machine closer to our imaginative thinking process. Nevertheless, the designer must engage the tools in a larger, collaborative creative process and not be driven by them to create faster and less relevant work.

Mastering All of the Tools of Design

If digital tools only work best in a balanced engagement of human hands and minds, then what creative input must the designer bring to the tools? All innovative sensory statements are defined by a creative process that turns an abstract idea into a material realization. How that process unfolds is an ongoing matter of discussion for artists and neurologists but, historically, most creative people have been able to classify their creative engagement into two stages – an initial surge of abstract inspiration followed by a period of practical work using the tools of their trade.

This same process also is common in other fields, such as musical composition. Wolfgang Amadeus Mozart once wrote to his father: "I must finish now because I've got to write at breakneck speed – everything's composed – but not written yet." Although Mozart was a genius, he still applied an iterative process of writing down musical sketches, starting with pieces of the melodies and drafting scores that described the instruments in the piece and how they should play the music. Finally, he wrote down – very beautifully, as you can see in the Mozart museums in Vienna and Salzburg – the master score, with all the notes, voices, and harmonies. Mozart, in other words, was the master of both his art and its tools.

Unlike physical materials, digital tools don't offer any resistance to manipulation – other than the technical difficulties involved in their use. As a result, they don't show the user his or her mistakes like, say, a carpentry tool might reveal a flawed skill when the user is shaping a block of wood or foam by hand. Such a resistance-free approach to creative shaping can be a huge handicap in the creative process because designers can be fooled into thinking they have created a world-class design when actually they have created nothing more than a pretty picture. In other words, the digital tool is powerful, but it also can only create an illusion of reality. The designer's judgment as to what is essential and relevant and what is not, therefore, must remain more important than the technology he or she uses. For example, virtually anyone can make a realistic image or video of anything visible to the naked eye. But if it lacks concept, this overwhelming amount of visual information doesn't serve much purpose and becomes little more than a meaningless waste of time, energy, and material – a new source of visual pollution. Copy-pasted imagery is rampant. And with all due respect to YouTube and its minions, original content in professional quality is as rare as a four-leaf clover.

Design is often considered a profession for individuals, but the real imaginative process – one that results not just in conceptual creativity but in true innovation and tangible results – comes when individual thoughts collide in group discussions and brainstorming. One of the tools we used at frog to initiate the creative process was called frogThink – a session of exploratory steps we initiated with our clients to get at the root of what needs to happen and why. As we have seen in this process, the magic of creativity comes from openness, non-definition, and a certain amount of ambiguity – none of which is a strength of computing. That's why freethinking and an interactive-creative dialogue are vital to the creative process. Heinrich von Kleist describes this back-and-forth verbal process best in his famous essay "Über die allmähliche Verfertigung der Gedanken beim Reden" [The Gradual Completion of Thought during Conversation].[3] "By talking with someone and exchanging points of view," he writes, "ideas gel and take shape."

TOOLS, TECHNOLOGY, AND CONTROL

As science advances, so must design. Designers must accept that technology is no longer limited to physical mechanics and electronics but has expanded into chemistry and biology – the decoding of the human genome by Craig Venter being just one example. For designers these advancements offer multifaceted challenges. The most important one is that of making any of these scientific advances humanistic; the second is to convert this expansion of knowledge and capabilities into new tools and opportunities, so that we humans define what is human, rather than having machines define the best machine. That comment might make skeptics smile, but we already have a "Terminator-like" scenario in the financial markets, where computer programs influence the dynamics of trading to the point that, after machines squeeze the last drop out of the stock, bond, and futures markets, they cause collapses when they all make a similar decision to get out of them. Tools must remain tools in the hands of humans, but humans must be capable of using them.

SONY WEGA FOAM MODEL, 1975

Taking Our Tools to the Next Level: Virtual Reality Simulations

One digital tool that has revolutionized the process of design and architecture is virtual reality (VR). VR is a viable and safe tool for product development and user simulation. The automobile industry uses it for automotive interior simulation, and it has long been valuable to the health-care industry where it is used for surgical simulations. However, because these kinds of applications are still mostly controlled by and designed for technocrats, the opportunities for the rest of us are what will make VR the next big thing – and perhaps provide us with the most humanistic tool we've ever experienced.

Jaron Lanier – Silicon Valley digital Renaissance man, computer scientist, composer, visual artist, author, and professor at University of California, Berkeley – invented publicly accessible VR about twenty-five years ago. I had the privilege to work with Jaron on the frox hypermedia system – a frog venture from the late 1980s – and I have rarely met a more radical and ethically committed person. Jaron expanded digital computer interactions and interfaces from line-based or icon-based screens to three-dimensional virtual spaces. Like a novelist researching characters for a book, Jaron is always making mental notes about how people react to situations so that he can create more realistic VR interactions. Once, during a trip to New York, I was walking down the street in Manhattan and happened upon Jaron sitting at a street-side table in front of a restaurant. I joined him, just as a huge rainstorm turned south Central Park into flooded chaos. Sitting under the restaurant's canopy we observed how people reacted – some in panic, others with ultimate cool. A well-dressed middle-aged man carrying an attaché case walked down the sidewalk completely soaked from his tie to his wingtips, acting as if there was no rain at all. Jaron smiled and said, "He's an alien – a true New Yorker."

Jaron's first company was VPL Research Inc. In 1999, Sun Microsystems acquired VPL's seminal portfolio of patents related to virtual reality and networked 3D graphics. The technology Jaron and his team developed at VPL Research Inc. was a defined virtual space comparable to a CAD space but with totally interactive "objects." He also created the first usable software platform architecture for immersive virtual reality applications as well as the first *avatars* or "representations of users" within digital systems. Jaron also created the dynamic user interface for a VR prototype that used a data glove and 3D head-mounted displays. The glove would track the movement of a user's arm, hand, and fingers while the helmet-like monitor would allow multiple users to move and act in an artificial three-dimensional space. The user could select from a menu of geometric elements (three-dimensional objects, such as cubes and spheres) by grabbing the objects and placing them in the virtual space, then change their size, color, and material. The user could also move within the space by walking or flying.

In addition to creating the foundation for VR, Jaron's work has influenced movies such as *Minority Report* and *Tron Legacy* and, of course, video games. In an interview with Java software developers way back in 1990 Jaron made this important point: "What most people are curious about," he said, " [...] isn't so much these industrial uses; rather, they want to experience some new level of cultural expression that arises out of virtual worlds. [... Ones] that you can change from the inside; a world that people use as a form of expression, in which they're creating things together. [...] They would make up little realities and visit each other's realities, or co-create them. And I think that level of activity would give rise to really, really wonderful new sorts of human relationships and experiences."

In my opinion, this concept of virtual reality opens up new opportunities for designers. It certainly advances the still primitive choices of Web 2.0, such as those we have seen in video games, websites like Second Life, and special effects for movies. And yet, we have a way to go before we realize the true potential of virtual reality. The technology still lacks the expressive power necessary to make virtual interactions between humans or between humans and objects relevant. Fortunately, Jaron's advice for our next generation of digital artists and designers also applies to creative strategists – the entrepreneurs of the future. "Technology offers convenience, but people are searching for meaning," he says. "Most digital developments offer neither, for the simple reason that the creators are confused about what a computer is. A skeptical appraisal of computers and the psychology of relating to them can break through the blandness barrier that confines most digital creations."

Shaping the Way Forward

Young designers will have all kinds of tools at their disposal. It will be their responsibility to resist the temptations of the shortcuts some of these tools – especially the digital tools – offer them. In light of the many challenges before them, I believe that emerging designers will have to improve their analog-shaping capabilities. Today, virtually all young designers and design students are digitally literate, having grown up in a digital environment, both at school and at home, in which using computer technologies for creative purposes has become second nature. Without proper mentoring and training, these students too often confuse noise (in this case, images) with the signal (a concept), and are in essence "silicon doodling."

I believe it's time to bring our design students back into the model shop. They have to learn the core skills necessary to be able to function as true professionals – skills such as typography, tension and resolution, shapes, balanced proportions, and the integration of esthetics versus ergonomics. The quick-and-easy approach has long-lasting and regrettable precedents in design. When Paul Hildinger, the model-shop master at the legendary design school HfG Ulm, for example, discovered the quick and easy process of gluing together polystyrene sheets to create design models, students happily stopped building models from clay and wood. But the new material didn't work well with complex, rounded, or large shapes, so suddenly, everyone was designing small, square boxes. By simplifying the modelmaking process, the HfG modelmakers had inadvertently unleashed a style that came to dominate nearly every new design. Add shades of gray along with a yellow, orange, or soft-green button and you have German design of the 1960s and 1970s.

The magical formula is to apply all tools the best way and where they make sense. The ability of computers to create bionic shapes defined by the creative application of mathematical formulas and non-resolvable chaos equations is one of the bright spots on design's horizon. Today, we can run samples off algorithms or programs, wait for the results, and then chose, modify, rerun, and so on. While the results of this work will always boil down to the human ability to judge and choose the final product, it doesn't hurt to have quality options from which to choose. And digital tools are great at the end of the process, as well, when it comes to document a design into the supply chain for production.

Finally, it's important to remember that there isn't an ideal way to design. Actually, the vast space it leaves us for individuality and exploration is the most beautiful aspect of our profession. Of course, all of us operate within professional environments and therefore must be aware of the budgetary pitfalls within this open landscape. Yes, digital tools may entice some designers into believing that they can save time and money by skipping the analog phase of their process, shunning the modelmakers as little more than an unnecessary cost. Ironically, however, the differences between these approaches are fading, as advanced user interface design increasingly eliminates the borders that separate physical and digital design processes. In the end, every design is physical because we humans interact by physical means. To illustrate this point, take a look at the work of frog's Colin Cole, who established his great "digital models" for our first SAP project in 1998 (his work is included in "Chapter 5: frog Classics of Strategic Designs").

For all of these reasons, I reestablished a small model shop during the six years I spent teaching at the University of Applied Art in Vienna, just as I will be installing a perfectly equipped model shop in my new Master Class studio in Shanghai. It fills me with great satisfaction that my Chinese partners understand the true value of a balanced convergence between digital and analog tools and processes in the work of design.

My message to new designers is simple, but important: We must use digital tools to the best of our abilities, but we also must avoid their curse of easy, early design successes and the complacency that can follow. This path inevitably leads into mediocrity the same way that excessive TV viewing kills creativity. And, without question, I believe that our creative excellence is vanishing, as our modern-day digital design software helps us pump out zillions of repetitive and bland products. Charlie Chaplin's "modern times" are entering the world of creative design – and this is a fate we, as designers and as members of society, cannot accept.

The true way of design is only achievable by combining all the tools and methods available to us: dreaming, thinking, collaborating, sketching, creative modelmaking, and experimental prototyping. All design tools – both analog and digital – connect our mind with the real world. They enable us to define shapes in such ways that even their limitations enhance our deep involvement, forcing us to hone our required skills into simple and true mastership. Yoda said, "Do or do not; don't try." We designers, on the other hand, must both "do and try."

1   See www.classicsonline.com/composerbio/Arthur__Kusterer/.

2   *The Law of Accelerating Returns* was written by Ray Kurzweil in March of 2001. Available in its entirety online at:
    www.kurzweilai.net/the-law-of-accelerating-returns.

3   Heinrich von Kleist, "On the Gradual Production of Thoughts Whilst Speaking," in: *Selected Writings*, edited and
    translated by David Constantine, Indianapolis: Hackett Publishing, 2004.

ALCATEL DIGITAL TELEPHONE, 1987. PHOTO: DIETMAR HENNEKA

5 FROG CLASSICS OF STRATEGIC DESIGN

"You can't connect the dots looking forward; you can only connect them looking backwards. So you have to trust that the dots will somehow connect in your future." STEVE JOBS

It always is difficult to prove an idea before it has been worked out and refined through real-world testing. This book is very much about the idea of design as a key driver in achieving great success in a balanced way, but many still consider design as a costly add-on – an inessential embellishment that adds time and expense to production. Well, when they treat design like that, that is what it becomes. I, however, never accepted this concept of "beautification," but always saw esthetics as just one means for a higher goal, that of providing humanistic products for people – objects or processes that are socially and ecologically balanced and that create happiness and build achievement. That's a challenging goal, but one that I have pursued for more than forty years. I believe that my success should also inspire others to undertake that pursuit.

Together with my peers at frog, I have worked on and helped to launch thousands of products. In the process, I have received hundreds of awards and my work is in the most prestigious art museums in the world. But more importantly, my work has improved the lives of millions of people who interact with it on a daily basis. As a company, frog has evolved from a one-person garage-based venture into a global organization with more than 1,000 employees. We have been able to achieve this growth by always trying to do the right thing, no matter how difficult, never looking for easy approval, and willingly accepting our share of scorn and ridicule along the way. I have never cared about my personal success, but I care deeply that my work creates success for all who use it. Creating that success is an ongoing goal for all work in Strategic Design.

To prove the relevance and value of Strategic Design, this chapter illustrates and explains some examples from my own professional and frog's history. These examples share one or more of the following characteristics, which define them as products of Strategic Design and have contributed to their success:

- Top management and/or entrepreneurs involved with these projects made design a core element of their strategy.

- The products and projects were/are highly influential on a global scale.

- The designs prove that even as technologies come and go, strong "brands by design" last.

- The designs have created or will create new markets and inspire innovative business models.

- They have enabled sustainable growth and achieved excellent financial results.

- They prove that customers care and pay for world-class products and experiences.

- They demonstrate that problems must be resolved by moving forward.

- They illustrate how businesses, such as frog, evolve by facing complex challenges.

It seems that we are living in an ever-accelerating world. We humans, however, have a long history, over which we have developed our genetic code, our behaviors, and our own speed – and human speed is slow. No matter what progressive technology will provide, we humans will advance at our own rate and use developments for our own purposes. The Internet has opened new channels of communication, which have enabled positive developments even as they helped amplify the dark side of man. I hope that the examples of Strategic Design in this chapter will help light a pathway that leads toward a more positive, human-centric future for technology and the ways we use it.

WEGA SYSTEM 3000, 1969, NEUE SAMMLUNG, MUNICH. PHOTO: DIETMAR HENNEKA

WEGA TV 3022, 1969, NEUE SAMMLUNG, MUNICH. PHOTO: DIETMAR HENNEKA

WEGA

"Reality leaves a lot to the imagination." JOHN LENNON

While studying to be a designer, I often passed a nice looking building in Stuttgart-Fellbach with a sign saying "WEGA RADIO." I knew that Wega had created a nice orange music system with Danish architect Verner Panton and that they also made cool television sets, which were sold by Braun. When I started to look into Wega's products at the IFA, I was amazed by the love of detail that their design exhibited but shocked by their bourgeois presentation. Wega's products lacked any type of cutting-edge expression of high tech. Their products looked more closely associated with bland chamber music than with the beefy splendor of Beethoven and rock 'n' roll.

So, in the spring of 1968 – one year before finishing my studies – I decided to become Wega's chief designer. I sent the company a letter explaining my intention, along with some photos of my work, which landed me an appointment with CEO Dieter Motte, grandson of the company's founder. Motte turned out to be a true believer in design. He liked my work and told me that he wasn't really happy with his designers. But, he also laughed a bit at my pitch for the top design slot and instead offered me an internship, explaining that he was impressed that I understood the technical side of consumer electronics.

I left Motte's office feeling a bit frustrated but decided to use some of his insights to upgrade the foldable radio I was designing as my entry in the very first Bundespreis Gute Form [German Federal Design Award]. Working during semester break, I actually forgot about the design contest, until one day I received a letter and a round-trip Pan Am ticket for Stuttgart-Berlin – I had won the award, and the German Secretary of Economy, Carl Schiller, was going to present it to me at a special ceremony.

Many design luminaries attended the event, including Dieter Motte. After the ceremony, he ran after me and said, "Sorry for my earlier rejection, but we really have to work together." I was excited but uncertain how this arrangement would work out. Then, one week later, I received a letter from Motte in which he outlined a very cool briefing. In it, he asked that I come up with a breakthrough design for a new line of Wega audio and television products – and he included a time plan and a fee proposal of DM8.000. At first I couldn't believe his offer was real. But after calling him from a public pay phone, I was on my way to Fellbach. After talking with his engineering and marketing executives, touring Wega's fine and flexible production facility, and discussing their showroom products and their competition, I proposed that we should focus on some radical approaches to design that would enable Wega to leap ahead of its chief competitors Braun and Brionvega. Motte also agreed that Wega would pay for an extra model so that I could design "my way" for each product. We shook hands, and my work began.

Stage One: Wega System 3000

In the late 1960s, the housings of consumer electronic products were made from either metal or wood, which made any sculpted shapes prohibitively expensive. We looked, therefore, at new technologies such as structural plastic foam and thin-wall metal injection as well as at electronic components we could modify for better usability. Our analysis of the user interaction also revealed lots of space for improvement. Instead of hiding flimsy buttons and levers behind obscure lids, we decided to make the physical experience "high touch." That decision required that we design our own levers, buttons, scales, and field-effect instruments, which was quite an investment for a company with revenues of around DM5 million. But Dieter Motte liked the uniqueness of this approach, and given the competitive strength of Braun and the up-and-coming Japanese contenders such as Sony, Sansuii, and Pioneer, he agreed to take on the extra investment.

When we developed the first radical concepts, Motte realized that Wega also needed an updated approach to communication and advertising, so he invited Germany's top advertising agencies to pitch their ideas. Initially reluctant due to the project's tiny budget, when the agencies saw the designs, they were in a frenzy to participate. Eventually, we convinced the powerhouse agency of Leonhardt & Kern (www.leonhardt-kern.de/) to put Wega on the map. They created an incredible campaign, which made the products – photographed by world-class photographers that included Peter Vogt and Dietmar Henneka and described by smart, targeted copy – the central star of the advertising pieces. The ads were all emotion. They began running two weeks before the 1971 IFA in Berlin, and when I arrived at the show, people were standing ten rows deep around the booth. Across the aisle, Braun's visitor space was empty. When a journalist asked how Wega compared to Braun, I said: "Braun is the Modern Jazz Quartet and Wega is the Beatles." (I still love Django by MJQ, but the White Album was way above it, in my opinion.) "But Braun isn't our competitor; our competition is the 95% of tasteless products out there."

We discovered that Wega appealed to non-design people as it did to celebrities and politicians. Wega's products became a common sight in the background of interviews with actors, soccer stars, or even members of parliament. Wega also won a public vote for Product of the Year in 1972, and the company also presented a Wega collection to a twelve-year old boy living in an orphanage. Wega went on to win design awards all over the world, and the company had grown tenfold by 1974 when it was acquired by Sony for its patents and innovative products, its access to the European market, and its design-based brand. Dieter Motte stayed on for one year after the sale, and when he parted we both had tears in our eyes. He said, "Take care of our culture; you will need access to Wega's top management in order to do that."

WEGA TV 3025, WEGA RECEIVER 3135, WEGA SPEAKER 3435, 1973, NEUE SAMMLUNG, MUNICH. PHOTO: DIETMAR HENNEKA

WEGA LAB ZERO, ULTRA HI-FI, 1976, NEUE SAMMLUNG, MUNICH. PHOTO: DIETMAR HENNEKA

Stage Two: Wega and Sony

In a funny twist of fate, Sony had offered me a position with them in November 1973, explaining that they wanted me to help bring a European feel to their products. Originally, Sony planned to build a new factory in Unna, Germany, but when the company realized that Wega's owners were in negotiations with Philips, Sony's former president and chairman Norio Ohga took the initiative and acquired Wega. He offered me a long-term contract with the charter, specifying that I would remain in charge of Wega's design and help Sony build a Japanese global brand, which would be second to none by "doing what only Sony can do."

This new arrangement meant that we at Wega could use our innovations in combination with Sony's technical background in electronic components, and we could also benefit from Sony's scale and superior manufacturing system. Norio Ohga's vision was that Wega would be the elite brand of the Sony family, but this turned out to be an emotional challenge for some of Sony's product teams. Fate was on our side for a while, however; our new CEO, Gerhard Schulmeyer, came from Braun, and Georg E. Huehne (audio) and Marcus Nurdin (video) took over product management. On Sony's side, Hideo Nakamura made miracles work, and Wega's own chief engineer, Rudolph Herzog, continued to excel. The products we created were seamless; we even defined the specifications of their electronic components, such as amplifying chips, FM-tuner sets, and speaker chassis.

Sony had a carefully developed audio design. Its television sets had achieved cult status, so we kept the design but retooled, modernized, and upgraded the products. We were the first who applied LEDs as field-effect and power indicators and, with LAB ZERO, we created the world's best FM tuner and discrete amplifiers for each speaker system in order to avoid any crossover. We also developed one revolutionary product, the music system Wega Concept 51K, which eventually was accepted into the permanent collection of the Museum of Modern Art in New York. We converted Sony's technology for mobile and wearable products into avant-garde concepts, such as the "frogpit" study and fashionable Walkman portable cassette players.

In spite of these successes, frog's time with Sony eventually fell under the shadow of internal politics. In 1978, Wega – with nearly DM1 billion in revenue – outperformed Sony, especially in the German market. In the aftermath of that market success, Sony's German managers – led by Jack Schmuckli – lobbied against CEO Gerhard Schulmeyer, who eventually left in frustration. Gerhard was a product fanatic, who always had seen design as Wega's centerpiece, and he knew how to spend money to make money. His loss was a dramatic blow to Wega.

The German Sony executives who took over after Gerhard's departure had a trader mentality. Aside from a few top executives in Tokyo, support for Wega weakened, signaling the beginning of the end: in 1980 Wega ceased to exist as a unique brand. Today's successful dual-branding strategies by companies such as Toyota with Lexus illustrate the absolute stupidity of Sony's decision to allow Wega's exit to happen.

WEGA SPEAKER 3440, 1970, NEUE SAMMLUNG, MUNICH. PHOTO: DIETMAR HENNEKA

WEGA HI-FI 3120, 1969, AND WEGA MODEL 42, 1975. PHOTO: DIETMAR HENNEKA

TOP: WEGA CONCEPT 51K, 1976, MUSEUM OF MODERN ART NEW YORK. BOTTOM: WEGA MODULAR TV, SYSTEM 5000, 1980.
PHOTOS: DIETMAR HENNEKA

TOP: WEGA DIGITAL AUDIO 5000, 1982. BOTTOM: WEGA HOME LAB 5000 WITH PERSONAL COMPUTER, PRINTER AND VIDEO, 1982.
PHOTOS: DIETMAR HENNEKA

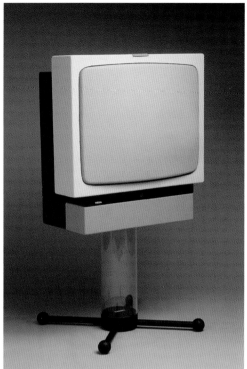

WEGA MODULAR TV AND VIDEO, 1976

WEGA DIGITAL MULTIMEDIA, 1987. PHOTO: DIETMAR HENNEKA

Stage Three: Sony

In 1974, working with Sony was an incredible learning experience. The company had near infinite technical abilities, but the designs, with the exception of some cool cassette recorders and portable radios, were just plain awful. Trinitron TVs were monsters, and Sony's hi-fi products were uber-technical metal boxes. The colors were flat or gunmetal gray with wooden veneer, and the designs were overloaded with unrelated shapes, strange edges, and decorative elements. Because Sony was very export oriented, the company's designers had looked for inspiration to middle-of-the-road brands such as Zenith in the United States and Grundig in Germany. Norio Ohga and Akio Morita, however, understood that bad taste isn't a base for sustainable success. Following the Japanese principle "Simple is Best" – where best means most difficult to achieve – we set out to create a new design language, which we ultimately called the "International Style" as an homage to the Bauhaus.

In contrast to the design's we had created for Wega, shapes in the new style were much more subdued. Because most products changed every year, we established overriding principles, rules, and a process for implementation. We designers were located on the top management floor of Sony's Shibaura headquarters. When a product went into implementation, we designers went to the factories – for example, to Osaki, where the company manufactured its Trinitron TVs – and worked with their engineers, but we kept the project centered at company headquarters.

With my Sony partner and friend Aki Amanuma, we created design templates, which included basic technical component layouts drawn on vellum; whenever a new product was being planned, the product team would receive a new transparent vellum copy so they could start work with the most accurate information. For a totally new product, such as the Walkman, we used the same process but created magnified templates in 2:1 scale.

The next step was to work with Sony's suppliers. Inspired by the tooling processes at Munekata, we created the concept of modular tooling, which enabled us to design products with thinner walls and, most importantly, with dramatically shorter turnaround times due to more toolmakers being able to work on smaller tools. Our concept enabled Sony to decide in the first days of the new year which product they would launch in April. The entirely new frogline TV system with various design elements and two screen sizes, for example, just took five months from technology analysis, market intelligence, and briefing to launch.

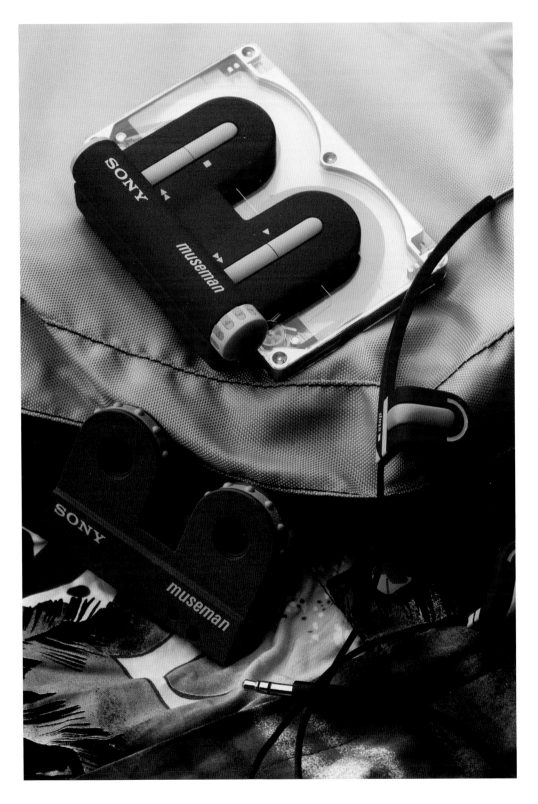

SONY WALKMAN STUDY, 1984 (BASED UPON DIPLOMA PROJECT BY JOERG RATZLAFF). PHOTO: VICTOR GOICO

TOP LEFT: SONY CAMCORDER, 1983. TOP RIGHT: SONY PORTABLE TRINITRON, 1975. BOTTOM: SONY BETAMAX (FIRST FRONT LOADING VCR)

SONY MODULAR TRINITRON, FROGLINE 3 AND FROGLINE 1, 1979. PHOTOS: VICTOR GOICO AND DIETMAR HENNEKA

TOP: SONY TRINITRON FORUM SERIES, 1985. BOTTOM: SONY BLACK TRINITRON, 1985. PHOTOS: DIETMAR HENNEKA

From a historic point of view, many of Sony's firsts were with technologies that have subsequently been phased out, such as Trinitron CRTs, the Betamax VCR – we designed the world's first compact, front-loading machine – the Walkman, and CD players, just to name a few. Our intense working relationship lasted until about 1986, after which frog worked with Sony on a project-by-project basis. After the founders Masaru Ibuka and Akio Morita left the company, and after Norio Ohga's death, the company lost its edge. In 2012, it entered its fourth year of financial trouble. In my view, Sony needs a top-level, design-centric strategy that extends across outside technology platforms (like Microsoft and Google) so it can provide convergent and seductive products again. The future of branding is in the digital experience domain.

SONY TRINITRON PORTABLE, 1977.

COMPUTER TECHNIK MUELLER (CTM)

"I do not fear computers; I fear the lack of them." ISAAC ASIMOV

Helmut Henssler, one of my high-school band members, studied computer science and became a programmer at a spin-off from Nixdorf called Computer Technik Mueller (CTM), named after its founders, husband-and-wife team Otto and Ilse Mueller. When the Mueller's company started to design a small-size "mid-class" computer for business administration in 1972, Helmut convinced them to visit me in my newly equipped garage shop. They looked at my work, loved the Wega stuff we were working on, and then said, "Let's begin!" Otto Mueller explained the layout and the usage scenarios for the new computer, and the peripherals CTM would use from companies such as Shugart and other Silicon Valley companies. Those peripherals included huge hard disks, tape storage, punch card readers and a printer from Daisy, and a 16-inch by 16-inch magnetic memory board with 64KB of memory. Mueller also pointed out that his machine would have the first client-server architecture in Europe.

Other than Nixdorf, which had a very hard-edge sheet-metal design, there was little competition for CTM. American companies such as IBM or Burroughs were counting on the ongoing popularity of refrigerator-sized machines. We agreed that the CTM machine should fit well in an office environment, and we played around with some quick models. Over lunch, we decided that there would be three units, with a standing box for the central processing unit (CPU), a table-like unit with keyboard and printer for the user, and a slim peripheral box for optional functions that would rest on the floor. Within two weeks the first sketches were ready, and the CTM people – working on the ground floor of a rented house where the Muellers lived upstairs – really loved them. We designed a structure to be made of steel tubing enclosed by thermo-formed plastic panels produced by a furniture supply company called Duratherm. I built the first four units in my garage, and we took them straight away to the Hannover CeBit Fair, one of the world's largest IT trade shows, in May of 1973. Our booth at CeBit was tiny, but traffic was heavy and the CTM 70 System became a success. Sales of machines quickly gave birth to a multimillion business.

As the company grew, so did its capital needs. In 1976, the Muellers sold the majority of their business to Diehl Data Systems, which also owned the Triumph company. With more financial muscle, we designed the second CTM series in structural foam (similar to the Wega televisions) and added visual screens for displaying output. In 1978, we designed the first freestanding desktop terminal with an integrated, tilting screen. CTM became a serious player in the German European market.

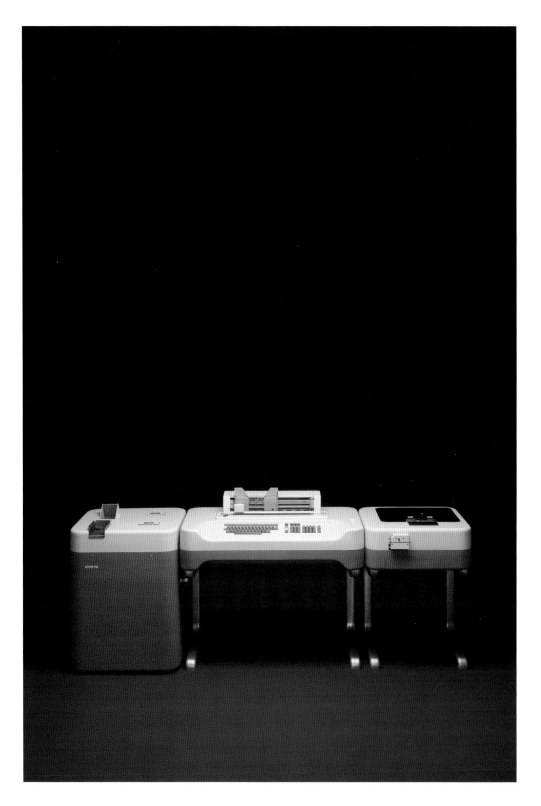

CTM 70, 1972. PHOTO: DIETMAR HENNEKA

frog's relationship with CTM ended when I negotiated a contract with Apple. When my partner Georg Spreng, who had worked on the CTM account for years, decided to leave our agency, I asked him to take the account with him. This was easier for me as Otto and Ilse Mueller had already left the company and started Hyperstone, which developed micro controllers for portable devices and worked closely with Hitachi. In 1992, Ilse Mueller was awarded the Rudolf Eberle Award of the state of Baden-Wuerttemberg, as she was the first female top executive and entrepreneur in Germany.

For me, the CTM experience was fun, and its steep learning curve prepared me for the Apple challenge. CTM's designs were highly influential, won multiple design awards, and were copied worldwide – all the way to Silicon Valley. In the Japanese way of thinking, this was a big compliment.

CTM 70-2, 1976. PHOTO: GERD SPRENG

ESSLINGER DESIGN CLIENTS:

CBOX SYSTEM AG, Chur, Schweiz
CTM GMBH, Konstanz
HÄFELE KG, Nagold
HANSGROHE KG, Schiltach
CHRISTIAN HOLZAPFEL GMBH, Horb
HILLEBRAND LEUCHTEN, Arnsberg
INDUSCO INC., Auburn Heights, Michigan, U.S.A.
INTERLÜBKE, Rheda-Wiedenbrück
FRANZ KALDEWEI GMBH & CO, Ahlen
KALTENBACH & VOIGT, Biberach
KAVO-ITALIA S.P.A., Genova-Nervi, Italia
KEUCO PAUL KEUNE & CO, Hemer
KÖNIG + NEURATH, Karben
MESSMA-KELCH GMBH, Schorndorf
METRONIC ELECTRONIC GMBH, Rottweil
ROSENTHAL EINRICHTUNG KG, Selb
SONY CORPORATION, Tokyo, Japan
TEXAS INSTRUMENTS, Villeneuve-Loubet, France
VEBA-GLAS AG, Essen
VOLKSWAGENWERK AG, Wolfsburg
LOUIS VUITTON, Paris, France
WEGA ELEKTRONIK GMBH, Köln_

CTM 70 NETWORKSTATION. PHOTO: GERD SPRENG

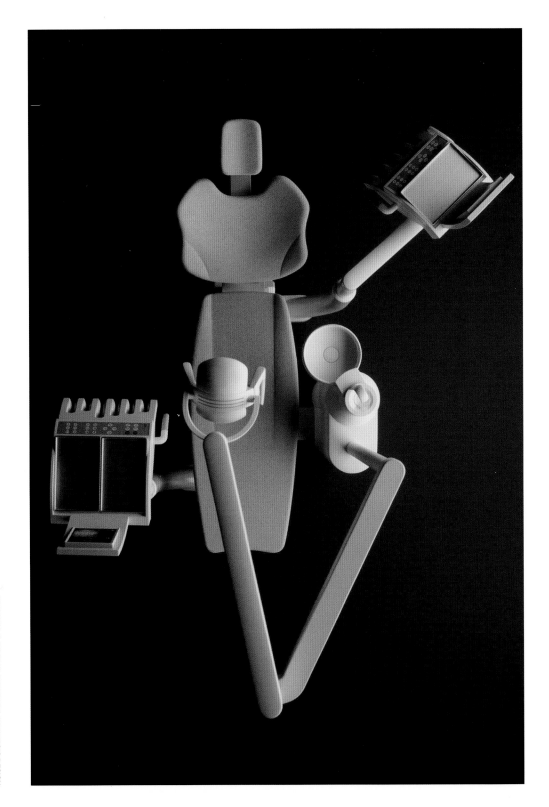

KAVO ESPETICA, 1050. PHOTO: DIETMAR HENNEKA

KALTENBACH & VOIGT (KAVO)

"I don't pay good wages because I have a lot of money; I have a lot of money because I pay good wages." ROBERT BOSCH

Just when the first Wega products had been launched, I got a call from Martin Saupe, chief technology officer at KaVo in Biberach, a German, family-owned company in the dental systems business, who had co-invented air-turbine drills and advanced electric dental instruments. Martin asked me for a proposal for a new dental light, and it soon became obvious that he had previous experience with designers – which wasn't entirely good news. When we toured the factory, I was impressed by the quality of the machinery, the processes, and the people. When we toured the showroom and the Research and Development (R&D) department, however, I was shocked by the company's brutal designs, both in the market and under development.

My aunt Wilhelmine Esslinger was a dentist, so I knew about the physical and emotional challenges for dentists. Dental visits aren't fun for anyone, but patients are there only for brief periods of time while the dentist is there throughout the entire workday. Driving home, I decided that we would create a holistic concept for an entire dental system that would be more ergonomic and emotionally appealing for dentist and patient alike.

So we set to work in frog's garage; I sketched, built small models, and shaped 1:1 foam studies. After a week, I was back on my way to Biberach, with a 1:1 foam model of the treatment element and 1:5 models of the system. I also had a nice slide show to illustrate the designs in full scale. Martin Saupe liked the work but was non-committal. When he opened a closet in his office, I immediately understood the reason behind his lack of enthusiasm. We were looking at a veritable design cemetery, about twenty small-scale models of dental units that would never be produced. I explained to Saupe that design must define the strategy of a company, and I told him that I would like to talk to the CEO – a request I felt justified in making, after having spent the previous seven days and nights working with my partners on designs for his company. Saupe called Karl Kaltenbach, the CEO and son of the company's founder, who was in a meeting with his chief financial officer. The two gave me "ten minutes."

After viewing the first of my slides, Mr. Kaltenbach jumped up and said, "This is what I always wanted." When he saw the models, he instructed Martin Saupe to develop the design concepts into a new product line of dental systems. We agreed on a royalty of 1% on net sales for frog and a front-fee of DM40.000. When work began, it was incredibly fun to see the honest excitement of the company's developers and marketing people, who added their ideas. The production people also were huge supporters. The result was the first Estetica 1040 system, which went on to become a best seller, making KaVo a global leader in dental systems and dental chairs.

Sales volumes were about twenty times more than originally estimated, so the royalty fees became frog's biggest financial success in terms of absolute profits, even in comparison with the fees we were to receive from Sony, Vuitton, and Apple. frog reinvested some of the money into basic research and blue sky concepts, which again resulted in more successful products, such as a female-inspired instrument design in medical plastic for KaVo. After Martin Saupe left KaVo, Heiner Zinser became CTO, and under his leadership we created what I still consider the best overall product line-up in the dental industry. The CEOs Karl Kaltenbach and Juergen Hoffmeister (from the second owner-family) always took great interest in our work and came to see design as the main source for the company's success.

When the family decided to sell KaVo to the Danahaer Corporation in 2004, Heiner Zinser left and acquired a small specialty company that supplied high-tech mechanical components to large industrial companies. With the company's switch to American management principles, frog also was phased out of its work with KaVo; design wasn't at the top anymore and became relegated to product groups.

I think it's important to mention that frog's typewritten contract with KaVo from 1971 was just half a page long. When people work together with positive energy and trust, and actually enjoy the risks of innovation, success is a natural result. I learned so much by working with the KaVo people, and for that, I will be forever grateful.

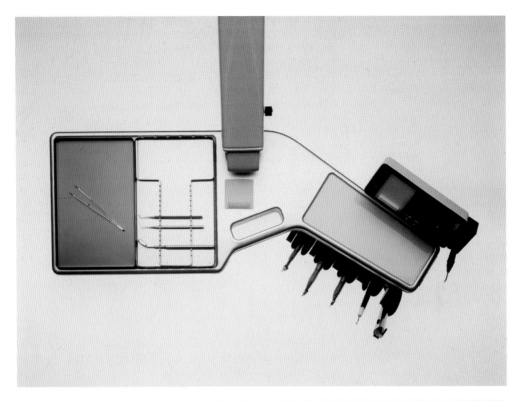

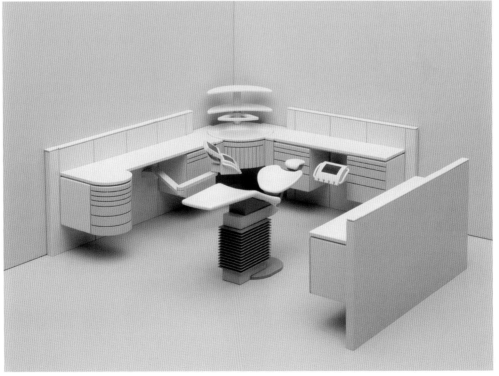

TOP: KAVO ESTETICA 1040, 1971. BOTTOM: KAVO ENVIRONMENT STUDY, 1999. PHOTOS: DIETMAR HENNEKA

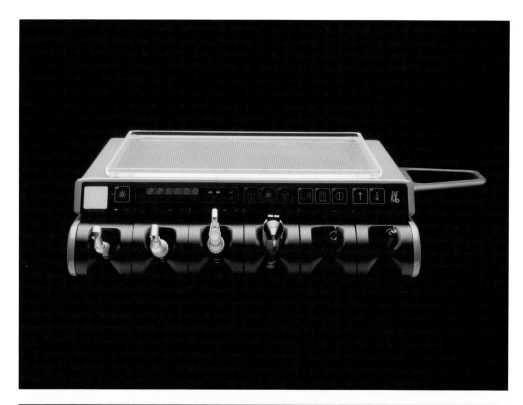

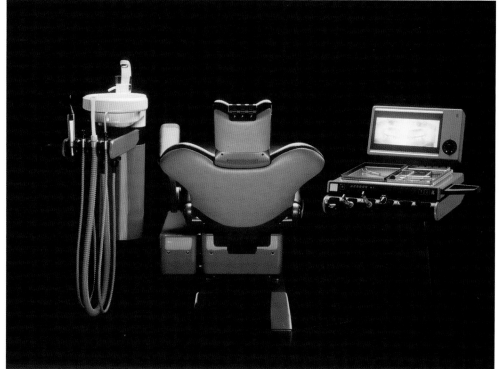

KAVO REGIE DENTAL SYSTEM, 1978. PHOTO: DIETMAR HENNEKA

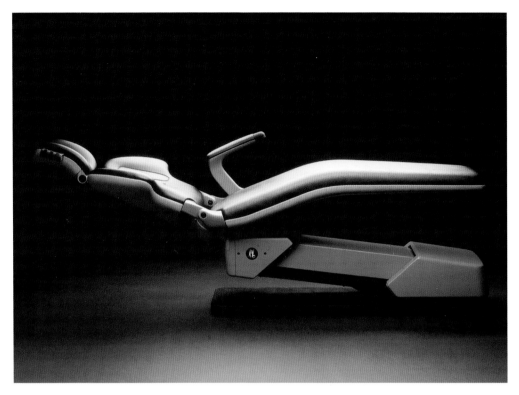

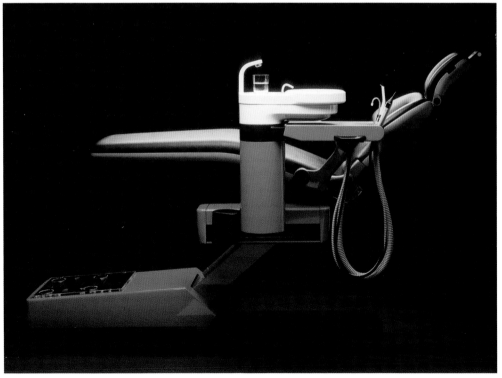

KAVO REGIE AND SIESTA CHAIR, 1978. PHOTO: DIETMAR HENNEKA

TOP: KAVO DENTAL LIGHT, 1976. BOTTOM: KAVO ESTETICA-3 DENTAL SYSTEM, 1993. PHOTOS: DIETMAR HENNEKA

TOP: KAVO SPYDER, BIONIC STUDIES. BOTTOM: KAVO KAPPA, DENTAL SYSTEM

HANSGROHE AND VILLEROY & BOCH

"Hollywood is like Picasso's bathroom." CANDICE BERGEN

Bathrooms are intimate and very private places surrounded by a lot of taboos. It became frog's task to make the bathroom space more appealing and livable when, in 1972, we agreed to work with Hansgrohe, a manufacturer of showers and faucets, and in 1979, with Villeroy & Boch, manufacturers of sinks, toilets, bathtubs, furniture, and tiles. The experiences these companies provide with their products are very basic and center upon water, cosmetics, and light — factors that influenced the designs frog created for these clients.

hansgrohe

hansgrohe is located in my father's birth town, Schiltach, in the heart of Black Forest. The then CEO, Klaus Grohe — son of the founder — called me in early 1972, to say that he had a design problem and, as I was basically a "local," he would like to come by and talk to me about it. One hour later he arrived with two of his engineers, who showed me a prototype of a handheld shower with a rotating head that produced three kinds of water sprays: regular, oxygen soft, and massage. The company's idea was to use the new device to compete with Water Pic's massage shower head. But, the design Klaus and his team showed me didn't look like anything you would want to get close to your naked body, and the prototype was made of melamine, which made it as heavy as a rock.

We at frog went into our garage, and within two hours we had some cool concepts — however some looked like male genitals, which wasn't exactly what was required. The big issues we faced in developing the design weren't just related to the way the showerhead looked but also to its technology. Showerheads are exposed to varying levels and types of chemical compounds in water around the world, and some of them can quite aggressively erode materials and destroy or block a showerhead's rotating parts. We also had to design the showerhead to give the maximum shower effect from the minimal amount of water. Because we were designing a three-dimensional object, we also needed to look for some semi-robotic equipment that could handle the production. Human labor was way too expensive, so we wanted to limit it to quality control and final packaging. Our task, in other words, was to design the shower for optimized production as well as for visual semantics, which were emotional and erotic — but not obscene.

Working with hansgrohe engineers, we found a small company, which took existing injection-molding machines and combined them with custom-made assembly devices. For our project, the company went one step further and combined an off-the-shelf machine with a very complex robotic assembler. The final machine enabled hansgrohe to produce the nine plastic parts of the shower head — housing in any color and the water jets in black — and

HANSGROHE TRIBEL SHOWER HEAD, 1972. PHOTO: DIETMAR HENNEKA

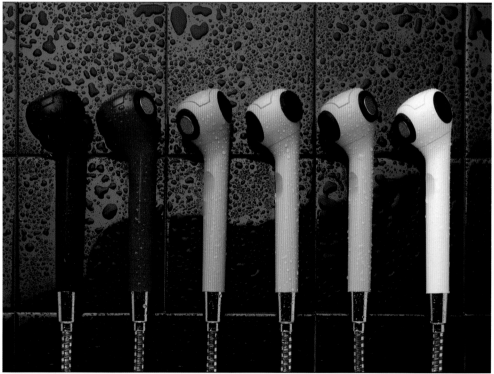

☂ TOP: HANSGROHE JUNIOR FAUCETS, 1981. BOTTOM: HANSGROHE TRIBEL SHOWER HEAD, 1972. PHOTOS: DIETMAR HENNEKA

immediately assemble them into a complete subset, which was then connected to the handle by hand. The machines produce the handle at the same time from the same material, so the tolerances of polymerization would be perfect. The code name actually survived and hansgrohe called the handheld shower "Tribel," which is Alemannic German slang for a rotating device.

The results were sensational. The new device was more than 50% less expensive to produce than a regular handheld shower, with a much better retail price. The design certainly was radical, but that was its major strength; it had no direct competition and its sales exceeded all expectations. To date, more than 25 million Tribel shower heads are in use. Over the years, hansgrohe became a global leader in bathroom lifestyle. My former partner Andreas Haug still works for them, along with Philippe Starck.

Villeroy & Boch (V&B)

Villeroy & Boch – the family still holds the majority of shares – has roots that go back 250 years to the time when Nicolas Villeroy and François Boch founded the company for ceramic ware in the French-German border area. After frog had made a name through its work for Hansgrohe, Kaldewei, and other bathroom fixture companies, Wolf Schmidt, a member of V&B's executive board, asked us for new concepts for the "bath as a living room." We created several lines of ceramic sinks, toilets, bathtubs, furniture, and tiles. Of these, the Magnum line became the biggest success, and V&B considered the Zenith line its undisputed design leader.

With Zenith, frog applied a new production technology, which gave us much more freedom: Instead of cutting clay molds with gypsum tooling, where the water gets sucked out and a hollow ceramic shape remains, we used a new method of slow injection molding to create a solid form. This allowed for more precise shapes, better transitions, and overall better control of the ceramic's shrinking factor during firing. We also designed sinks with combined materials, and the "reach" of the ceramic material was much more flexible, as the Zenith sinks shows. Naturally, our new designs required V&B to create a new communication and advertising campaign, which used Helmut Newton as the photographer. Working with that aspect of this product's development and launch was a sensational experience by itself. Helmut Newton actually took the name "Magnum" as an inspiration: in one of his shots, a lady holds a .44 Magnum with which she just has shot her lover's husband....

VILLEROY & BOCH SINK, 1987. PHOTO: DIETMAR HENNEKA

LOUIS VUITTON SEMISOFT, 1982. PHOTO: VICTOR GOICO

LOUIS VUITTON

"Fashion fades, only style remains the same." COCO CHANEL

Our work for Louis Vuitton, which began in 1976, isn't so visible in the company's product lines today – I think the stark colors we championed are the sole survivors. There's a reason for that, of course. Most of our designs were experimental, ideas that we created as we searched for a style concept that would transform Vuitton's image from that of a traditional French luggage maker (malletier) into a unique, luxury brand. What we discovered, oddly enough, was that if "nothing never matches" within a product line but consistently radiates high quality and a strong brand story, everything matches within that line – and among all of the brand's product lines, too. So, in our work with Vuitton, frog never tried to follow any trend, be it in lifestyles, fashion, or art.

We also researched new materials, such as Kevlar, and new production technologies, including pattern-oriented laser cutting. As I describe in a fine line, I worked directly with Vuitton CEO Henri Racamier and Philippe Legrand, who later joined frog as well. Philippe, a designer himself, was a brilliant project manager. Here, I want to show three projects, which we developed over ten years.

Challenge

This project reflected all of our initial research about Vuitton. It ended up as a top-of-the-line luggage series, made from Kevlar sheets and manufactured by processes pioneered by the French aircraft industry. The suitcases were indestructible – which was, however, a problem because minor repairs took a huge effort. The nicest detail of this line was its custom lock with special keys and handmade coding of the key patterns.

SemiSoft

This project built on Vuitton's successful semi-soft line of luggage and was made from plywood frames with soft covers. We, again, used a Kevlar fabric and connected the soft covers via a structural foam frame, which also served as a buffer. We used the visual treatment of the corners and the custom designed locks and zippers in other Vuitton products, such as bags.

LOUIS VUITTON CHALLENGE, STUDIES, 1976

LOUIS VUITTON CHALLENGE, 1976. PHOTO: DIETMAR HENNEKA

⁝ LOUIS VUITTON VOYAGER, 1985

Voyager

This was a truly innovative project in which a central frame could be housed in various combinations of optional side covers and shells, and accessories such as casters and handles could be mounted into the frame wherever users would like them. We designed the interior to make it easy for the traveler to access the luggage contents with a minimum of unfolding or disturbing their order. We used a shape that tested as "superior" in the International Air Transport Association test drum, and colors that reflected the new style of the products co-branded by Louis Vuitton Cup (America's Cup qualification races).

Ironically, the product was ready for production when Louis Vuitton/ Moet Hennessy (LVMH) was taken over by Bernard Arnault, who decided to build LVMH into a luxury empire through the acquisition of Dior and other fashion brands. However, he also expanded Vuitton's original strategy of creating brand shops in the tradition of the first store at Avenue Marceau in Paris.

APPLE IIC, 1983, WHITNEY MUSEUM OF AMERICAN ART, NEW YORK. PHOTO: VICTOR GOICO

APPLE

"I want Apple's design not just to be the best in the computer industry but to be the very best in the entire world." STEVE JOBS (1982)

In 1982, Apple was in its sixth year of existence, and Steve Jobs, Apple's cofounder and Chairman, was twenty-eight years old. Steve, intuitive and fanatical about great design, realized that the company was in crisis. With the exception of the aging Apple IIe, the company's products were failing against IBM's PCs. And they all were ugly, especially the Apple III and soon-to-be-released Apple Lisa. The company's previous CEO, Michael Scott, had created different "business divisions" for each product line, including accessories such as monitors and memory-drives. Each division had its own head of design and developed its product line any way it wanted to. As a result, Apple's products shared little in the way of a common design language or overall synthesis. In essence, bad design was both the symptom and a contributing cause of Apple's corporate disease. Steve's desire to end this disjointed approach gave birth to a strategic design project that would revolutionize Apple's brand and product lines, change the trajectory of the company's future, and eventually redefine the way the world thinks about and uses consumer electronics and communication technologies.

The idea for the project was inspired by the work of the Richardson Smith design agency (later acquired by Fitch) for Xerox in which the designers collaborated with multiple divisions within Xerox to create a single high-level "design language" that the company could implement throughout its organization. Jerry Manock, the designer of the Apple II and head of design in Apple's Macintosh division, and Rob Gemmell, head of design in the Apple II division, created a plan in which they would invite global designers to Apple headquarters and, after interviewing all of them, stage a competition between the two top candidates. Apple would choose a final winner and then use that design as the framework for its new design language. No one knew at that time, however, that we were in the process of transforming Apple into a company whose design-based strategy and innovation-over-money approach would make it a global success.

Snow White Meets frog

Early in 1982 I met with Steve Jobs in Cupertino, California. In comparison to Sony's well-established (and well-funded) Design and Product Planning Center and R&D departments, Apple was just a start-up. But meeting Steve Jobs was a life-changing and career-transforming event. We began by talking about my work – Steve was especially taken by frog's designs for Sony, all of which had become globally successful products. Then, he explained what he wanted Apple to achieve with its design: "We want to sell one million plus Macs" – more than ten times the number of Apple II computers the company had shipped. I explained that great design alone wouldn't get him to that number.

⌃ TOP: APPLE SNOW WHITE 1, "SONY STYLE," 1982. BOTTOM: APPLE SNOW WHITE 2, "AMERICANA," 1982

TOP: APPLE SNOW WHITE 1, "WORKBENCH," 1982. BOTTOM: APPLE SNOW WHITE 2, "APPLE II," 1982

TOP: APPLE SNOW WHITE 1, "SLATE," 1982. BOTTOM: APPLE SNOW WHITE 2, "MACINTOSH STUDIES," 1982

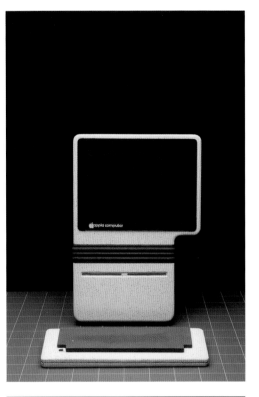

TOP: APPLE SNOW WHITE 2, "MACINTOSH STUDIES," 1982. BOTTOM: APPLE SNOW WHITE 2, "MACBOOK," 1982

I offered Steve a number of proposals for meeting his goal. First, Apple would need totally different systems for engineering, third-party partnerships, manufacturing and logistics as well as design. I also proposed that Apple could compensate for its lack of world-class mechanical engineering by using Sony, Canon, Samsung, and other electronic consumer companies in Asia as development and manufacturing partners. Most importantly, I explained, Apple needed one design team that directly reported to him, and that design had to be involved far ahead of any actual product development in Apple's strategic planning. This system would enable Apple to project new technologies and consumer interactions for years ahead, which would avoid short-sighted ad-hoc developments.

frog had yet to win the competition, but Steve agreed with my ideas about his company. He promised that when the competition was over, design would move up in Apple's hierarchy and report directly to him. He also promised that if frog won the competition and I became a consultant to Apple, he would name me the company's corporate manager of design – a promise Steve went on to keep. Naturally, this promise was both motivating and inspiring, but I knew it upped the ante of the challenge I was facing. Neither Apple's division managers nor its designers would accept this restructuring without a fight. Steve said, "That's your task, now." And so, my work began.

Phase One: Searching for the Design DNA

Each design project starts with research to discover what's out there and to explore the possibilities of what could be, but isn't yet. When we launched the Snow White project, computers offered little in the way of design, but their technologies were advancing rapidly. Performance was growing, physical sizes were shrinking, and – thanks to "professional" pricing versus "consumer" pricing – profit margins were still healthy. Personal computers were in their infancy, and Apple had an edge with its use of Xerox Parc's bitmap user interface, which appealed to everybody, not just professional computer users. However, most of Apple's products were primitive in their mechanical design, and their manufacturing costs were absurd. By leveraging the advanced electronics production methods being used in Germany or Japan, I projected that we could lower housing costs by 70 to 90%. So, we decided to use the same technically radical design approach for Apple's products that we used for Sony's. In fact, we could make the designs even better and more ecologically sound by using a case-production technique that resulted in a world-class, high-quality surface that didn't require paint.

We had no clear demographic market data, as there was no true precedent for our new approach in the technical market. We had to create a new paradigm for computers as the first industrial, mass-produced form of artificial intelligence for use by general consumers. As I explored ideas for designing the "face" of this new form, I looked at history, in particular Native American mythology, because I thought that Apple's design should be rooted in the West Coast's past. This search lead us to the geometric sand paintings of the Navajo, then on to the art of the Aztecs, whose carved stone reliefs often resembled astronauts. Those images inspired us to design Apple's computers to look like little people and to transform the display screen into a face.

After many talks with Steve and other Apple executives, we determined three directions for further exploration:

- Concept 1 was defined by "what Sony would do if it built computers." I didn't like this idea, as it could create conflicts with Sony, but Steve insisted. He felt that Sony's simple, cool design language should be a good benchmark, and Sony was the current pacesetter in making high-tech consumer products smarter, smaller, and more portable.

- Concept 2 would express "Americana," reconnecting high-tech design with classical American design statements, especially Raymond Loewy's streamlined designs for Studebaker and other automotive clients, the Electrolux line of household appliances, Gestetner's office products, and (naturally) the Coke bottle.

- Concept 3 was left to me. It could be as radical as possible – and that made it the best kind of challenge. Concept A and B were well-founded in proven statements, so Concept C was my ticket for a voyage toward a mysterious destination. It also would become the winner.

Working on Concept 1 was easy because I "knew" Sony's design strategy. I didn't copy that strategy but used it rather as a starting point as I conceptualized a system of modular elements that would allow Apple to create many different products with fewer parts. But this concept had drawbacks: the assembly costs were high and the result simply wasn't cool enough. Clearly, creating nice shapes was only one aspect of the challenge we were facing.

Working on Concept 2 was great in the beginning, and we got quick results. But the concept's retro-futuristic approach was not innovative enough. We designed some beautiful shapes but with little conceptual content, and the entire concept simply didn't express the new semantics we were aiming for. I began to wonder whether the streamline design was too young to feel historic. I understood the attraction of the concept; people are quick to reject any true innovation and so always want to find something familiar in anything new. Nevertheless, the idea behind Concept 2 simply didn't work, and so we moved on.

Concept 3 offered a golden opportunity to create and visualize a revolution – and I got stuck. Due to my work for electronics companies such as Wega and Sony, I knew that I was going to have to stretch myself beyond my comfort level. Looking at Mario Bellini's and Ettore Sottsass's work for Olivetti didn't help: their designs were too expressive, and their elitist style wouldn't appeal to the mass audience we were targeting. Steve Jobs liked Dieter Rams's design for Braun, and I admired Dieter's understated approach to design, but I found it a bit too exclusive

TOP: APPLE SNOW WHITE 1, "LISA WORKSTATION," 1982. BOTTOM: APPLE SNOW WHITE 2, "FLAT SCREEN WORKSTATION," 1982

TOP: APPLE SNOW WHITE 2, "MAC & APPLE II," 1982. BOTTOM: APPLE SNOW WHITE 2, "WORKBENCH & MUSIC MAC," 1982

TOP: APPLE SNOW WHITE 1, "MODULAR MAC," 1982. BOTTOM: APPLE SNOW WHITE 2, "TABLET MAC," 1982

APPLE IIC, 1983

TOP: APPLE SNOW WHITE 3, "APPLE II," 1984. BOTTOM: APPLE SNOW WHITE 3, "MACBOOK," 1984

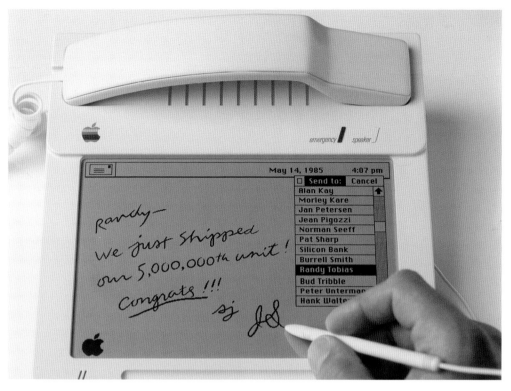

May 14, 1985   4:07 pm

☐ Send to: Cancel

Alan Kay
Morley Kare
Jan Petersen
Jean Pigozzi
Norman Seeff
Pat Sharp
Silicon Bank
Burrell Smith
Randy Tobias
Bud Tribble
Peter Unterman
Hank Walter

randy—
We just shipped
our 5,000,000th unit!
Congrats !!!
                sj   JS

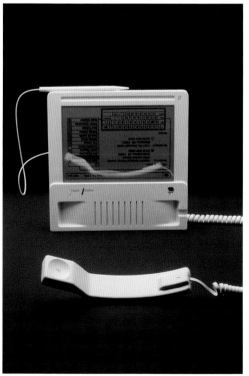

APPLE SNOW WHITE 3, "MACPHONE," 1984

for the time. In fact, Apple wasn't a "computer company." Apple was about a new paradigm: artificial intelligence products for consumers – children, seniors, and everybody in between. My past work didn't inform this project.

What helped me to catch the right spirit was the time I spent hanging out with programmers like Andy Hertzfeld and Bill Atkinson. They talked of software almost poetically while their screens just showed lines of abstract-looking code. Those lines became a key inspiration for my work. The second inspiration was Bill's prediction that all bulky, physical technology, from monitors to CPU boxes, would eventually give way to elegant "slates." So the visual DNA for Concept 3 was "lines and slates," which also meant "no angles," just transitions. And the color had to be white – or as white as possible.

Phase 2: The Snow White Design Language

We shipped the first set of models to California, and after discussions with all of Apple's teams, we agreed that Concept 3 "lines, slates, and no angles" – a design language we would name "Snow White" – was the way to go. We also created a brief description of the concept's signature elements and visual treatments:

- Slates with a zero-draft character shape, minimal surface texture, no paint, minimal transitional angles when needed (monitors), and volumes/sizes as small as possible.

- Symmetry, whenever possible.

- Thin lines from front to rear, 2 mm wide, 2 mm deep, grid 10 mm, recessed at front = 30 mm, recessed at rear = 4-10mm.

- Color = white, soft olive gray as a contrast [in late 1984 the lone color would become a light gray called "platinum"].

- Branding = solitary Apple logo badge with seamless inlay into the design. Product naming in tampon-print, dark gray. Typestyle: Adrian Frutiger's Univers condensed italic and Garamond condensed.

After discussing the technology and possible trends with Apple's managers and engineers, Bill Atkinson challenged me to include projections about future developments like flat screens, touch interfaces, and the merging of telephones into computers. Back in Germany, frog went to work again, and I used Bill's input to go beyond the basic Snow White project requirements and conceptualize possible new future products as well. Bill even combined a European vacation with a work session in our Black Forest studio. The results were probably the world's first concept of a wireless mobile flip-phone, a touch-pad computer, and a laptop computer with a screen as large as a keyboard and touch interface. When Steve presented the laptop Mac model to the Mac team during the final recess in 1983 as "the next Macintosh we will build," they gasped in disbelief. But, I knew this work was extremely important. After more than a decade in electronic design, I had seen many technologies and companies come and go, and I was sure that Apple needed a design strategy that went beyond computer boxes, keyboards, mice, and monitors.

For the final presentation, we turned a room at Apple's Mariani building into a showroom. Even by today's standards, it was one of the best presentations I can remember. Steve Jobs was really excited and so were Apple's board members, who also had the treat of viewing the slides show and models, and hearing us discuss our concept. frog won, and to make our success complete, Apple awarded us an annual $2 million contract and put us in charge of all Apple designs. Even though I remained a consultant, I was named corporate manager of design – as Steve had promised. Now, the real work would begin.

Steve Jobs had acquired much more than a new look; our collaboration had resulted in a new direction for Apple, as the world's first digital consumer electronics company. And Steve had also advanced his understanding of products and their effects in the marketplace. He had embraced the new concept of simple, additive shapes, presented in white with no added color. In fact, when he spoke at the 1983 Aspen Design Conference later that year, he even condemned Sony's "dark metallic paint." For Steve, everything was black or white. That kind of direct, no-prisoners mentality combined with his unique ability to listen and eventually change direction when confronted with a better way made him an ideal partner for progress.

Phase 3: Putting Snow White to Work

Even though I had the full backing of Steve Jobs, most of Apple's designers still considered themselves to be in charge of design, and nearly all of them refused to cooperate with me. I felt that the company was still in crisis mode in view of the Apple III flop and the growing Lisa disaster, and it could not afford such a lack of professional discipline. So, I didn't budge. As a result of our standoff, some designers – including Jerry Manock – left Apple, and others had to be asked to leave or moved to other departments, including Rob Gemmell, to whom I am still thankful. John Sculley – Apple's new CEO – didn't help the situation, either. His response to any dispute brought before him was to ask in full corporate voice, "Is this professional or personal?" It all was professional, as far as I was concerned. So I was incredibly grateful for the support by Steve Jobs and determined to repay him with my own commitment to excellence. He had asked for the world's best design, and he would get it. It was a simple as that.

When the "whimsical" Apple IIc won Time Magazine's recognition as 1984's Design of the Year, Steve's vision was validated in a way that went beyond great sales numbers. Unfortunately, Apple's overall performance wasn't strong that year. Macintosh sales were well below expectations, due to the computer's subpar design and sharply higher price, which John

APPLE IIGS SYSTEM, 1985. PHOTO: DIETMAR HENNEKA

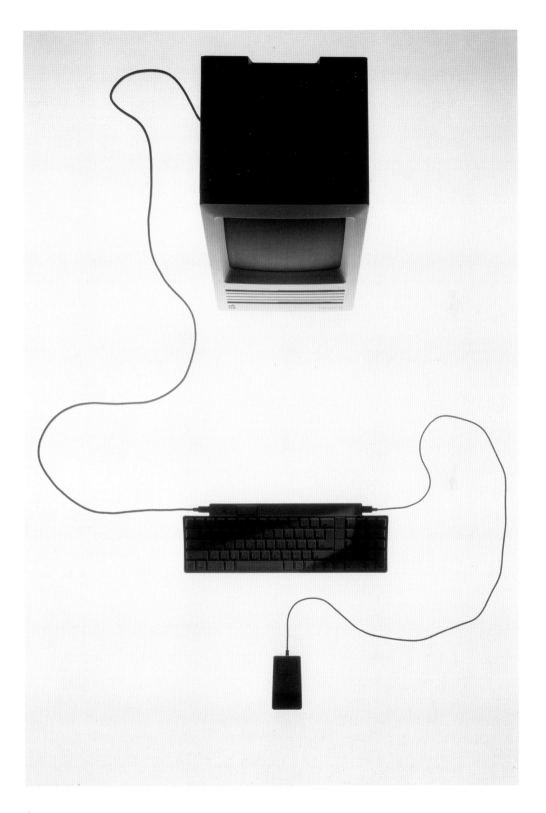

APPLE MACINTOSH SE, 1983. PHOTO: DIETMAR HENNEKA

Sculley had ratcheted up from $1,900 to $2,500. In spite of the Apple IIc success, therefore, we were in no position to sit down and take a breather. Now, we had to keep feeding the Snow White design into Apple's other product lines.

We next shifted our focus to Apple's printers and a final redesign of the Apple II desktop line. In close collaboration with Canon, we launched a major innovation breakthrough with the LaserWriter. To get away from the ugly "dot-matrix" printing that was the accepted norm at that time, Steve licensed typesetting-quality typestyles from the Berthold type foundry in Berlin. Apple's developer improved anti-alias technology so much that the PostScript programming became the new standard of desktop publishing.

As we moved more deeply into Apple's future product development, we felt that the Snow White design language was a bit too soft and a bit too complex in its details. To make the design more competitive, we sharpened the details and extended its application to smaller products and new technologies. As our "show cars," we created telephones (in collaboration with AT&T), TV-connectable Macs, and a collection of products that could become viable for future digital electronic development, such as music and video players. At Steve's insistence, we added the color "black-anthracite" to our spectrum.

The studies we created for this Snow White 2 initiative were actually quite dramatic and somehow timeless, as was proven when Jonathan Ive picked up on the design again with the iPod and subsequent Apple products. The line-up for the Apple II GS with CPU, keyboard, mouse, connectors, cables, and printers (made by Tokyo Electronics) was the first full implementation of the Snow White 2 design language. Ironically, these were the last products in the life of the Apple II line, but their great economic success was vital for Apple; the Mac didn't sell well enough to carry the company. In hindsight, I am very happy about the Apple II GS line because it brought a long journey to a close.

We then determined that the next generation of a compact and "insanely great" Mac – dubbed BigMac and Baby Mac – had to bring Apple to the absolute forefront as a source of cool and friendly digital machines that everyone could use. We worked with Toshiba on a new cathode ray tube (CRT) front in order to avoid the cheap look of a regular CRT screen, and we also looked at flat-screen technology. To make the Mac as small as possible, we experimented with wireless keyboard and mouse connections. During the development of the Baby Mac, Steve brought on prominent new team member Allan Kay. Given the great progress we were making with both our software team and Susan Kare's work on the user-interface side, I felt that the Baby Mac would become one of the greatest products ever. But fate was against Steve and me; he lost a power struggle with John Sculley and was kicked out of Apple. With that, Baby Mac became my best design never to be produced. And with Steve gone, Apple had lost its soul, only to regain it twelve years later, when Steve returned in 1997.

APPLE MACINTOSH SE, 1983. PHOTO: DIETMAR HENNEKA

NeXT

"The Web as I envisaged it, we have not seen it yet. The future is still so much bigger than the past." TIM BERNERS-LEE

After Steve Jobs had been kicked out of Apple, he and some friends from Apple started NeXT, a company dedicated to producing a superior "smart-station" computer for use in higher education. The NeXT OS was based upon UNIX and the hardware was a next-generation version of Apple's, using Motorola's 6800 family microprocessor with Cycle Instruction Set Computing (CISC). The CISC technology wasn't as beefy as the new generation chip with Reduced Instruction Set Computing (RISC) used by Sun Microsystem's SPARC, but it was much easier to program with graphic languages. Because it used the CISC chip, NeXT's CPU was too slow to run Unix at speeds comparable to Sun's Solaris OS. The graphic NeXT Step OS had superior usability, multitasking, and rock-solid performance, however, which motivated Tim Berners-Lee to write the code for the Internet at CERN on a NeXT machine, which is now on exhibit at the Computer History Museum in Mountain View, Silicon Valley.

After Steve's departure, frog continued to work with Apple, so I didn't want to take on any assignments for NeXT. But when Apple began breaching our contract as part of their extortion tactics, I agreed to work individually (not as frog) for NeXT. Apple actually helped me come to that decision, with its absurd reaction to a very nice letter Steve sent them to ask that they allow me to work for him. Apple refused, and they put Rich Jordan – their company "bloodhound" – on my heels. Nevertheless, Steve and I, along with David Kelley, NeXT's mechanical engineering consultant, got together on a Saturday morning to talk about the concept they were developing. The layout of the CPU with a mainframe-like backplane was really cool.

NeXT CUBE, 1986, MUSEUM OF MODERN ART, SAN FRANCISCO. PHOTO: DIETMAR HENNEKA

NeXT CUBE, EARLY MODEL, 1986

TOP: NeXT STATION, 1988. BOTTOM: NEXT COMPUTER BOARD, 1977

NeXT MONITOR, EARLY MODEL, 1986

NeXT CUBE, GRANITE STUDY, 1986. PHOTO: DIETMAR HENNEKA

Steve already had asked a London-based design firm to do a study, but their concept of designing the NeXT machine as a huge human head was a bit bizarre. After some discussion and some sketching on my side, we agreed on a direction. So, I went home and went to work in our family kitchen; by the Sunday evening, I went back to Steve with a preliminary design that totally excited him; the CPU would be a cube and the monitor two slabs, one facing the user with the screen and the other facing backward, to contain the neck of the CRT and electronics. Because Sony would engineer and manufacture the monitor, we didn't have to accommodate the "typical" restrictions of the day that made monitors look cheap and clumsy. David Kelley engineered the cantilever stand as a very nice piece of craftsmanship. I then went to Germany to build detailed models at a friend's model shop, producing one cube in granite and one cube in black-anthracite. Naturally, Steve went for black. Finally, I converted Paul Rand's cube logo into 3D. Within two months, the design was ready for final engineering.

I wouldn't have missed the NeXT experience for anything. Working with Steve in a smaller setting was fantastic, and we had the perfect processes. After Steve returned to Apple, NeXT survived only through the Mac OS. And strangely, its design was a bit funky. So, I was quite happy when it got converted to Apple's "aqua" design . . . and my NeXT stock options converted into Apple shares.

NeXT STATION, 1988

HELEN HAMLYN FOUNDATION: CORDLESS IRON, 1986

THE HELEN HAMLYN FOUNDATION

"Old age is no place for Sissies." BETTE DAVIS

In 1986, we were approached by Helen Hamlyn who had started a foundation to help improve the lives of senior people through design.[1] Helen invited several designers and design agencies to create an environment that would inspire seniors and provide a positive atmosphere. frog decided to design three items for the new environment, which were commodities not at all tailored for older people:

- The Bed: Older people have problems getting out of bed, so we created a height-adjustable concept for a bed that combined safe ergonomics with an elegant and optimistic style. The bed's tilting handle is both practical and decorative, and the canopy's soft colors create a pleasant atmosphere.

- Inductive Iron: Handling heavy objects is a problem for seniors, and cords are dangerous for anyone who lacks vision and mobility. So we decided to design an inductive, cordless iron with a handle that clearly communicates where the user is to hold it. The energy comes from inductive coils in the ironing board, which heat up the iron's soleplate.

- Rotating TV: This concept was inspired by a 1968 German comedy movie Zur Sache Schaetzchen (English title: Love Illusions) in which the male lead had tilted his TV by ninety degrees so he can watch lying on his side. We expanded this idea by controlling the rotation with a disc on the remote control, which otherwise reacts to voice. The device's buttons are sensors embedded in waves so they are easy to feel.

Many of the designers Helen invited to participate in the project had created serious tools for overcoming physical limitation, and the designs all looked very orthopedic. In stark contrast, our contributions were colorful and cheerful, but still functional. The fact that we had used technical innovations, rather than simply boosting functionality, made our contributions a big hit with senior Londoners. It was another triumph for frog's guiding principle that "form follows emotion."

HELEN HAMLYN FOUNDATION, ROTATING REMOTE, 1986. PHOTO: DIETMAR HENNEKA

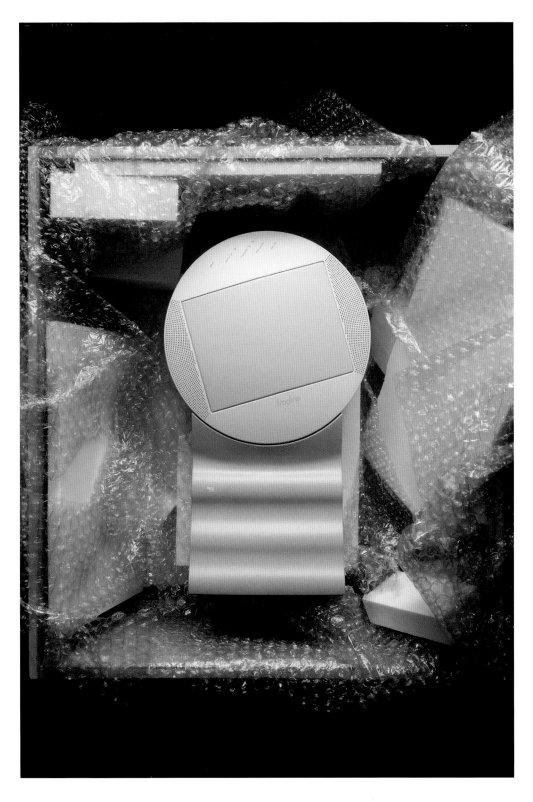

HELEN HAMLYN FOUNDATION, ROTATING TV, 1986. PHOTO: DIETMAR HENNEKA

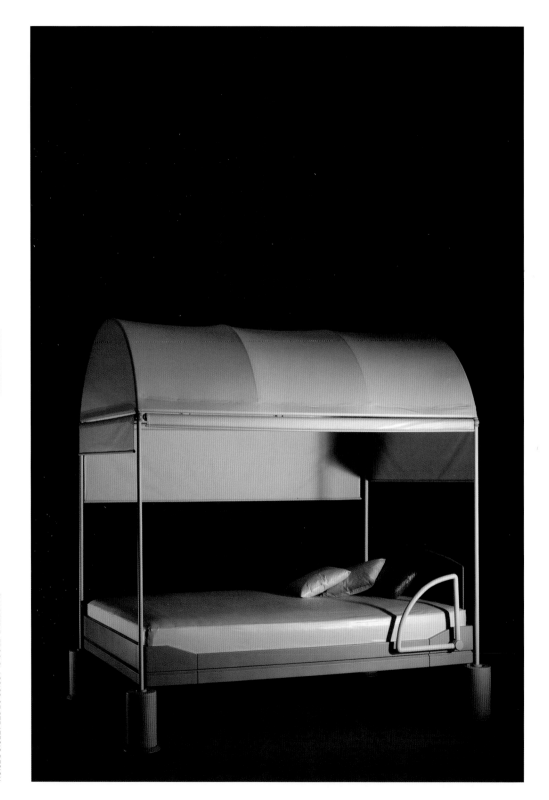

HELEN HAMLYN FOUNDATION ERGONOMIC BED, 1986. PHOTO: DIETMAR HENNEKA

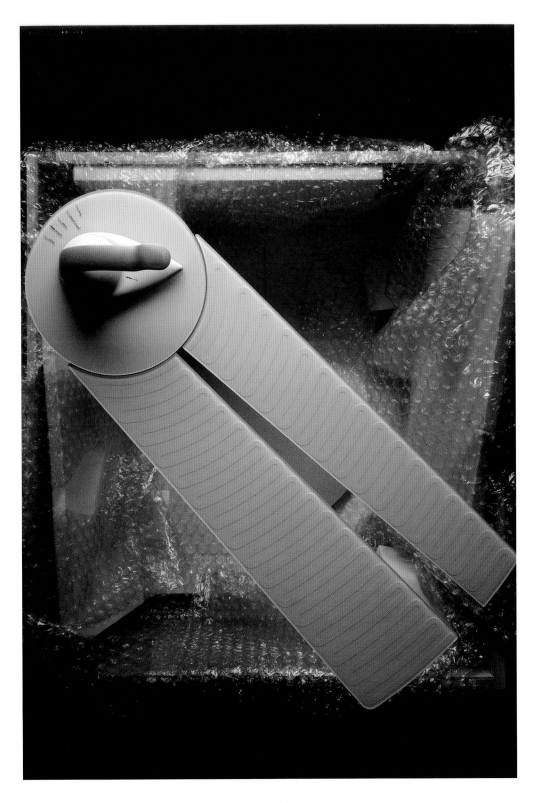

HELEN HAMLYN FOUNDATION INDUCTIVE IRON, 1986, MUSEUM OF MODERN ART, MILWAUKEE. PHOTO: DIETMAR HENNEKA

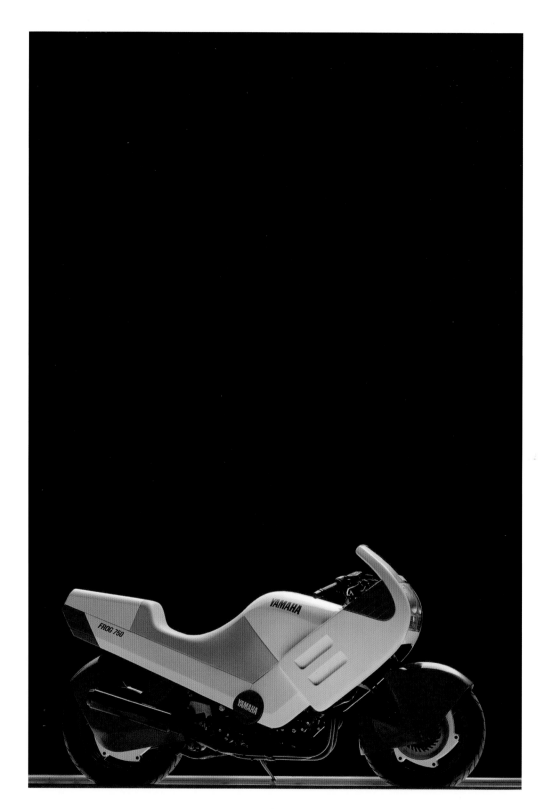

YAMAHA, FROG 750 STUDY, 1986, MUSEUM OF MODERN ART, SAN FRANCISCO. PHOTO: DIETMAR HENNEKA

YAMAHA

"The best safety lies in fear." WILLIAM SHAKESPEARE

The Yamaha Frog FZ 750 project was inspired by the German bike magazine *MOTORRAD*'s 1986 call for a safer and more beautiful bike and by California legislation against very dangerous motorcycles (the magazine's editors and California's legislators both cited the Yamaha's FZ 750 as a major culprit behind their decisions). I decided to participate in *MOTORRAD*'s competition, and as soon as Yamaha USA got wind of my interest, they told me that they would be happy to collaborate.

We made a foam study on a scale of 1:2.5 (which made it on the cover of *MOTORRAD*), and then, with the support of Yamaha USA, went on to design and build a 1:1 prototype based upon the FZ 750. Next, we imported a real FZ 750 from Japan – with no pistons and holes in the cylinder head to make it undrivable and, therefore, legal within California – and set to work. In addition to creating a retro-futuristic design language in that project, we also integrated features stemming from safety research by the University of Bochum in Germany, including bodywork that helped protect the rider in side falls and a more secure seat/tank. Because many accidents in the United States are caused by a car cutting into a bike's way, we also increased side visibility. Our design included double headlights – by now an industry standard – and lightweight rims with a carbon-fiber core in order to reduce the mass of the wheels, which back then was quite a challenging proposal.

We finished the prototype in frog's German studio and shipped it to Yamaha's headquarters in Hamamatsu, Japan. They liked it very much but decided not to build it. We got Yamaha's permission to publish the bike, however, and the global effect was tremendous. The biggest compliment then came from Honda, when its design team dedicated their Hurricane design to the Frog FZ 750. They even offered me one as a gift.

Today, most people know the Frog FZ 750 from Dietmar Henneka's beautiful photographs of it. After having been the main attraction in frog's San Francisco lobby for many years, the Frog FZ 750 has gained loftier recognition, having been "knighted" as art by the Museum of Modern Art, San Francisco.

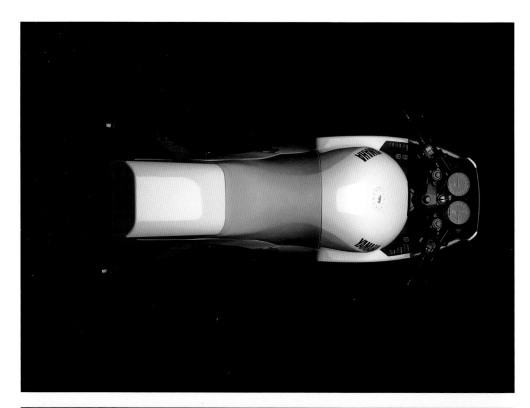

↑ YAMAHA, FROG 750 STUDY, 1986. PHOTO: DIETMAR HENNEKA

YAMAHA, FROG 750 STUDY, 1986. PHOTO: DIETMAR HENNEKA

OLYMPUS

"Look, I'm not an intellectual – I just take pictures." HELMUT NEWTON

Photography is one of my passions. I studied it and learned a lot from my friend Dietmar Henneka, and I have been lucky enough to afford all of the cameras I love to use. After I redesigned the Minox 35mm camera, Olympus presented frog with a dream project: designing a new paradigm for digital cameras, as well as a scientific microscope. frog convinced Olympus that the design DNA of the project should be rooted in the Japanese principle of simplicity and the perfect usage of tools.

The LiOM1

The move from film to digital technology liberated handheld cameras from the body shape required to handle the roll of film and the mechanism used for pulling the film across the back of the optical lenses. In digital photography, the only fixed needs are a sensor chip behind the lenses, the lenses themselves, and the elements necessary for handling the camera. Because people were accustomed to using film cameras, we wanted the camera we were designing – which we named the LiOM1 – to have a similar user experience. Think, for example, of a car's steering wheel that is augmented by additional buttons; it has new functionality, but it is still a steering wheel.

The LiOM2

Based on our research, we knew that people love holding slate-shaped objects. So, in the more fashionable design of the LiOM2, we exaggerated the slab as well as the lens. We also provided a lanyard, making the camera akin to high-tech jewelry. The LiOM2 received enthusiastic reactions from those who viewed it, but the managers at Olympus didn't have the courage to implement the design. In a sort of back-handed compliment, Samsung launched similar concepts after our publication of the LiOM2, but the copies were very bad.

The Olympus Microscope

Designing a microscope requires that you begin using one and then diving into "micro-world." Whatever I put under the lens of a microscope makes me wonder at how beautiful, complex, and strange the world is. When we did user testing for the Olympus microscope project, it became clear that the scope's architecture had to be changed to make it easier to access and use. Eventually, we created a vertical Y-profile, which allowed most access to the microscope's controls and gave it good stability. We also put a ventilation system in the back so hot air from the lamps wouldn't bother the user. Finally, we reworked and improved all the elements of its physical interface. The microscope achieved almost instant success in the marketplace, and the design won many awards.

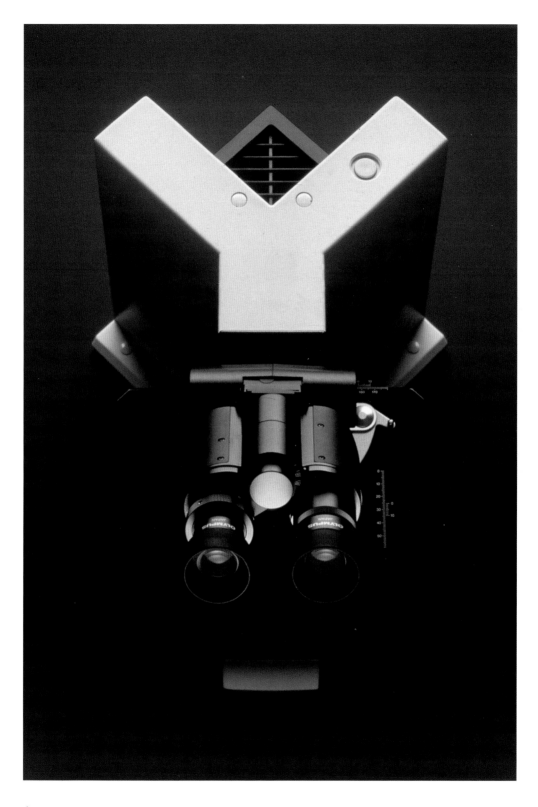

OLYMPUS SCIENTIFIC MICROSCOPE, 1988

OLYMPUS LIOM DIGITAL CAMERA, 1988

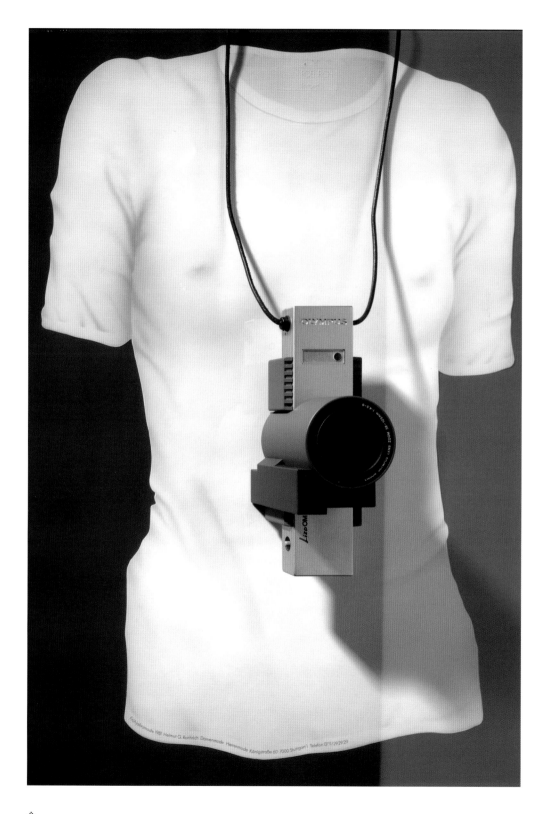

OLYMPUS LIOM-2 DIGITAL CAMERA, 1988

LUFTHANSA, FRANKFURT AIRPORT, GATE, 1994

LUFTHANSA

"Flying dreams mean that you're doing the right thing with your life."

DOUG COUPLAND

Over my career of forty plus years, I have flown millions of miles, sometimes making three trips a month from Germany via the North Pole to Tokyo and back, or to Hong Kong for a meeting. I feel at home in airplanes, and when I don't sleep or read, I love to look out of the window. Icarus's dream still is alive in me. Because I grew up in Germany, I liked Lufthansa, but more for its safety record than its design. The cabin interiors looked like a German office: gray and boring. Then, in 1993 I got a call from Hemjoe Klein, executive vice president for Lufthansa's passenger business. He had seen a California-produced TV special about frog and me, and he felt that we could help Lufthansa become more likable.

I met with Klein, and we discussed what would be needed to transform the airline's image. Lufthansa just had decided to remodel Terminal 1 in Frankfurt and to lease new terminals in Munich and at New York's JFK airport; that meant there was an opportunity with this project to recreate the airport experience. In addition, Lufthansa had placed huge new plane orders with Airbus, so we would be able to design their interiors from scratch. Lufthansa also planned to refurbish its fleet of Boeing planes—especially its 747s. (Interestingly, back then, Southwest Airlines was the main buyer of Lufthansa's used but still top-notch 737s.) So, frog went to work for Lufthansa, and here are the key elements, which have been in constant use since 1997:

- The Design DNA: Lufthansa was officially founded in 1953, when the Allies (the United States, United Kingdom, and France) gave Germany permission to create a new airline. The real founding date for Lufthansa, however, was 1919. Naturally, we had to eliminate any association with the Nazi era, and therefore we decided to make the Junkers JU 52—the last pre-Nazi plane developed in Germany—the genetic icon. Like the Ford Tristar, the JU 52's fuselage and wings were covered with corrugated metal, which provided more stability with less weight (aerodynamics have relegated corrugated metal to the past, but we still liked the emotional message it transmitted). Based on the much-loved JU 52, our new design DNA was defined by sinuous curves, waves, and mechanical semantics, rather than sleek streamlines.

- The Airport: The main physical interaction point between passengers and an airline is the counter. Even though we also designed self-check-in kiosks, we wanted the Lufthansa counter experience to be both functionally satisfying and emotionally appealing for flyers. I don't want to dive into the details of our counter design, but the most important issue for the employee is the position

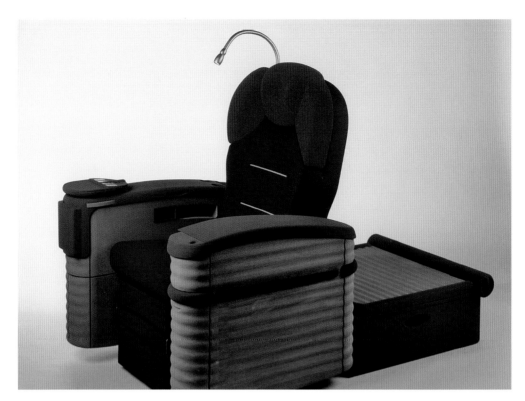
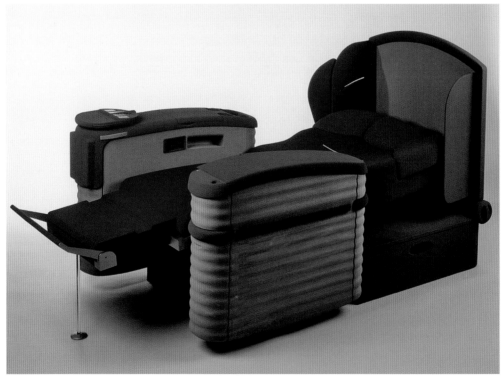

⇡ LUFTHANSA, FIRST CLASS SLEEPER SEAT, 1994

LUFTHANSA, FRANKFURT AIRPORT, LOUNGE, 1994

of the passenger in front of the counter. To address that issue, we created a wave design with a concave pocket in stainless steel forming the place to stand, and a convex "shield" carrying the brand image and keeping passengers a comfortable distance from each other. Redesigning the waiting areas and the lounges in the airport was an especially fun part of frog's work. Guided by the design elements of American Deco, Michael MacDonnel, an architect from New York, helped us to convert the JU 52 into interiors that had an optimistic touch.

- Plane Interiors: Plane interiors contain two main elements: space and seats. Our influence on the space was limited because the materials are dictated by weight and safety issues, yet we had more freedom with the seats. The first-class seat was a special challenge because we had to use the mechanisms of the old seats, which declined seventy-five degrees, and then modify them so the backrest and the footrest would move ninety degrees to create a horizontal bed. The shapes were curvy and comfortable, and we combined armrests with containers for the passenger's belongings. The solid surfaces were lightweight, corrugated plastic, which brought the JU 52's sensibility into the plane. After flying on our frog-designed seats for more than fifteen years, I still like them. Their days are numbered, however, as the new planes will have a seat design similar to those of Singapore Airlines or Emirates Airline (but then looking like a living room isn't exactly a cool thing for an airplane).

LUFTHANSA, FRANKFURT AIRPORT, TUNNEL AND SIGNAGE, 1994

SAP, LOGO AND CORPORATE IDENTITY, 2000

SAP

"From my earliest days developing business software, I have always believed that design has to start with the user." HASSO PLATTNER

One company nobody would have connected with great design fifteen years ago was the German software company SAP (Software Application Programs), the world's leader in enterprise software (also called ERP, for Enterprise Resource Planning). SAP had its own discrete operating system (ABAP), and its R/3 applications involved more than 50,000 different screens. Doing an expense report required an employee to go through a total of eight different screens with the data designation often miles away from the active input field. The visual elements of the program were gray-on-gray.

Even as the company gained success during the mid-1990s, cofounder and CEO Hasso Plattner felt that there was a need for major initiative in order to create "software that works like people" instead of requiring "people to work like software." Matthias Vering, group leader for software design, contacted frog to help with the redesign.[2] After a couple of work sessions at SAP's headquarters in Waldorf, Germany, and at frog's offices in Austin, Texas, with SAP's designers Leif Jensen-Pistorius and Peer Hilgers, we assigned frog's Mark Rolston and Collin Cole as the project's key designers. The main problem the designers faced wasn't looks but interaction and legacy. The SAP functions were structured for easiest programming rather than logical work flow. And, at first, the active fields on the R/3 screens were locked and couldn't be moved. So, we decided on a two-step process: First, we would improve usability with a graphic system that would give the user quicker access to on-screen functions. We also could integrate multiple screens – such as those for expense reports – into one new screen by designing a system that would launch all "old screens" in the memory and then build the new screen from its contents.

Results for the first step were great. Tests by the University of Mannheim showed that the new graphic system reduced mistakes by 73% and the learning time for new R/3 users by 82%. We also designed a new corporate logo, new collateral materials, and an online design guild (www.sapdesignguild.org/), which supported and accelerated development of new applications both with in-house and third-party developers.

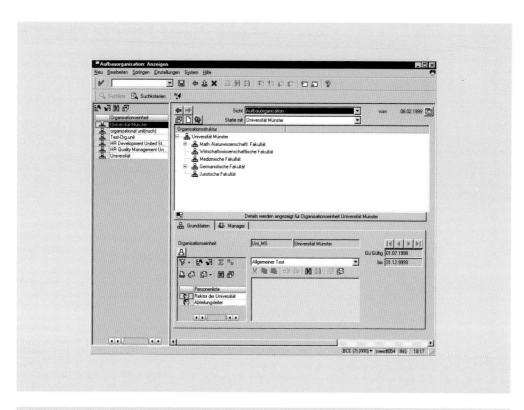

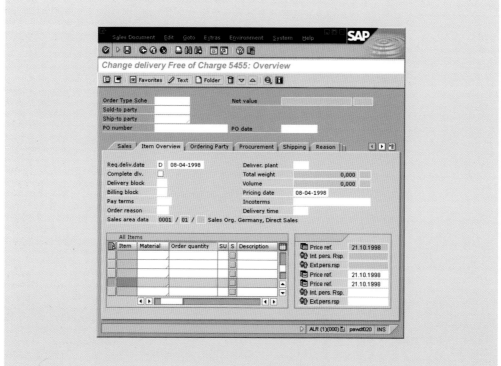

TOP: SAP, R/3 SOFTWARE "BEFORE," AS OF ~1989. BOTTOM: SAP, R/3 SOFTWARE "FROGGED," 1999

The second step was the development and design of mySAP.com, an internet-based portal which took R/3's applications online and expanded their functionality, usability, and accessibility. Because SAP didn't have the technology capable of handling the portal, frog scouted and found an American-Israeli company called TopTier that initially worked on the project as a partner before being acquired by SAP. Shai Agassi, TopTier's founder, joined SAP as its chief technical officer but left a year later after both sides learned that Shai didn't want to adjust to life and work in a large corporation. The new products were a big improvement for SAP and opened new markets. SAP's inner organization struggled to deal with the challenges of those changes, and Hasso asked me to serve for one year as interim chief marketing officer. Working with Ogilvy Mather, I implemented a more emotional communication strategy: "The best run SAP," and "Porsche runs SAP." After one year, we hired Marty Homlish from Sony, who did a great job in further changing SAP's approach to its customers.[3]

SAP, R/3 SOFTWARE "FROGGED," 1999

DUAL CD PLAYER, 1994

DUAL

"Success consists of going from failure to failure without loss of enthusiasm." WINSTON CHURCHILL

Around 1995, frog was asked by Wolfgang Momberger – then a member of the executive board of German retail giant Karstadt – to help in relaunching the Dual brand. The Dual company had once been a global leader in turntables for vinyl records but went bankrupt in 1982, and the brand was subsequently "shipped around" before finally being acquired by Karstadt. Even though the venture wasn't a financial success, it is of historic relevance due to its convergent solutions and because it represents a rare example of a retailer who decided to design a complete user experience for a consumer-tech brand. All of us involved in the project learned about the importance of a sound strategy (Karstadt decided early on to use Dual as an exclusive shop brand) and about project management. Both Karstadt and frog were too optimistic from the beginning, however, and went into unknown territory without preparing each other for the realities of such a complex endeavor.

Karstadt's management still was thinking "procurement," and the management task force didn't understand the added complexities of product development. Working with ODMs in Europe and Asia requires a professional and respectful partnership where the goals are set and the work starts as teamwork. In contrast, the ever-present price negotiations, which typically "bookend" such projects, will poison those important relationships. In one case, a Korean company miraculously pulled together a celebratory dinner, complete with toasts and a great atmosphere, which went very well . . . until a Karstadt executive said: "Now we have to talk about price again." Karstadt's managers also made way too aggressive revenue plans driven by stock keeping units. They believed that "more product equals more revenue." So the product line-up mushroomed, but the development budgets for engineering, tooling, and inventory financing weren't realistic anymore. On frog's side, the design aspects were no problem, but we were overwhelmed with the engineering and logistics of the project. In order to fill the voids, we were hiring outside consultants, especially for hardware engineering and software coding, which not only added operational complexity but also made the project hard to control. The results were partially worthless and a waste of money.

TOP: DUAL TV SET, 1994. BOTTOM: DUAL BOOMBOX, 1994

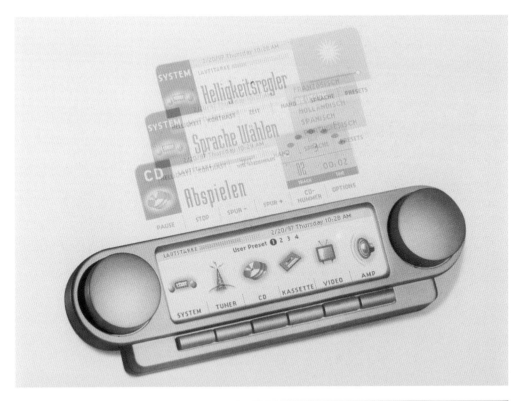

TOP: DUAL DETACHABLE SOFTWARE UI, 1994. BOTTOM: DUAL DIGITAL AUDIO SYSTEM, 1994

Still, there were some real breakthrough products – most notably, a portable digital boom box and the world's first software-operated hi-fi system, which demonstrated and defined convergence even before Apple launched its first audio and video products. In addition, the system's hardware and software were integrated into a discrete unit, which plugged into the front of the pre-amplifier and also could be taken out as a remote control. The physical user interface combined the classic car-radio concept of two rotary knobs and some push buttons. The digital user interface worked with real-life icons, which users could understand without having to study a manual. Together with its retro-futuristic brand design, products, and ecological packaging, the program's strong features became a trailblazer for many competitors.

Without the insufficient strategic preparation and operational mistakes, the Dual hi-fi system could have been a modest but healthy success that the company could have built upon. But, when the numbers didn't add up, Karstadt divested the brand in 2004, and it is now owned by DGC GmbH in Munich. As in so many cases, less would have been more.

DUAL BESTSELLING BOOMBOX, 1995

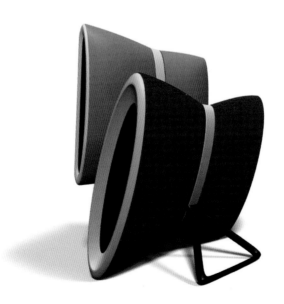

DISNEY PC STUDY, 2003

DISNEY

"What you can dream, you can do." WALT DISNEY

I have been a Disney fan since I first laid hands and eyes on their magazine as a young boy. As nice as the cartoons with Donald and Mickey were, however, it was the center section of the magazine, where Walt Disney illustrated his vision of "Futureland," that I found most fascinating. I loved the monorail, the automated kitchens, the flying cars. Our family also cherished the ritual of our visits to Disneyland in Anaheim — when our children were young, this also served as proof of a solid marriage — and we watched Disney movies and shopped in the Disney stores. But I never associated Disney with high tech, so the call I received from Disney's headquarter in 2000 was the last thing I expected.

On the phone was Simon May, an executive in charge of licensing the Disney brand into adjacent marketing areas. After having expanded into logical branches like strollers, clothing, and baby accessories, Simon explained that Disney would love to venture into consumer electronics for children and families. They hadn't found any company with a design that would represent and actually build the Disney brand; he was looking for a licensee who could create a "high-tech Disney design DNA," develop products with third-party manufacturers, and then place these products into retail outlets. May had talked with other design firms, including Ideo, but frog's industry experience, network, and especially our experience co-designing with retailers encouraged May to give us the nod. The team for "Disney CE" was led by Harry Dolman, executive vice president of Disney Consumer Products; Simon May, director of licensing; and Bob Bacon, product manager. We had direct access to top management, enabling us to make quick decisions.

Work started with a joint workshop with Disney Imagineering — one of the most creative teams in the world — and our frog team with Chris Green as lead designer. The product would have to strike a balance between playfulness and performance, so we created a design language connected to Disney characters. Then we traveled to Asia, to meet with manufacturers, including Philips, Samsung, and Panasonic. Management at those firms all liked our ideas, but I saw no way to realize such a program within their corporate structures. Then, we talked to retailers at Best Buy, Target Stores, and Circuit City. They loved the concept but gave us low price points, which seemed impossible to achieve, and they wanted a higher margin than with Sony's products. Finally, we talked to kids and parents, who also loved the idea but insisted that the products should be good quality and, above all, easy to use. After all of this input, we went back home to analyze and think.

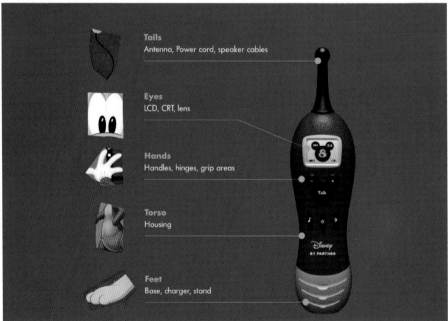

TOP: DISNEY CHARACTERS, 2002. BOTTOM: DISNEY DESIGN LANGUAGE, 2002

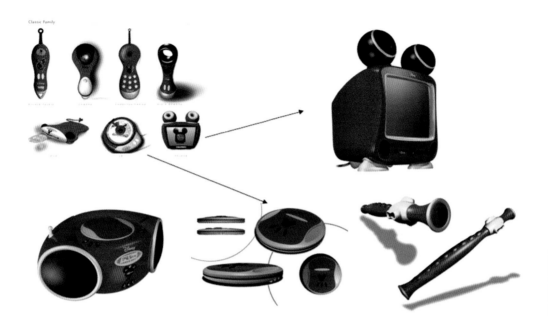

We decided that we would develop the products directly with ODMs in Asia who worked for brands such as Sony, Samsung, and Philips. But we still had to reduce costs, which seemed possible, considering that the children and parents we targeted as customers valued simplicity over a glut of features. We eliminated the shuffle function in the CD player, for example, because it actually irritated young users. As a result, we saved about $5 in materials over the Sony version.

We also had to provide extra financial space for Disney and frog's joint royalty, which averaged around 8%. That space had to be carved out in the supply chain because retailers didn't agree that consumers would pay an additional 30% for the Disney brand. Looking at a TV set, the math was simple: Assuming a retail price of $100, we had to design a product with a bill of materials of just $25 (instead of $35), we had to provide about 3% extra for the distribution partners (Memorex/Americas and Medion/Europe), and we also had to factor in a marketing budget. After we had established the benchmarks, we went back and forth between retailers, factories, and Disney who would create the packaging, and MarCom materials.

And we succeeded. The products were an instant success and created more than $200 million in revenue in their second year after launch. The success turned out to be a windfall and, with the business model established, Disney decided to make the business a new division of Disney Consumer Products, led by one of my favorite former frogs: Chris Heatherly, vice president of technology and innovation.

SHARP

"You're going to have to out-innovate the innovators." GARY HAMEL

How do you compete with Apple's iPhone? You don't! frog's work for Sharp takes it own path to achieve user-delight, which naturally is especially challenging in the cluttered and complex space of Google's Android Operating System for Smart Phones. The goal was to design a new mobile user-experience model, called Feel_UX, that is uncluttered and effortless to organize and use. Unlike other Google-related mobile handset manufacturers who historically customize Android by simply adding another visual layer on top of the platform, the frog team went more than skin-deep and carefully curated the experience to create a new device that is straightforward for beginners, yet has the flexibility in customization that advanced users love. Improvements were made in simple but smart usage and personalization. E.g. the lock screen concept, which traditionally served its purpose of securing personal data, was redesigned to give users faster access to their most cherished content, such as photos, music or stock quotes. The frog team also analyzed real-life situations instead of retreating to easy-to-program features: the less clicks the better.

Paul Pugh, frog's vice president for software innovation insisted "When you visit a store, it's very difficult to distinguish between the different Android models – they all look and interact alike. To create a special screen experience is crucial to making a great first impression." Another innovative feature includes an animated weather motion experience that dynamically changes as the weather patterns do, giving real-time visual information to the customers. The launcher was elevated into a streamlined home space for users to easily manage their applications, widgets and shortcuts. Contrary to other Android phones with a harsh techno-look, which normally appeal to early adopters and techies, the team introduced flashes of colors and opted for a softer, more accessible look-and-feel to cater to a wide range of users. The radical, minimal visual design of Feel_UX also does away with conventions, and is nothing less than a top-to-bottom rethink of the entire Android user experience: where a user normally sees a desktop-style screen with widgets and app icons, Feel_UX will always go one level deeper, and the need to launch a separate list of apps is an unnecessary barrier to some of the phone's most useful and frequently-accessed functionality. Research showed that most users didn't really understand what widgets (small applications) and shortcuts are. In Feel_UX, widgets have their own dedicated screen and can be easily placed anywhere in a sheet, and its never-ending nature means users won't ever have to rearrange their phone's home screen just to find a place for a new app. Paul Pugh again: "We thought widgets were some of the more unique features of Android versus competitor handsets, so we wanted to kind of celebrate them by giving them their own space. We think we've taken the best of Android and elevated it." Simplicity is a Japanese ideal and Feel_UX is intended to reach as wide an audience as possible, including those upgrading from basic-feature phones for the first time. That doesn't mean it'll be limited to entry-level phones, however – Sharp is launching it on a range of seven devices from the radiation-sensing Pantone 5 to premium Aquos Phones like Docomo's Zeta, AU's Serie, and SoftBank's Xx.

Aside of the visible results and the instant success, this project is a great example of frog's collaborative teamwork across the globe, lead by Mark Rolston and Collin Cole – frog's original digital design leaders since 1996. Sharp is located in Hiroshima/Japan, the lead design team was in Austin/Texas, supported by digital design teams in Bangalore/India and Kiev/Ukraine. This allowed frog and Sharp to create a tremendous amount of great concepts, detailed design, production assets, motion studies and design specifications in record time – nine months from the first concepts to market-ready handsets. The level of fidelity in the design is a result of frog's vertical structure, which enables extremely accurate engineering implementation.

Peter Vogt photographed WEGA 3020 CTV by **frogdesign**, Grenzweg 33, D-7272 Altensteig, Grenzweg 33, telephone +49. (0)7453-8000

Eldorado.

FROG AD: PETER VOIGT, WEGA 3020

frog ADVERTISING CAMPAIGN

"Don't bunt. Aim out of the ball park. Aim for the company of immortals." DAVID OGILVY

Looking at frog's achievements, one also has to mention our daring advertising campaign, which not only changed the way a creative design agency had to communicate, but it also turned into an inspirational tool both for designers and companies. Naturally, it was a bit crazy for a back then tiny company to spend hundreds of thousands dollars, but the campaign was a game changer: frog's work was recognized around World, other design firms also were forced to follow us, and we attracted both the best companies and the best talent. And the campaign also was a motivation for us to excel to the point, where we couldn't afford anything less then to create absolutely cutting edge work. So, why and how did this start?

When I started my own company in 1969, designers weren't supposed to act as entrepreneurs. Even the great ones were either employed like Dieter Rams at Braun, or they had relatively small studios like Mario Bellini or Joe Colombo in Milan. And in the United States, design had become a stale formula for product differentiation, and even bigger studios like Henry Dreyfuss Design had to abide the rules of corporate America, which means their work was nice but not breathtaking. In Germany star designer Luigi Colani – creating wonderful and sometimes controversial concepts – was a master of self promotion, but he failed to create a solid design company based on his fame. I understood that to create a relevant design company beyond the typical design firms of five to fifteen people – who then split due to ego clashes – it was important to build a brand beyond single persons. Dieter Motte's Wega Campaign also was a great motivation: despite being the smallest competitor, Wega became a cult and outgrew the competition. And to be honest, I always dreamed to create a design company which would be globally relevant. After I had some good successes with premium clients such as Wega, Sony,hansgrohe, KaVo and Vuitton, I decided to lay the foundation for a global quest (I know this sounds crazy and it was...). We started slow with the back cover of the German "form" magazine and our first ads weren't really great. We wanted to show too much, the photography was mediocre and the message was confused. I decided against all logic to act like my clients: only the best! As design has a strong visual element, I invited the World's best photographers to take my objects and to de-code them so people would understand the philosophy. Naturally, this was a bit insane, as frog design just was a small agency of five people in the German Black Forest. But as we were highly profitable, I felt that this was the best way to go, and after some shaky start, I could win some real masters. My idea was to give them full freedom of interpretation, and also to pay them the top money they requested – up to 80,000 dollars in today's money per shot – and so stars such as Helmut Newton, Dietmar Henneka, Hans Hansen and Victor Goico were creating their visual magic. And with Swiss Urs Schwertzmann, I also contracted a world-class advertising designer. Regarding placement, I only went for the back covers, even as the cost were a multiple of the inside spreads, and I also committed to long-term contracts, always with a first-buy again option. After some years and the establishment of frog's American studio, frog had acquired the back covers of virtually all good design magazines back then: *from* and *design report* in Germany, Design in UK, *ID Magazine* in the United States, *Design* in Australia and *AXIS Magazine* in Japan. Also very important was consistency – the design of the ads went unchanged for twenty years – and world-class photographers finally *wanted* to work with frog. The outcome was, that frog design attracted the very best people, the very best clients and we also established frog design as a global leader. Yes, we invested a lot of money, but it created a fantastic return: frog wouldn't have established such a dominant presence especially in the pre-Internet age and superior brand value without the campaign.

Helmut Newton photographed Villeroy & Boch and hansgrohe products by frogdesign, Grenzweg 33, D-7272 Altensteig, Grenzweg 33, telephone +49. (0)7453-8000

The American Dream.

PAUL MONTGOMERY DIGITAL CAMERA, FROG JUNIOR, 1988

frog junior

"The old pond
       a frog jumps in:
   Plop!" BASHÔ

Mentoring young designers always has been a priority in frog, starting with hiring graduates right out of school, where companies and our competitors always required five years of professional experience. And for many designers who made a great name for themselves, frog has been the first station of their professional life: Ross Lovegrove, Stephen Peart, Herbie Pfeiffer, Yves Behar of fuse project, Andreas Haug and Tom Schoenherr of Phoenix Design, Friedhelm Engler, design leader at General Motors, Fritz Frenkler, Professor at the Technical University in Munich, Sigmar Willnauer, Professor at the College of Design in Schwaebisch Gmuend and Anthony Guido, Associate Professor at the University of the Arts in Philadelphia – just to name a few.

So it was quite logical, when we started our "frog junior" program in 1984: we invited each year two design schools in the United States and Europe, and then supported the teaching staff by working visits, seminars and workshops. The theme of the projects was left to the school and at the end of the semester we chose the three winners of each school which then were promoted on a page in the design magazines frog was advertising on the back cover. In addition, frog designed an ad for the first prize winner, which was published at frog's expense in the German *form* magazine as well as in the American *ID Magazine*. Due to the quality of the work, we also could acquire a lot of positive public relations in general interest magazines and newspapers around the World. Some of the winners got a job at frog – like Paul Montgomery and Dan Sturgess – and some would accelerate their career like Thomas Bley would later become one of frog's General Managers or Grant Larsen who became a key designer for the Boxster at Porsche.

However, after ten-plus years frog junior ran into an unexpected problem: there weren't enough design schools anymore, and with the advent of the worldwide web, students had other opportunities to promote themselves. However, frog's creative leaders continued to mentor young talents by visiting design schools and universities for guest lectures and workshops, and will do so in the future.

1 Today, the Paul Hamlyn Foundation – named after Helen's husband, publisher of Penguin books, who died in 2001 – focuses on serving young and disadvantaged people.

2 In 1996, frog had expanded into digital design by acquiring Virtual Studio in Austin, Texas. Two of the Virtual Studio partners, Marl Rolston and Collin Cole, are members of frog's global leadership team. After acquiring Microsoft as our first "digital" customer (frog helped Microsoft develop the user interface of Windows XP), SAP's R/3 was our first strategic software user-interface project. Our work with SAP helped us leapfrog into convergent design in which frog became a global leader.

3 Marty Homlish has been HP's executive vice president and chief marketing officer since April 2011.

6 BUILDING TOMORROW'S DESIGN LEADERS

"Leaders are made rather than born." WARREN G. BENNIS (ADVISOR TO FOUR PRESIDENTS)

To change the world, we first have to change the world's people. On a personal basis, change is difficult but manageable. Changing others, however, is nearly impossible unless they are young, talented, and motivated. To harness – or rather, unleash – that transformative potential, I have passionately immersed myself in the work of education, training young, creative people to become competent and responsible leaders in the field of design and in business.

My first teaching experience was from 1989 to 1994, when the governor of my German home state asked me to become one of the ten founding professors for the HfG Karlsruhe in Germany, which was associated with the ZKM. Led by Heinrich Klotz, the ZKM was the first museum to collect digital art and media installations. My vision for my students at the HfG was to integrate the concept of convergence into their approach to design, which meant teaching them to design products with both physical and virtual qualities. I also wanted to help redefine the ideals and methods of the Bauhaus and the progressive HfG Ulm for the digital age.

The university was new, so my class was very small. And it stayed small because I believe that an elite education requires close attention and intense mentorship by the teacher. The class was very successful, garnering international awards for our designs of digital interfaces for an integrated digital media space. The students, who were well-prepared and ready to change the world, went on to establish successful careers. Some became leaders, either by leading design departments at major companies or by building their own design agencies.

MY VIENNA STUDENTS 2011. PHOTO: THEMSELVES

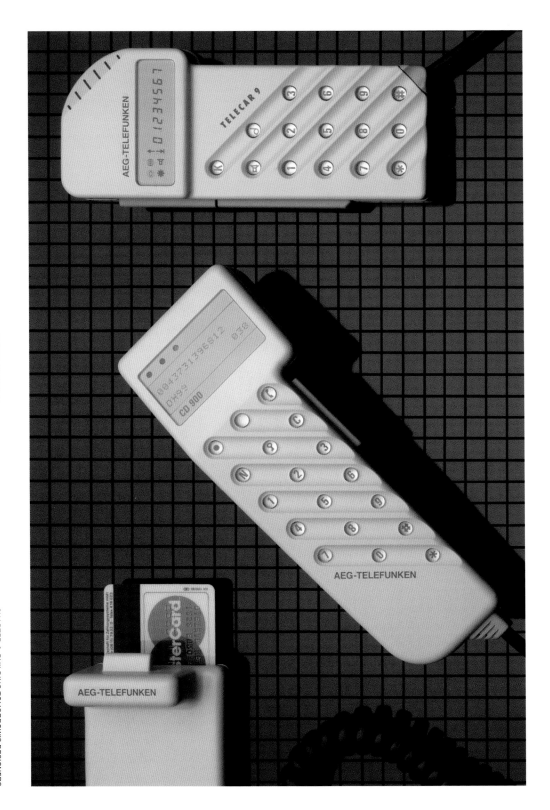

The class also was an apprenticeship for me. I learned that teaching students to design for professional clients in an agency like frog requires building their social skills and developing their ability to interact with people with different backgrounds, training, and interests. And I also learned that students must be prepared for stepping into a professional future that involves leveraging scientific developments and technologies that don't yet exist.

With the experiences I gained in that first teaching assignment, I had begun to develop a new vision for design education, one that I have continued to explore and define in all of my subsequent work. In this chapter, I'd like to explain a bit about my experiences in this work, how I have shaped my educational approach, and how I believe we can (and must) use the educational process to prepare a new generation of design leaders—innovative designers, entrepreneurs, and business-savvy collaborators—who will be capable of creating a better, more sustainable future.

SEEING THE FUTURE BY LOOKING TO THE PAST

As science and technology progress at an ever-accelerating pace, students need to know how to look back in order to understand future trends. To anticipate progress over the next five years and to put that progress into perspective, I teach my students to survey the developments that occurred over the past twenty to thirty years. Whatever process or formula they use, design students have to learn from history in order to project, simulate, and design the future today. And this principle isn't limited to science and technology; it also applies to social trends and, in particular, to ecological sustainability.

Developing the Master Class ID2

My second teaching engagement began in 2005, when Ross Lovegrove, one of my very early frog colleagues, was professor for the Master Class ID2 at the University of Applied Arts in Vienna. Frustrated by lack of support for his curriculum focus on bionic and ecological design, Ross resigned after only one semester, and so the university asked me to help out as a visiting professor. When the university then asked me to commit to a longer-term teaching position, their offer came with some unique challenges. The university had no international standing in the field of design, and the internal situation at ID2 was chaotic, with no students present and studios full of trash and broken equipment. Other professors living in Vienna were barely present, leaving the frustrated assistant teams to function on their own. There was basically no money available for providing the technical support for design classes such as model making, in spite of the nearly $30,000 per student provided by the tax-paying citizens of Austria. In other words, the situation was an absolute nightmare.

I wasn't discouraged by these challenges. I was starting to phase out my operative role at frog, and I believed this new teaching position offered the perfect opportunity to prove that any creative person can succeed with an open-minded but disciplined education. Living in California, this had to work with just four working sessions of two weeks each per semester, and I knew that accomplishing this monumental task would require a new kind of digital teacher-student interaction. With the approval of my family, and after some intense discussions with the assistant team of Stefan Zinell, Nikolas Heep, Martina Fineder, Matthias Pfeffer and later also Peter Knobloch, we were ready to begin the journey of change.

Developing our Mission: Convergent, Social, Sustainable Design

The team began by defining a new mission. In Austria, as in many places, Design (that is, the field and concept of design) remains very connected to its roots in arts and crafts. A carpenter might function as an interior designer, a tailor a fashion designer, a typesetter a graphic designer, and a metalworker or silversmith an industrial designer. So, in our mission statement, we needed to update our educational approach to prepare students for excelling in the profession as it is today and for transforming it into what it must be in the future. That meant teaching convergent, strategic design—no matter what physical or virtual manifestation it might assume. To set the stage for that teaching model, we created this mission manifesto:

"The holistic challenge for Design is to create physical and virtual objects, which are useful, artful, and capable of inspiring spiritual values while using as few atoms and bits as possible. Design is our modern-day continuation of technical functionality converted into historic and metaphysical symbolism. When designers create a new and better object, a mechanism, a software application, or a more inspiring experience, that creation will become a branding symbol in itself, characterized by meaningful innovation, good quality, and ethical behavior. People will recognize the resulting visual symbols as a cultural expression of humanized technology and subconsciously connect it with historically transmitted visual shapes and patterns. Design cannot be just a fashion statement but must advance our industrial culture by providing sustainable innovation, cultural identity, and consistency, and by creating emotional and social belonging.

"Designers have a social responsibility to connect and coordinate human needs and dreams with new opportunities in science, technology, and business, so that the results of their efforts are culturally relevant, economically productive, politically beneficial, and ecologically sustainable. Accelerated globalization poses huge challenges and offers new opportunities, which demand that designers be both talented and capable of identifying and influencing new trends. They must use their skills to master the complicated issues surrounding outsourcing and to reverse the current overproduction of generic and hard-to-use products.

ZENITH DATA SYSTEMS LAPTOP, 1994. PHOTO: DIETMAR HENNEKA

Designers also need to invent new concepts for home-sourcing by helping local and tribal cultures convert traditional practices into beneficial new concepts. To succeed as competent and respected executive partners in the rational world of business, designers must become creative entrepreneurs and executives themselves. Ultimately, Design must rise above all commercial-functional benchmarks and aspire to near-eternal cultural relevance and spirituality."

ADJACENT DISCIPLINES AND INFLUENCERS OF STRATEGIC DESIGN

Setting Up Teams, Themes, and Processes

Design is a team sport. Nobody can solve complex challenges alone, and designers have to work with professionals in other disciplines. Therefore – except for their diploma projects – we determined that the students had to work in teams of three or four. The leader of each team had to be a senior student, and every team also had to include at least one freshman, an arrangement that promoted cross-learning within the team and tamed potentially destructive egos. At the end of each semester, we assigned the students themes for the next semester, so they could prepare ideas for meaningful project proposals, which, at minimum, had to be convergent, social, and sustainable. The semester themes always included a social and an ecological challenge – for example, "Safe and Clean Personal Space," "Human Tools," "Our Blue Ark," or just "Green." At the start of the semester, each student made a brief presentation and, through a semi-democratic process, we selected which projects would be the twelve winners (one for each team). With the teams set up, the work could begin the same day. This process kicked off the semester on a high note and inspired all of us – students and teachers alike.

In keeping with processes in business planning, engineering, and marketing, we divided the semester into three four-week phases:

- Discover Phase: Any design process must start with research and focus on human behaviors, social trends, market-relevant desires, and emerging opportunities in science and technology. During the Discover phase, students gained a good understanding of the space in which they were designing and what the project would achieve for the potential users. At the end of this phase, the team documented their findings and presented them to the entire class, an experience that developed their presentation skills, sparked further discussion, and promoted mutual learning.

- Design Phase: The briefing was the basis for this phase of conceptual and esthetic ideation. The students now had to create new ideas and concepts to explore all feasible options. In addition to sketches, the students created concept models and user scenarios. At the end of this phase, the teams presented two to four concepts to the entire class. After a discussion, each team selected its winning concept.

- Define Phase: In this final phase, the students refined their chosen design concept by creating a series of models and CAD renderings. Even in my earliest classes, I expected students to produce professional-grade models, which we paid for with money earned by the students in workshops with companies (you read about these workshops later in the chapter) that also provided necessary equipment, such as a 3D printer. The result of this phase was an original design suitable for commercial implementation. The final documentation and presentation of the design had to be in adequate forms of media, such as drawings, renderings, models, digital animations, and prototypes.

Realizing that modern business and industry is global and that design is a globally networked profession, I brought the lessons I had learned at frog right into the class. When I wasn't in Vienna, the students had to upload their weekly progress report onto a secure shared website. By Monday morning in Vienna, my assistant team had my feedback and then presented it to the entire class. Students could email questions to me and I would answer them immediately, no matter where I was. Later, I always tried to follow up my email response with a phone call. In my view, communication skills are vital for success in design, and so even these communication processes offered important training to my students. After a slow start, this process resulted in a "perfect machine."

Teaching Through Real-World Experiences
Within their academic education, I wanted our design students to have the opportunity to work in realistic scenarios with good companies. My goal was to give the students firsthand, real-world experience as well as an opportunity to make important personal contacts and to position themselves for paid internships or their first job – or even to kick-start their own design agency.

I told the companies we would participate in the workshop for a donation fee of about $45,000. I also made it very clear that the class wasn't a design studio, but that academic goals were paramount. Companies such as Flextronics, Telefunken, XXXLutz, Arcelik-Beko, and T-Mobile accepted these terms and later confirmed that the workshop process also helped them to rethink their own approaches to design. Everyone saw a great value in this exercise.

With any company, the task for the class was to inspire the executives who worked with them, to demonstrate new market potential, and to moderate the transfer of ideas and concepts into convincing proposals for new convergent products, services, and content. Each workshop ran parallel to regular semester projects. At its core was a three-day session in a modified format of an ideation process we had developed at frog called frogThink. The students worked in six teams (different than the semester teams) and went through three focused ideation sessions – Association, Alternative, and Provocation – themed by a starting statement, which became more important with each phase.

Each day, the teams worked for six hours and then presented their work to the executives and the class. From each team, the group selected the three best ideas, so at the end of the three days, we had nine ideas from each team, or a total of fifty-four ideas. Then, we discussed with the executives which three to six ideas were the best overall. Through the end of the semester, we communicated back and forth with the company while the students converted the ideas into a professional presentation. When the company chose an idea for production, we recommended a professional studio or, in some cases, the company hired an alumnus from our class.

Seeing the world is vital for designers, and for me, every design student should visit three critical centers of creativity and design: Japan, Holland, and California. Because our student workshops had earned the means to pay for most of the flights and hotels, our class could venture out to meet key people and companies in these destinations, which are normally not accessible for students. In Japan, we visited Kenji Ekuan at GK Design, Toyota's advanced design studio as well as Panasonic, Tama Art University, Fumi Matsuda at Tokyo Zokei University, Katsutoshi Ishibashi at AXIS magazine, Kyoto Seika University, Kyoto Manga Museum, and Yamaha. In Holland, we met with Stefano Marzano at Philips and visited Technical University Eindhoven and Delft.

In California, the class was able to visit a number of leading designers and design studios, including CCA San Francisco, Stanford d. school, Carnegie Mellon University, Art Center College of Design in Pasadena, Jonathan Ive and Rico Zorkendorfer at Apple, Dan Harden at Whipsaw, frog, Ideo, the Computer History Museum in Mountain View, Google, Specialized, Disney Imagineering, BMW Designworks, and the Volkswagen/Audi Advanced Studio in Santa Monica. We also had an opportunity to explore the venture incubator Mind The Bridge, San Francisco, which helps bring European entrepreneurs to Silicon Valley. These field trips were both rewards for the students' hard work and further motivation. Much more importantly, however, they offered students a glimpse at the reality of global design at the highest level – a level my students had to aspire to.

Demanding a Commitment to Excellence

In terms of design, the University of Applied Art in Vienna wasn't a first-rate school when I joined it. I knew that this had to change – beginning with my class. In addition to subjecting applicants to my class to a thorough three-day entry exam in which they had to do a quick project, I also shared with each of them the realities of the design business, so that everyone entering the class was fully prepared for the work – and profession – ahead of them. When necessary, I helped them work through their personal blocks and, in some cases, asked them to commit in writing to giving their best in the class.

In my view, we educational elders are responsible for building the next generation of creative leaders, so our responsibilities aren't limited to lecturing. Another important element in achieving excellence is discipline – or, as I call it, "always showing up." A design leader can't quit, and students must accept the responsibilities that come with the task of designing products for millions of people all over the world. My wife, Patricia, summed up this idea in her own formula for success in design: 1% idea, 90% process and discipline, and 9% luck. Ideas certainly are the spark that lights the creative fire, but the fuel comes from perfect operations. Any shortcoming in these elements demands more luck – which can run out fast. For all of these reasons, I set a high standard for disciplined, professional habits in my class.

In order to generate visibility for the Master Class ID2, the students had to send their work to design competitions. I also funneled their work into my own professional network, to help generate internships and jobs for the students. We all worked hard to improve the class, and success came slowly. But after about four years, the class had reached a level I felt comfortable with. And then, the awards began rolling in: First place in the Global Electrolux Award, multiple Austrian Staatspreise (National Design Awards), and multiple awards in design competitions in Germany and Japan. The students also got the attention of creativity-minded websites such as Boing Boing, Gizmodo, C.Net, and Core77. Finally, the American magazine Bloomberg Business Week ranked the Master Class ID2 among the world's top thirty design programs in elite education. Equally important was the recognition of world-class companies such as Audi, which made a grant to the class in order to research "mobility of young families in Vienna" and to design proposals.

Today, my students have been accepted in world-class companies and design agencies around the world. And, I want to point out that my students – and my assistant team – achieved all of this success within a mediocre and even hostile environment. As Albert Einstein once noted: "Great spirits have often encountered violent opposition from weak minds." Because the class drew such positive attention – for example, the ten minutes Austrian President Fischer spent at my students' booth in the annual degree show – envy set in. The jury sessions for diploma students at the end of each semester were a scandalous display of incompetence, envy, and personal payback. Some of my fellow professors expressed their hostility towards me by trying to punish my students with bad grades. In one case, I submitted a student project that another professor had panned to a National Design competition, where it won the Grand Prize. Nevertheless, the class has generated more good news than bad. Through the initiative of Christoph Thun-Hohenstein, the new director of the Museum of Applied Art next door to the University in Vienna, I have helped to curate an exhibition called MADE4YOU. It includes key works by my students in a section called Future Lab, which certainly will help to document the students' talent and inspire a continued drive for excellence throughout our field – a goal I also hold for this book. Some of my students have proven that they are well on their way to becoming true leaders, and for that, I am both optimistic and thankful.

Moving Forward: The DeTao Master Academy

Toward the end of my teaching in Vienna, I was approached by the DeTao Master Academy in Beijing, China. It was scouting for foreign creative leaders in the areas of design, architecture, and cinema in order to help promote and educate a new creative elite in China. There, Design is considered a subset of the arts, and there is an obvious disconnect between business and the nation's high-tech industry. While China strives for global recognition as a business and high-tech leader, Chinese design students are creating vases, chairs, and art objects. During my discussion with representatives of the DeTao Master Academy, one official convinced me of his understanding of the work I had done as a teacher in Vienna when he said that "both Austria and China are developing countries in design, but Austria doesn't know it."

While these discussions were unfolding, I was also offered some opportunities at home, and many of my friends in Silicon Valley questioned the logic of accepting a teaching position in China. But, in my observation, America is far from a designer's (or an educator's) paradise. Most executives in America are just chasing money, and most politicians paralyze any positive move towards a more humanistic model of business and industry through their idiotic partisanship and overweening desire to get reelected. Our nation's radicalized electorate fails to understand that the current financial and economic crisis is also a crisis of ethics. We neglect the critical work of liberating our country of its addiction to oil, which enriches countries that are hostile to us and pollutes the air we breathe. In addition our manufacturing jobs continue to vanish into Asia. When it comes to education, all our elected politicians can think of is to cut funding – and this in light of absurdly high bonuses on Wall Street and billions wasted for wars that never should have been started. And, to say the least, strategic design isn't high on anyone's professional or educational agenda.

Make no mistake, I'm not blind to the problems in China. A lot of products coming from China are badly designed and often of questionable quality. But these products are typically designed by designers in America and Europe, or they are requested by executives who are just looking for the cheapest possible price, with no regard for quality and ecological impact. After taking all of this into account and, again, with the support of my wife and family, I decided to accept the challenge. Today, I am working to educate China's creative designers, leaders who will help to make design a keystone of Chinese development and who will develop new methods for achieving more success with less. The timing of this work is critical because the Chinese economy is evolving from one in which high growth is driven by low prices to one in which strong growth is fueled by quality. The ideas and techniques developed by graduates of the DeTao Academy program also will help reduce the all too common exploitation of Chinese workers and natural resources. My goal for Design in China is to reduce production, to increase profits, and to increase product life cycles (and thereby reduce waste).

As with the Master Class ID2 in Vienna, my first task for the DeTao Academy program was to craft a mission statement. Here is the mission we will pursue:

Building a sustainable, creative elite community both with Chinese and global talent, by educating, training, and mentoring design leaders for education, business, and government agencies – and helping to convert Chinese industry and companies from "the world's biggest workshop" into creativity-driven design and brand leaders.

After several good discussions and a search for the best location, my studio has found a home at the Shanghai Institute of Visual Arts of the Fudan University, located in Songjiang University Town in western Shanghai. The building is new and is host to many colleagues from all over the world. The facilities will include a state-of-the-art design studio, furnished with original work from design leaders such as Vitra, Herman Miller, and Artemide – for one cannot educate great designers in an environment of bad equipment or shabby copies. And, of course, we have also designed some of our own pieces to use within our space. We have a cutting-edge model shop – probably the first of its kind in Chinese education – equipped with German machinery and tools. The facility includes an ecologically safe color system and spray booth, a standard set by frog and happily adapted by Apple and other companies.

The first hire for my five-member team is Benjamin Cselley. Benjamin was one of my very best students in Vienna, so ID2 will remain a part of my professional life. In order to achieve the best possible results, ours will be a post-graduate program with a maximum of thirty students.

THE DETAO MASTER PROGRAM

Here is a detailed overview of the DeTao Master program:

Status of Program	Post-Graduate – DeTao Master Program (not sanctioned by Government)
Strategic Design	Analog-Digital Convergent Products, Human-Machine Interfaces, Content Integration of Innovation and Business, Social and Ecological Sustainability
Industry Focus	Wireless and mobile, Digital consumer electronics, Mobility, White goods and appliances, Wellness and health, Machinery and robotics
Duration	1 or 2 years (depending on student and decision by teaching staff)
Semesters	March-June and October-January (8 months)
	Internships recommended during 3-month summer break
Method of Studies	Seminars and lectures, Modelmaking central to project work
	Semester projects (teams, 3 months)
	"Quickie" projects (individual, 1 week)
	Workshops with companies (parallel to regular schedule)
	Final project (individual, 3 months)
Students/Applicants	Design undergraduates
	Professionals with a degree in Design
Application	(to be delivered to the studio 1 month before entry exam):
	Personal portfolio
	Personal letter of motivation
	Records of undergraduate degree in Design
	Letter(s) of recommendation
3-Day Entry Exam	(at start of each semester):
	Personal interview
	Sculpting and sketching of objects
	Test project over 48 hours
Ratio	Max. 8 students per teacher
Tuition	RMB 120K/year

Preparing Designers to Lead the Future

The world is constantly changing and so are the requirements for strategic designers. As I have stressed in other chapters of this book, the challenges we are facing in regard to ecology, social balance, and sustainable development are paramount to our work as designers and central to our creative education. As we work to design a better future, we must be fully aware of the past, especially in the way it has been reflected in the emotional and functional issues of consumer behavior. One of my favorite koans (Zen riddle) distills the essentials of past, present, and future, in the simple words "already here and tomorrow." In keeping with that wisdom, I would like to conclude this chapter with a list that I think may help illuminate our future challenges through a historic perspective:

- 1960–1970: As customers looked for products, the mantra was "Satisfy me," and brands had to inform consumers. A good example is the utilitarian and practical Volkswagen Beetle.

- 1980–1990: As products had to look for customers, the mantra was "Seduce me," and brands had to attract consumers. A good example is the freewheeling fun of the Sony Walkman.

- 2000–2010: As products became a tool for a lifestyle, the mantra was "Change me" (or even better, "Change us"), and brands had to be personal statements. A good example is Apple's iPhone.

- ~2020: Looking ahead, customers and products will become one, and the mantra will be "Know me." Brands will have to be "the way."

As I contemplate the last item in this list, which lays out what I believe is the future direction of strategic design, I am reminded of the words of Lao Tzu: "Life is a series of natural and spontaneous changes. Don't resist them; that only creates sorrow. Let reality be reality. Let things flow naturally forward in whatever way they like." I think of this statement often in response to the question I so frequently hear from friends and colleagues who learn of my newest educational venture: "Why China?"

DORIAN

you are the content

eternal youth is the ultimate perversion

be honest with yourself

ZEIT

determine your future

I ♥ NICOTINE

OSKAR WILDE

Discover

The "Dorian Gray Book" is a communication tool for social networking. It's based on the moral principles of the book written by Oskar Wilde 1890.

Eternal youth - Data storage   Multiple identity - different accounts   self awareness - looking beautiful   Motivation - Data storage   Craving for beauty and love - Body transfer

Design

Local information
The system also allows contacts to see your current geographic information, making it easier to meet with you and eliminating those "where are you?" phone calls.

Data expiration
Everything you upload on dorian can be given an expiration date. The data is fully deleted when the date is reached.

Brand relations
Brands have the ability to create an interactive relationship with their customers. You can get information from your favorite brands and have access to a contact person to help you.

Analysis
The whole system offers a special prognosis tool, which is helpful in situations like writing a message and getting a useful link or you can also use it as a Timeline to see the development of a relationship – and the system will predict how it might develop in the future.

3 Layers with ranking
Your contacts can be sorted into three different layers. You have control over who can see what information about you. Your contacts are ranked according to communication frequency – like in real life.

Define

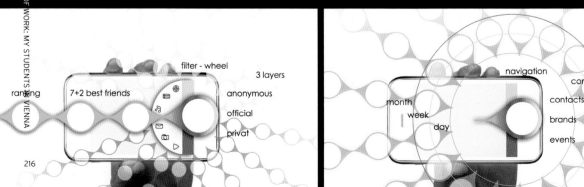

filter - wheel

7+2 best friends

3 layers
anonymous
official
privat

ranking

navigation
content
contacts
brands
events

month
week
day

7 A PORTFOLIO OF WORK: MY STUDENTS IN VIENNA

"No great thing is created suddenly." EPICTETUS

Here, I want to show you a small portfolio of some of the best work by students in the Master Class ID2. The brilliance of this work amply demonstrates that designers are made, not born. This work also proves that students are willing to take even the steepest road ahead when they are on a mission to improve and beautify the world.

These selected projects from the Master Class ID2 at the University of Applied Arts in Vienna demonstrate how a holistic design education can inspire students beyond their own expectations and also prepare them for a career as thoughtful and caring professionals. The projects are presented in six areas – all essential to people's lives. All of these projects had to qualify as social, sustainable, and convergent. Semester projects were conducted in teams while diploma projects were individual efforts, although the team spirit of the Master Class motivated students in all of their work. Students incorporated new technologies currently in development within their work, given that it may be five or more years before these students will be taking their places as leaders in industry, research, or executive management.

Credits: All projects of the Master Class ID2 were created by my former students, whose names appear with the illustrations of their projects, along with their own description of their work. Students conducted their work from 2005 to 2011 under the instruction and guidance by the teaching staff at the University of Applied Arts, Vienna, Austria.

Chair: Univ. Prof. Dr. Hartmut Esslinger | Conceptual instruction: Stefan Zinell, Nikolas Heep and, until 2008, Martina Fineder | Digital design and animation instruction: as of 2007 Peter Knobloch | Modelmaking and technology support: Univ. Prof. Matthias Pfeffer

DORIAN GRAY BOOK, A "FACEBOOK" WHICH CAN PROJECT AND FORGET.
STUDENTS: HARALD TREMMEL, NADINE VON SEELEN, ALEXANDER WURNIG

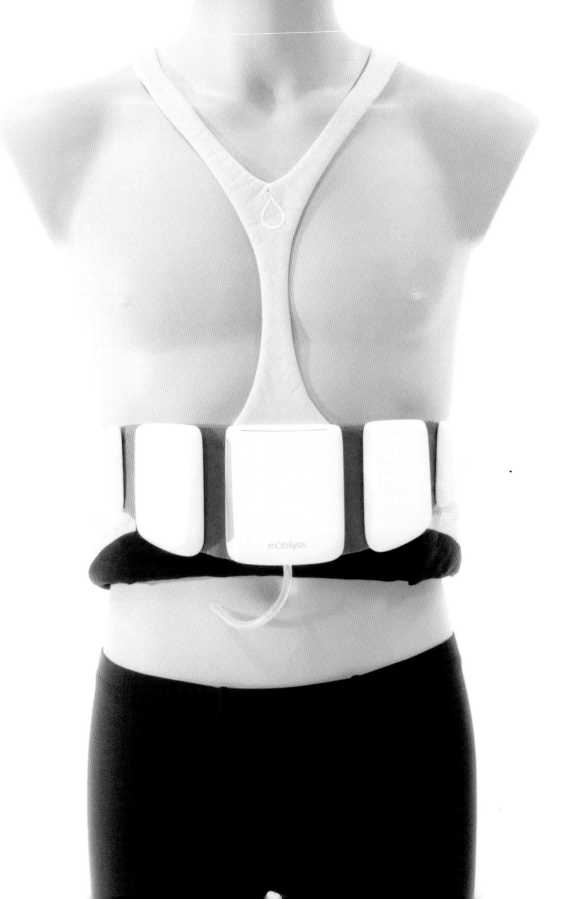

HEALTH

Mobile Dialysis

Winner of the Austrian National Design Award

Semester Project: Maria Gartner (lead), Nico Strobl, Stefan Silberfeld, Dimitar Genov

Living with the need for constant dialysis is a tough fate. After researching existing technology, the team devised a method for combining multiple dialysis technologies into one single system that can be worn by the patient. As the students explain, Mobilysis is a brand new mobile dialysis system aimed at people with kidney failure. By using Mobilysis, patients have the choice when and where to undergo vital blood cleaning, rather than spending hours of their time in specialized centers. Dialyzing liquid is pumped from the container belt into the abdominal cavity in multiple cycles, where it cleanses the blood through the peritoneum. Lethal urea is thereby transferred from the body into the liquid, through a process of simple osmosis. After every cycle the contaminated liquid is purified in the technical element and is thereby ready for the next cycle. With this system it is possible to carry out dialysis at home. The device consists of two parts: a flexible belt, divided into multiple membranes, which contains the dialysis liquid, and a hard-shell front piece housing the hardware, the catheter connector, and the intrarenal cleaning unit. The Mobilysis system is controlled via an intuitive and easy-to-use smartphone application. Basic safe manual operation is also possible through buttons on the front part.

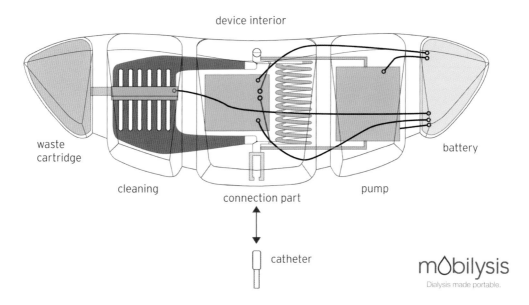

device interior

waste cartridge

cleaning

connection part

catheter

pump

battery

mobilysis
Dialysis made portable.

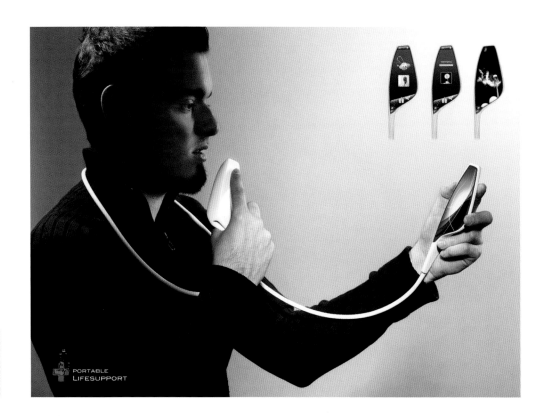

PORTABLE
LIFESUPPORT

HEALTH

Portable Life Support

Semester Project: Benjamin Cselley (lead), Niklas Wagner, Lukas Pressler, Oskar von Hanstein

According to medical reports, over 600 million people worldwide suffer from chronic obstructive pulmonary disease (COPD). COPD is the fourth leading cause of death in the United States and is projected to be the third leading cause of death for both sexes by the year 2020. To get a feeling for COPD* yourself, do as follows: Hold your breath, until you can't stand it any longer, continue to count to ten, and then breathe out! This should give you an idea what COPD feels like. An effective cure is to practice breathing, and the Portable Life Support system perfectly supports you in this practice. Portable Life Support also offers respiratory treatment and reports your progress via WLAN to your attending doctor.

High-Tech Arm Prosthesis

Semester Project: Helene Steiner (lead), Lukas Pressler, Nico Strobl

There are two challenges for hand and lower-arm prosthetics: function and semantics. The prosthesis shown here is a step toward a new robotics-friendly society, and the technology itself is designed as an attractive device. This device doesn't attempt to disguise itself as a simulated arm but rather transforms a handicap into a tool with more power and possibility than a human arm can offer. The wearer maneuvers the arm via myoelectric sensing and controls the tools with gestures combined with the display located at the "forearm" for fine tuning. The device includes the newest wireless technologies as well as handy tools, such as a camera, flashlight, screw driver, phone, bottle opener (!) and a USB stick for data exchange.

* Asthma sufferers should not attempt this experiment.

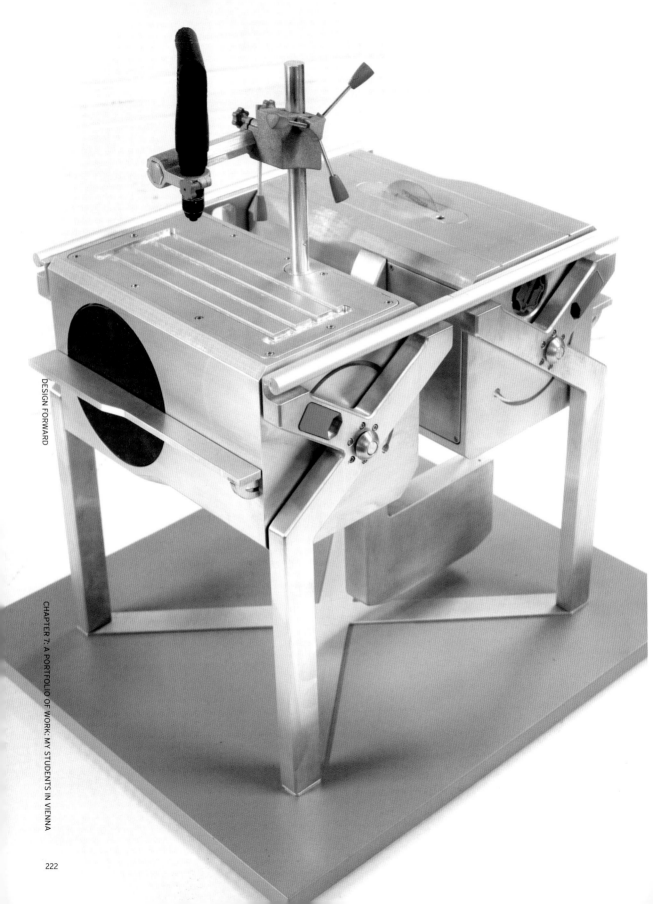

LIFE AND WORK

ModelMachine

Diploma Project: Bernhard Ranner

Besides sketches and renderings it is crucial for a designer to have real models to judge the ergonomics, haptics, and function of his work. The earlier in the design phase such quick models are built the better. Unfortunately only big companies and design agencies can afford to have a designated model shop. ModelMachine is designed to fill this void for the smaller agencies and start-ups. With a footprint no bigger than an office desk, ModelMachine offers everything one could ask for in a model shop. Actually, this is a dream-machine for modelmakers, created by a designer who loves to design by models.

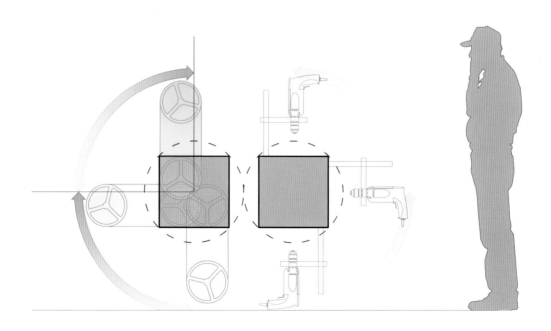

LIFE AND WORK

Flatshare Fridge

Winner of Global Electrolux Award

Semester Project: Stefan Buchberger (lead), Martin Faerber

The flatshare concept as a modern style of living offers a way – particularly for young people – to live cheaply and independently in common spaces. The idea of flatshare deals with the emerging problems of disorder and the need to create privacy in these urban living forms. Modular elements within the Flatshare Fridge allow each user individual customizations (skins, add-ons), systems of order, and mobility. The add-ons have different functions – a blackboard, a flower vase, a bottle opener, and so on – which users can add to the front of the elements. Every module (up to four pieces) is connected to cooling fluid and electricity through the base station, where a regulator controls the power of the compressor according to the number of used modules. All in one, one for all – saving energy and money! The dimensions are the same as conventional fridges, which enables the flatshare fridge to be used within a standard kitchen. On the top and bottom there are two bases to stack the modules perfectly together. Both sides are equipped with handles to be able to stack and separate the modules easily. The cubic capacity of each module is 84.3 liters, which is a bit more than the average storage capacity required by one person, as statistics have shown.

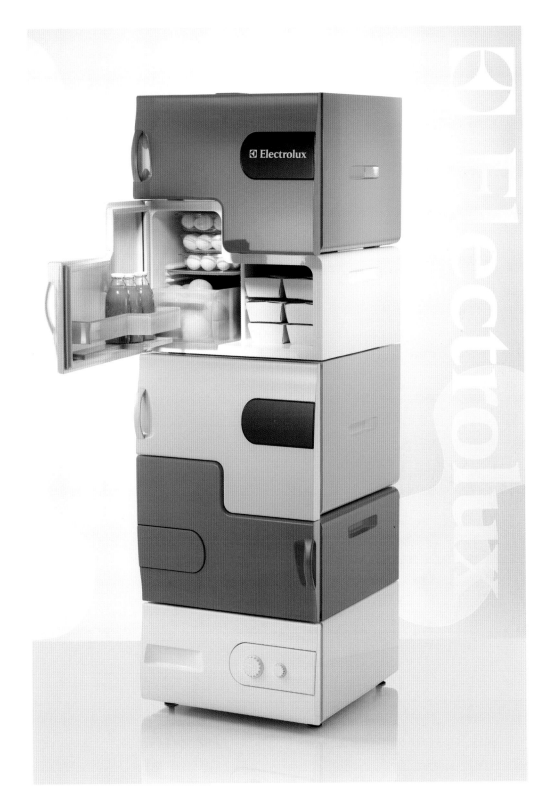

ENTERTAINMENT

Robotic Hero Bugs

Diploma Project: Benjamin Cselley

Following the motto "make videogames come alive," this project features nature-inspired robots equipped with the most advanced bionic muscle technology and artificial intelligence, operated via an application on a smartphone or a tablet computer. For ultimate entertainment, we present KOLO, SHO, AKU, NOMIA and TWIN, each of them having a unique ability. What do these "creatures" have in common? They are RoboBugs! And they might become HeroBugs, but in order to achieve that status they need a trainer – you! You, the user, prepare them for the performing three disciplines: sumo, parkour, and harvest. Overcoming these challenges demands absolute unity of trainer and bug, man and machine, adding a new a new level of fascination to "convergent gaming." The robots can be programmed with specific abilities, but then they act completely autonomously. The HeroBugs are the fighters, and the human player is the coach in the corner of the dojo.

The Heroes:

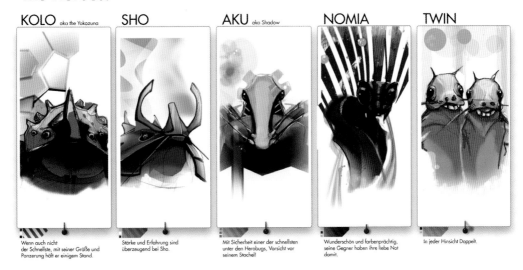

KOLO *aka the Yokozuna*   SHO   AKU *aka Shadow*   NOMIA   TWIN

Wenn auch nicht
der Schnellste, mit seiner Größe und
Panzerung hält er einigem Stand.

Stärke und Erfahrung sind
überzeugend bei Sho.

Mit Sicherheit einer der schnellsten
unter den Herobugs. Vorsicht vor
seinem Stachel!

Wunderschön und farbenprächtig,
seine Gegner haben ihre liebe Not
damit.

In jeder Hinsicht Doppelt.

ENTERTAINMENT

DiGuitar Synthesizer

Diploma Project: Anton Weichselbraun

Next to the flute, the guitar is the most popular musical instrument on the planet. The DiGuitar offers guitarists the combination of analog playability with the technology and methods of electronic music. It replaces strings, pickups, and frets with digital inputs, and it models a MIDI-Signal adaptable to sound like any given guitar and amp setup. A touch-sensitive neck analyzes and produces sounds based on finger positions, and liquid micro-channels rise above the surface to create variable fret positioning while piezoelectric actuators emulate frequencies of vibration corresponding to the played note. The brain recognizes these frequencies at the fingertips as the true sensation of physical strings.

Jelly Web, Hypermedia System with Touch Interface

Diploma Project: Konrad Kroenke

It's time that Internet-enabled devices become loveable, personal partners. These days it's common practice to use a lot of devices for daily business, such as communication, entertainment, and e-commerce, or simply to get information: one data stream – one interface. All the information, contacts, and business data we use should be available to us in a sensual form. Technically, Jelly Web is a simple computer with a small temporary storage and a good data transfer capability. The unit is always online, and contents like videos, music, and games placed on the servers of the supplier are shared with all other users. An intuitive, tactile user interface helps to break barriers and also activates the sense of hearing and seeing by handling its acoustic and visual contents. The design of the device's case differs from the usual appearance of electronic devices and encourages users to establish a personal relationship with the new family member. The user is in direct tactile contact with the sensitive surface of the "base," and this skin answers in the language of graphical representation. For the reproduction of high-grade video contents, an LED projector is integrated into the side of the body. To provide a brilliant audio-visual display, the base is supported by two majestic sound-generating units. These obelisks house cameras – the electronic eyes for interacting visually with others.

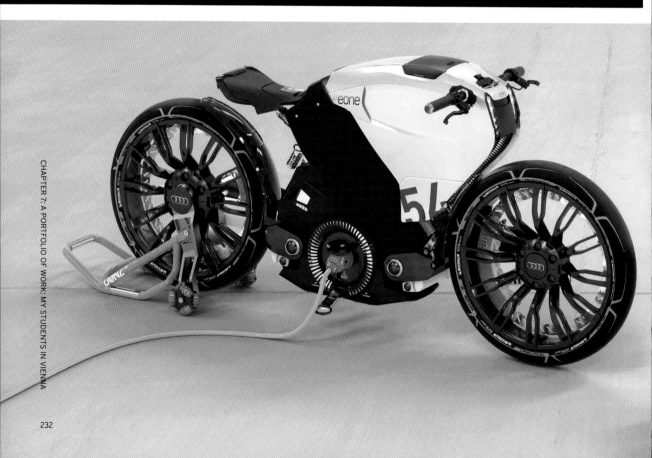

MOBILITY

Audi E1

Diploma Project: Lukas Doenz

It is not well known today, but the Audi Group has a long tradition in motorcycles. The brands DKW and NSU once were market leaders, and the 1955 NSU MAX was the first motorcycle designed with a monocoque from stamped and welded sheet metal. Looking ahead to electric drive trains and advanced telematics, the Audi E1 applies most advanced kinetic energy recovery system (KERS), digitally enabled safety features like stabilizer, lane change and distance controller, and drive-by-wire steering as well as all-wheel drive. Driving safety is also enhanced by cantilever suspensions for both wheels and a brake assistant. The ergonomics are adjustable to different heights of riders and to allow riders to choose between relaxed cruising and a sportier ride. The design defines new semantics for green energy, which radiate high emotional appeal, and it exposes all the new technology components, such as KERS, LED lights, battery packs, and other components, for easy customization.

MOBILITY

Digital Traffic Signs

Winner of multiple Design Awards in Austria and Germany

Semester Project: Erol Kursani (lead), Alexander Wurnig, Shirin Fani, Kristina Chudikova

There are more than 600 different traffic signs in use today and each one costs more than $400. At least one third of these signs are unnecessary, and it costs more to remove them than to keep them in place. Furthermore, many statistics show that people don't understand some traffic signs. In this design for digital traffic signs, control lines, which lead drivers through traffic, are projected on the windscreen yet appear to be a part of the street. The system is user friendly. A green line means "drive" and a red line means "stop." The yellow line in the middle provides the navigation system. Our aim is to reduce the chaos that rules the roads, make traffic flow fluent, organize traffic management, and eliminate visual clutter by physically removing the traffic signs. This design incorporates Head Up Display (HUD), which is controlled by satellite and projected onto the driver's windshield. With this design in use, streets are free of signs, traffic lights are reduced, and there is a Dynamic Traffic Light system dedicated for pedestrians. The system is also flexible: it adjusts to the actual traffic situation, for example, in low traffic, the light stays green.

Learning Cockpit

Winner of the Austrian National Design Award

Semester Project: Ewald Neuhofer (lead), Marco Doblanivic, Alex Gufler

As more than 50% of all traffic accidents are caused by drivers during their first five years of driving, this project focuses on learning to drive safely – and continuing to do so. In order to avoid any distraction from a screen on a center console, this concept concentrates all instruments and indicators in front of the driver. Instead of just informing the driver about speed, the software interaction provides advice, early warnings, and praise. When the driver demonstrates dangerous or distracted driving behavior, the device delivers negative feedback, such as unwanted music. The design and ergonomics of the "steering wheel" integrate all manual controls and also allows a more flexible configuration inspired by the yoke in airplanes or the joysticks used for video games.

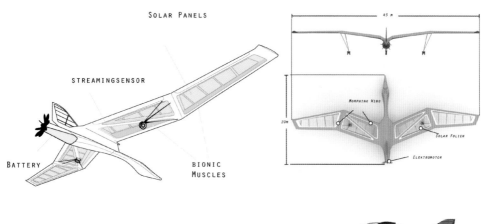

SOLAR PANELS

STREAMINGSENSOR

BATTERY

BIONIC
MUSCLES

45 M

MORPHING WING

20M

SOLAR FOLIEN

ELEKTROMOTOR

Leonardo
JUPIN.GHANBARI@JOOON.AT
ESSLINGER ___ DIPLOM 2011

DEFINE

„FOR ONCE YOU HAVE TASTED FLIGHT,
YOU WILL WALK THE EARTH,
WITH YOUR EYE TURNED SKYWARDS."

Leonardo
JUPIN.GHANBARI@JOOON.AT
ESSLINGER ___ DIPLOM 2011

MOBILITY

Leonardo Solar Plane

Diploma Project: Jupin Ganbari

The goal for this project was to get inspired by Leonardo da Vinci's sketches and models of "flying machines," and then to look for new solutions applying state-of-the-art solar flying technology by NASA and other companies to those early designs. Leonardo designed with materials known to him; with access to modern, hyper-strong materials, we can assume that he would have created more bionic and birdlike designs. The Leonardo Solar Plane is supposed to fly with minimal support by an electric propeller engine, which is located at the tail in order to avoid any turbulent drag along the fuselage by the airstream. The chosen configuration is for four people with luggage but can be increased for short-distance air-shuttle services.

PROJEKT IDEE:
Solar Bird Leonardo

HOW WOULD LEONARDO DESIGN A SOLAR BIRD?

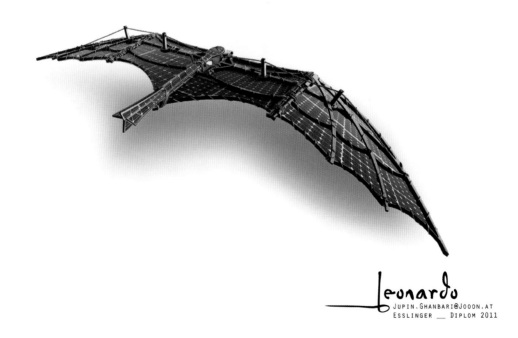

Leonardo
JUPIN.GHANBARI@JOOON.AT
ESSLINGER __ DIPLOM 2011

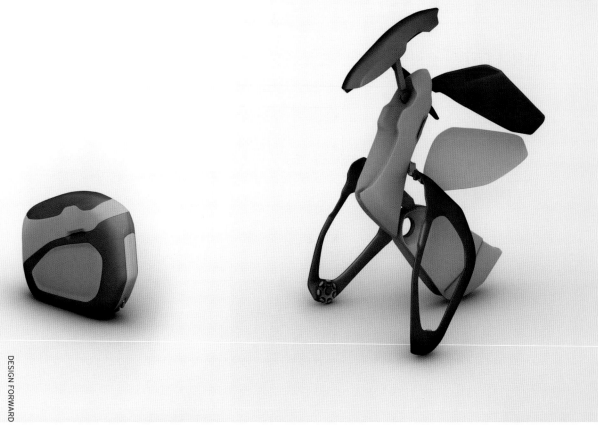

DIGITAL CONVERGENCE

Mariposa Transformer

Diploma Project: Florian Wille

The motivation behind this project was "what Steve Jobs would do in 2015." The resulting design is a convergent hybrid of a computer, communicator, and self-reliant bionic robot. As an MIT study showed, users are more likely to bond with a robotic interface than with a screen-based agent. I assumed that this must be especially true for people alien to technology, such as children and senior citizens. Mariposa is aware of its surroundings and is able to overlay the real world with digital information through its projector. This makes it possible to break the keyboard-screen paradigm, allowing for new ways of interaction.

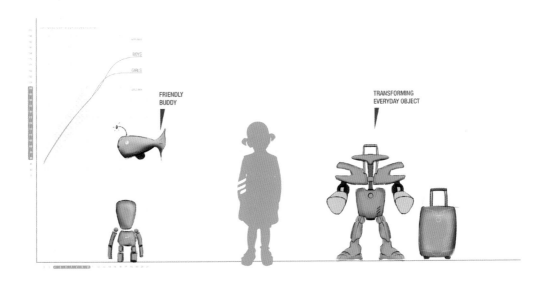

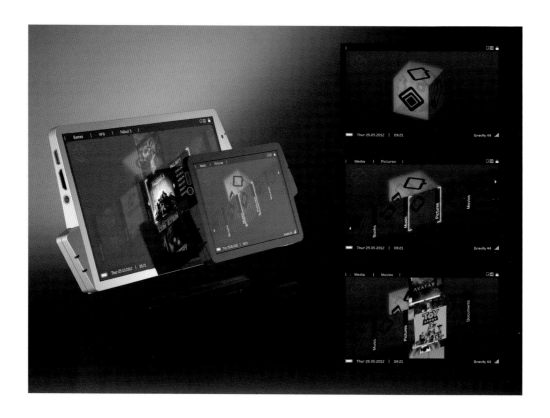

DIGITAL CONVERGENCE

Work Flow App

Semester Project: Minich David (lead), Martin Strohmeier, Marc Krenn, Stefan Kachaunov

Everybody knows that there is always a big difference between planning and execution. The basic problem is to decide about priorities and meaningful sequences of tasks. Extending beyond a simple calendar and organizational app, Workflow allows a user to break down project tasks according to three basic categories of importance: must do, should do, and want to do. The app allows users to give feedback on their own performance by filling in progress bars as various elements of a task are completed. In addition, contacts can be synced with the user's address book, grouped into categories, and linked to specific projects. This provides easy access to everyone involved in a particular project.

Gravity Phone & Cube UI

Semester Project: Claudia Bär, Maximilian Salesse, Peter Schanz

The provocation for this design was that Apple's iPhone and all its copies are too boring and do not allow physical user-interface expansion into applications – for example, medical, gaming, and applications for blind people. These expansions require specific haptic interfaces and, eventually, also will involve hardware such as a micro-switch display for Braille. Our goal for this product was to design a smartphone with a longer life cycle through modular architecture and improved usability. Therefore all components of the device are replaceable and upgradable, increasing the long-term and personal value of the digital tool. We also designed this concept to implement new technologies that optimize battery life, offer multi-touch experiences such as squeezing, and reduce negative environmental impact. The Cube user interface provides 3D navigations via the analogy of a "magical" box. As a result, the user will be able to access the desired application with fewer clicks and errors.

SURVIVAL

Aqualris Water Filter

Winner of the Austrian National Design Award

Diploma Project: Talia Radford Cryns

Aqualris is a portable water purifier for regions found near and within the tropics, where many suffer under the effects of natural or manmade catastrophes that limit the availability of access to clean and safe drinking water.

Aqualris combines the three steps to safe drinking water – collection, filtration, and neutralization of pathogens – together in one portable tool. This design aims at empowering people by providing them with safe, potable water independent of energy sources or infrastructure. After the water is collected, it is fed through a removable filter, which is then handily attached onto a lanyard that has instruction symbols printed onto it. The filtered water is gravitationally pulled under a layer of converter crystals that modulate the sun's rays to a UVC frequency with high germicidal qualities, which directly hit every water molecule passing under

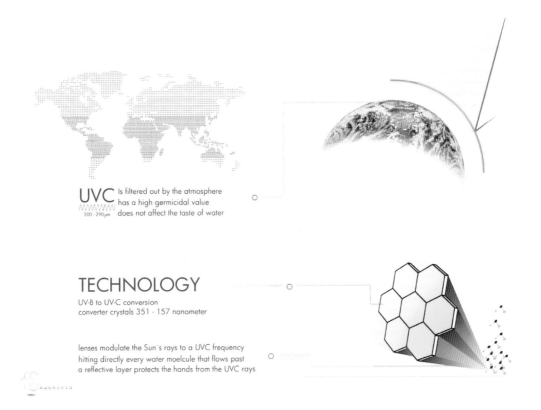

UVC Is filtered out by the atmosphere
/\/\/\/\/\/\ has a high germicidal value
200 - 290 μm does not affect the taste of water

TECHNOLOGY

UV-B to UV-C conversion
converter crystals 351 - 157 nanometer

lenses modulate the Sun's rays to a UVC frequency
hitting directly every water moelcule that flows past
a reflective layer protects the hands from the UVC rays

AQUALRIS

SURVIVAL

Beach Rescue

Semester Project: Joachim Kornauth (lead), Lukas Pressler, Lukas Vejnik, Joe Mueller

Drowning ranks third among the causes of unnatural deaths in Europe, with more than 20,000 cases reported every year. Statistics show that securing the victim in the first minutes of distress is crucial for a successful rescue. S-QUIP is a drone that automatically monitors waterfronts, harbor areas, or, when mounted on a ship's guardrail, the area around a ship. In case of emergency, the drone is autonomously launched from its beacon to reach a person in distress. It drops an inflatable life buoy and signals the victim's position, thus bridging the time gap till rescue teams arrive.

Invitro meat cultivation

Diploma Project: Oskar von Hanstein

The current common method of meat production is unsustainable due to its ecological side effects and cruel conditions for farm animals, which also result in threats of bacterial and viral epidemics. Scandals about mass-produced, contaminated meat are growing, as are the demands for an end to the system's unsustainable waste of natural resources. But new technologies for eliminating these problems are already in development, and we can assume that they will be applicable for growing markets very soon. Researchers are growing in vitro meat products, for example, using tissue culture technologies. *TIME* magazine identified in vitro meat production as one of the top fifty breakthrough ideas of 2009. This is not a vegetable protein imitation; it is a product derived from culturing real animal muscle tissue cells. The benefits of in vitro meat cultivation include ease of feeding a larger population, limited land use, more efficient water use, well-regulated quality, reduced greenhouse gas emissions, and reduced fuel-versus-food decision-making for food production.

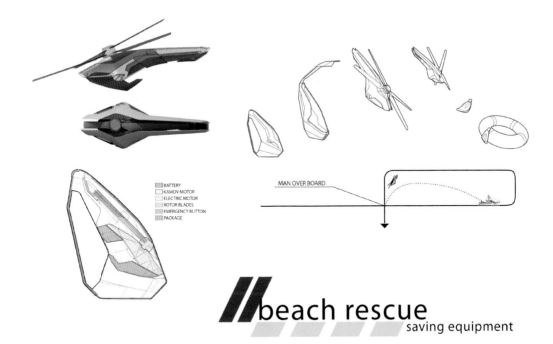

BATTERY
KAMOV MOTOR
ELECTRIC MOTOR
ROTOR BLADES
EMERGENCY BUTTON
PACKAGE

MAN OVER BOARD

beach rescue
saving equipment

MAN OVER BOARD

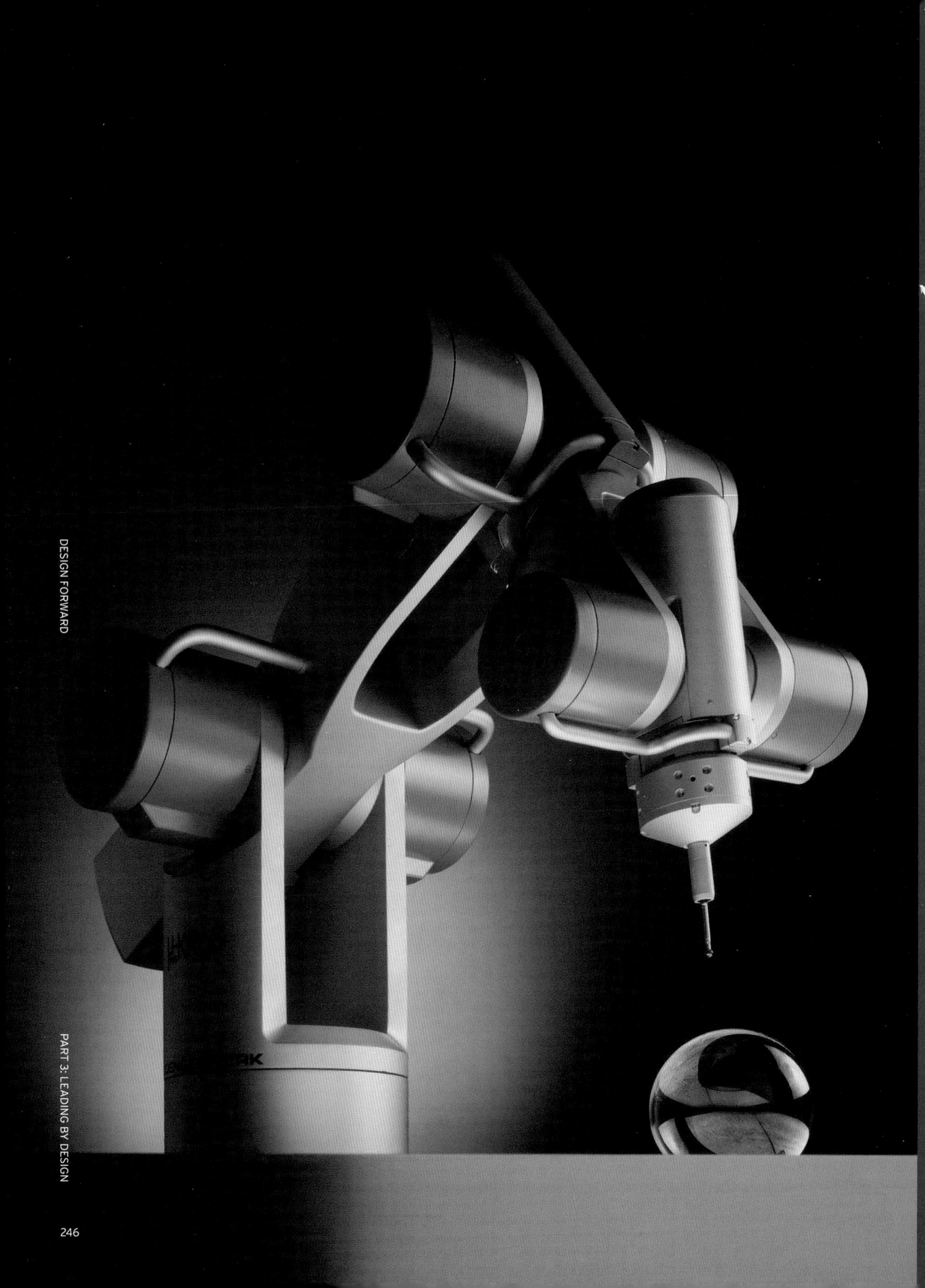

LEADING BY DESIGN

8 THE BOILING FROG

"If you drop a frog in a pot of boiling water, it will of course frantically try to clamber out. But if you place it gently in a pot of tepid water and turn the heat on low, it will float there quite placidly. As the water gradually heats up, the frog will sink into a tranquil stupor, exactly like one of us in a hot bath, and before long, with a smile on its face, it will unresistingly allow itself to be boiled to death."

BASED ON *THE STORY OF B* BY DANIEL QUINN

When I started frog (whose name is an acronym for the Federal Republic of Germany) in 1969, I was aware of the ecological challenges we were facing globally. When the Club of Rome published its first report, "The Limits of Growth," in 1972, I understood that we needed to change our industrial models from commodity-driven consumption to human-centric usage. As a species, frogs are extremely sensitive to imbalance. I think it's quite interesting, therefore, that the "boiling frog" metaphor offers a perfect illustration of how the majority of humans complacently shrug off the daily trickle of alarming news about the challenges we are facing today – pollution, global warming, financial brinkmanship, wasteful and populist-primitive politics, and human and social neglect. This same kind of fatal complacency seems to curse many companies who start out successfully but then fail to respond as their competitive environment heats up through technological, strategic, and cultural advances. Eventually, their failure to remain competitive dooms them to obsolescence.

If we want to avoid the fate of the boiling frog, we as people, communities, nations, and global mankind must become aware of gradual changes in order to avoid undesirable or even catastrophic consequences. The big question is, even when we become aware of growing threats, will we act upon them? And what are our options?

Given the failed global warming summits, the partisan strife in the United States Congress, and the helpless fatalism displayed at the World Economic Forum at Davos, the issues surrounding us are certainly heating up. Like it or not, we must accept that most executives and politicians currently in power cannot or do not want to switch gears in face of alarming news. They appear to be capable neither of recognizing the true nature of the challenges we face nor of "jumping out" through innovative ideas or initiatives. These facts offer disheartening answers to our most pressing social, economic, and environmental questions.

But, in reality, I believe that the deeper reason for the overriding complacency that grips so much of the world today is a behavioral and intellectual blindness. The complex problems we face today are defined by images, behaviors, and emotions, and solving such wicked problems requires creative thinking. Nearly all political, business, and educational leaders are rational, career-oriented left-brainers, however, who typically rely on logic for solving problems. We cannot expect much in terms of creative social solutions from these folks, especially since so many of them are hostages to their overblown egos and slaves to special interests.

On the other side we have a minority – about three in ten – of creative right-brainers, who are capable of thinking non-linearly as well as viscerally and therefore can provide creative and strategic solutions to these wicked problems. As I explained earlier, however, the overwhelming majority of them lack the professional skills necessary to work as equal partners with the people who are in power. If they want to claim their own fair share of power, pay, and influence, creative people must step up to the role of leadership.

Our most important task as creative leaders is to enable the rational leaders to understand that we all have to jump because we are in the same boiling water together. Therefore, I would like to use this chapter to outline my observations about the hurdles before us and how they have formed, and to offer some alternatives for overcoming them. In the course of that discussion, we will take a closer look at how some businesses have responded to the heating up of their own competitive environment, either by slowly sinking into a deadly slumber or by taking a creative leap into a new and more sustaining environment.

The Inevitable Evolution of Capitalism

In order to understand how we got here, we need to look at where we have come from. Since most people in the world today live and work in more or less capitalistic economic systems, we must look at the history of capitalism to understand how our current systems evolved. That history actually begins during the Renaissance and the Age of Enlightenment, when science, education, and individual human rights started to blossom. Just when ownership was becoming a more universally accepted idea, the Industrial Revolution came along, fed by the magical triangle of a trusted political system, better universities, and talented people who converted their ideas and visions into companies, industries, and new economies. Thus, capitalism was born.

While it is largely defined by a new attitude toward materialism, early capitalism also depended upon some fundamental cultural shifts in regard to philosophy and religion. As German philosopher Max Weber explained, these shifts began when the Christian Reformation in Europe (lead by Martin Luther, John Calvin, and Jan Hus) created more self-defined Christians who no longer relied on the Catholic Church's "buyable" promise of eternal salvation. As a result, the Puritans and Calvinistic Christians believed that they had to prove in this life that they were deserving of God's love and forgiveness. In the newly developing system of individual rights and ownership, more people began to work hard, live modestly, save their money, and reinvest it into their endeavors – behaviors that triggered a cycle of ever-increasing success.

This cycle created an extremely productive symbiosis between capitalism and religion – a fact Karl Marx recognized in his criticism of the suppression of the working classes through monetary means. But, when Marx called religion "opium for the masses," he missed the point: religion was the driving force behind capitalism. Ironically, communism also had the blessings of religion. Still, aside from the communist revolution in rural Russia, Marxism had a profound effect on the evolution of capitalism in Europe and the United States. Workers requested a fair share of the monetary and social rewards, went on strikes for better work and living conditions, organized themselves in labor unions, and gained political influence. At the same time, industrialists such as Henry Ford and Robert Bosch seemed to understand their social responsibility. They believed that their workers should make enough money so they could buy and enjoy the products they created – and these businessmen's companies became hugely successful.

In the twentieth century, products for personal use became an increasingly important industry, and mass production replaced individual manufacturing by both lowering prices and by providing better quality and design. The United States pioneered this advancement in manufacturing, but it was the international avant-garde architects, artists, and designers in the German Bauhaus University (1919–1933) who defined a new consumer culture liberated from "imperialistic-hierarchic" symbolism and functional compromises. The technology-inspired Bauhaus architecture, known as the International Style, promoted social change in urban living and shaped the skylines of modern cities.

With the advent of consumerism, capitalism and religion began to switch roles. Walter Benjamin – a German philosopher who committed suicide as the Nazis closed in on him in 1940 – thought that capitalism, which was only mildly tolerant of religion, had itself become a religion. About seventy-five years ago, while exiled in Paris, Benjamin stated that the new indoor shopping malls of Les Halles were modern-day cathedrals and temples, a thesis supported today by a comparison of medieval cathedrals to buildings such as the HSBC building in Hong Kong designed by Sir Norman Foster. Benjamin also observed that the act of buying had taken on a near religious character as a new form of spiritual worship. He even went so far as to posit that monetary debt had replaced ethical guilt (in German *debt* and *guilt* are the same word: *Schuld*), causing people to have to work to pay back their dues.[1] These ideas were in stark contrast to Max Weber's thesis that hope for salvation is the motivation for success.

THE HOLY ORDER OF APPLE

While Walter Benjamin's ideas about the blurring of religion and consumerism may sound radical, let us consider them in light of the commitment of Apple's customers (or, let's say, followers) to its products – a commitment with clearly religious characteristics. The BBC reported in 2011, that when an Apple fan's brain is scanned while viewing images of Apple products, it shows the same type of visual responses found in religious acolytes.[2]

Researchers found that the anticipation of the opening of an Apple store stimulated a response in the brains of those waiting outside (bottom row, center) similar to that of deeply religious people during intense prayers and rituals (bottom row, right).

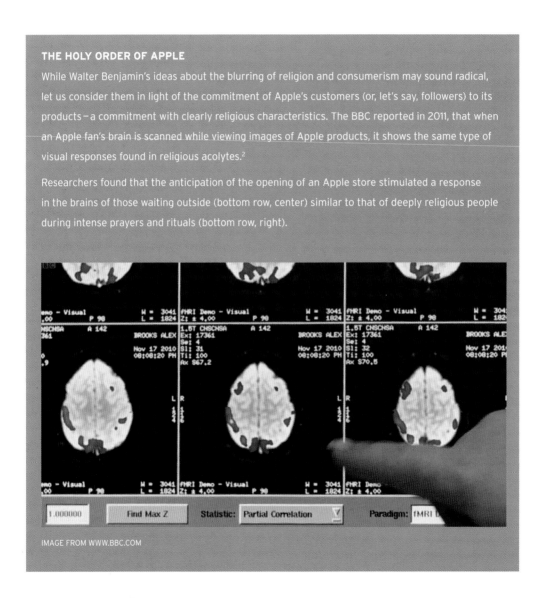

IMAGE FROM WWW.BBC.COM

From here, it doesn't take a radical leap to reach today's most prevalent form of capitalism. Money has become the god – with religion mostly a hypocritical excuse for fundamental ideologies of greed, environmental neglect, and systemic social imbalance. (Sadly, this perversion of spiritual religion is mirrored in many non-industrialized countries by fundamentalist intolerance and violence against women, children, and "infidels.") As a consequence, competition between most companies, industries, and countries no longer revolves around achievements such as great products and services but instead rests on abstract values derived from balance sheets and shareholder and market valuations. The financial industry (a cynical oxymoron of a term) is powerful enough to manipulate politics, as is proven by the United States' weak Wall Street reforms and the British government's retreat from the European Union despite the dire state of the productive British economy. In capitalism today, honest work loses out to exploitive speculation, and the rare leader such as Steve Jobs who pushes for "insanely great" products is seen as an aberration.

The Alternatives

In January of 2011, Harvard economist Michael E. Porter along with Mark R. Kramer wrote an interesting article in the *Harvard Business Review* titled "Creating Shared Value," in which they describe how capitalism might be reinvented and, subsequently, trigger a new wave of innovation growth (a stark departure from their previous ideology of a "clean capitalism"). Recognizing that people no longer buy into the ice-cold system of maximizing profit and success by any means, Porter and Kramer describe how investors and consumers today have lost trust in companies led by overpaid executives, even those who disingenuously tout corporate responsibility programs. As governments flounder in their attempts to try to correct abuses, the authors fear, companies and the economy will stall.

While a cynic could say that it takes time and effort to motivate unethical executives and companies to adapt to ethical conduct, Porter and Kramer make a convincing case that old-school executives and companies are losing out at an accelerated pace because they are incapable of innovating and leading any form of creative revolution. They also make it very clear that stupid and wasteful leadership is clearly recognizable. In their article, the authors ask why so many companies are wasting their resources, failing to follow a cogent strategy, alienating their customers, abusing their outsourcing partners, and – at the same time – wondering why a company like Apple is so successful and even loved. Porter and Kramer then go on to explain that a company must embed itself into culture and in turn have a positive impact on people's lives. While these ideas aren't revolutionary in creative circles, it is good to hear them coming from left-brainers.

As their final argument, Porter and Kramer propose that executives and companies have a holistic responsibility to humanize their practices and products. They foresee the next big transformation of "business thinking" as a movement aimed at integrating ethics, culture, and creative planning and implementation at center court, and positioning social progress above economic gain. Their concept of shared value acknowledges functional and emotional needs and envisions them as part of a new system, one which is founded in a more creative education and promoted by more compassionate leaders; a system in which individual human needs and desires trump mass marketing. Personally, I like their ideas. I just hope that we can accelerate the transformation process.

Of course, the abuses and excesses of capitalism have triggered responses from numerous radical thinkers and writers, such as Raj Patel, with his book *The Value of Nothing*.[3] The Austrian author and economic commentator Christian Felber proposes a somewhat utopian return to a form of basic capitalism in which community comes first and competition is replaced by a more socially balanced ranking of values, which, for example, define a company in terms of its contributions to the common good. Felber's ideas are similar to those of Rudolf Steiner, the founder of a human-centric philosophy called *anthroprosophy*, which is also the base of the education model in the Waldorf schools around the world.[4]

When it comes to operative details, Felber is at a loss, but I like his ethical zeal. We are in desperate need of radical ideas today, and we will also have to experiment with new and more creative socioeconomic models. Only through this kind of imaginative exploration of economic alternatives will we be able to overcome the current crisis of values, which, in essence, is a crisis of bad economics. We need a better way.

Money still seems to rule the world, but the most valuable technology company in the world – Apple – is at its core an idea company. Apple upended all of the accepted rules of corporate management. Where the company's competitors, from Sony to Samsung to HP, have hundreds of product lines, Apple just has four: Macintosh Personal computers, iPod music players, the iPhone, and the iPad – with these last two lines sharing the same architecture. Apple also was the first high-tech company to sells its products in its own brand stores – like the fashion brands Louis Vuitton or Chanel – while its competitors still have antiquated distribution models. In spite of this clear example of the power of idea-based strategies to succeed over those based on cost-cutting, most executives still don't get it. They fail to grasp the magnitude of this management revolution, and so they just keep trudging down the same old roads rather than making the leap to a new and better way. The "golden calf" continues to seduce way too many companies. With publicly traded stock or an impending initial public offering, leaders continue to be motivated by illogical goals such as looking good in quarterly reports, paying for statistical market gains instead of building true potential, or just plain riding on hype. Even organizations that are losing money enjoy high valuations and, in spite of the painful lessons we should have learned from the Internet bust and economic collapse, casino-like bets replace reason in the marketplace.

ACER ASPIRE, 1995. PHOTO: DIETMAR HENNEKA

SCITEX HIGH END SCANNER AND PLOTTER, 1991

by hiring world-class design agencies, such as frog, Ideo, and Smart Design, but then the initiative stalled as HP executives refused to take concerted action. Lucente had especially no say with the HP's computer group in Palo Alto or with Compaq in Houston, and there were no consequences for mediocre designs.

Fiorina's disconnect with HP's reality became obvious in 2003 when she tried to counter Apple's iPod success with a better HP answer, code-named Pavilion and conceived in cooperation with Napster, a company which infringed music copyrights. The following year, when it had become clear that HP couldn't deliver a credible alternative to the iPod, she made a deal with Apple to buy bought iPods from Apple and sell them with an HP logo on the back and different packaging. It never occurred to her that an HP customer wouldn't want to buy an Apple product from HP. When the deal was canceled in mid-2005, HP had only reached about 5% of Apple's numbers. And to add insult to this defeat, Apple enforced that HP was not allowed to market any other music player until August 2006.

Carly Fiorina's worst decision was the 2001 acquisition of Compaq, a company that was already at the end of its life cycle. After price wars and botched acquisitions of the failing Tandem Computers and Digital Equipment Corporation, Compaq's CEO Michael Capellas was running for cover – and into HP's arms. In fact, Compaq was a hollow shell of marketing – nearly all products were outsourced, designed, and manufactured in the Far East. HP, on the other hand, had a successful printer business, but it was a "me, too" company with no unique strengths in personal computers. According to Fortune Magazine in 2005: "The HP-Compaq merger was a big bet that didn't pay off, that didn't even come close to what Fiorina and HP's board said was in store. At bottom, they made a huge error in asserting that the merger of two losing computer operations, HP and Compaq, would produce a financially fit computer business."[6] Finally, HP's board decided to let her go, but not without a scandal, triggered by at least one director who spilled his disagreement with Fiorina to journalists. And what about Wall Street? When Carly Fiorina joined HP, the stock traded at $52, when she was dismissed it traded at $21.

Mark Hurd, CEO from 2005 to 2010. Then CFO Robert Wayman served as interim CEO until 2005, when the board hired Mark Hurd, who had spent twenty-five years at NCR. Hurd's first action was to push short-term profits by cutting investment for R&D (as share of revenues) from ~4.3% in 2005 to a low of ~2.2% at the end of his tenure in 2010. In the process, he laid off thousands of highly qualified employees while leaving the positions of many mediocre people untouched (again, in total disregard for the principles set forth by Dave Packard in the HP Way). Strategically, Mark Hurd not only damaged HP's intellectual assets but he also acted as a stone-cold money capitalist.

At first Wall Street applauded and the stock went up – at one time rising close to $42. But then cash problems occurred as HP's long-term debt grew from $3.4 billion to $14 billion (as of March 2012, it had grown to $23 billion), and HP's average net profit margin of

legendary HP brand is badly damaged, thousands of people have lost their jobs, billions of corporate assets have evaporated, and way too many employees are demoralized. Whitman's first decision was a good one: HP is keeping the PC business. And the company is certainly rebuilding itself. In February 2012 – Meg Whitman's first reporting quarter as CEO – HP beat Wall Street's expectations. But HP still hasn't resurrected its once great image. At the time of writing this chapter in 2012, numbers remain down from 2011 (sales $30B, down 7%; profit $1.5B, down 44%). Business in HP's most important areas, such as personal computers, printers, and gear for data centers, are still in trouble, and only software shows an increase due to the multibillion-dollar acquisition of the enterprise information management software company Autonomy. Whitman says that her main goal is to rebuild Hewlett-Packard's long-term health instead of looking for quick fixes. When announcing HP's first quarterly results on February 22, 2012, she said, "We are taking the necessary steps to improve execution, increase effectiveness, and capitalize on emerging opportunities to reassert HP's technology leadership."[9]

However, in my opinion, regaining its previous glory isn't enough to make any company great again. What HP really needs is new glory. The company's past successes were defined by absolutely superior, inventive, powerful, and trailblazing new products which, in turn, created new markets. To match those achievements, HP must become a leader in design and hire the world's most talented people instead of relying on its current design team. Meg Whitman will have to reestablish a culture of fearless innovation at HP. The company certainly has great engineers, so Whitman must provide a creative environment in which they can do their best work, making HP a place where risks can be taken without fear of failure and where the brightest minds can shine. HP also needs to become a cult brand for today's high tech-high touch generation, which is defined by its social media interaction, transparency, and unforgiving judgment. In order to achieve economic performance, HP also needs to create unique and emotional appeal.

In other words, Meg Whitman – and the board – must understand the power shift towards creative and human-minded design that has happened elsewhere within HP's industry. Operational face-lifts won't cut it; she has to build a company that can invent and not just acquire the future. A first step toward that goal might be putting at least one world-class design leader on HP's board of directors. As Steve Jobs and Apple proved, design is a top-down matter. And for all the great people at HP, my biggest wish is that products will win again over money.

The Creative Capitalism Alternative: Apple

We've never worried about numbers. In the market place, Apple is trying to focus the spotlight on products because products really make a difference. [...] You can't con people in this business. The products speak for themselves. STEVE JOBS, 1985

Much has been written (even by me) about the founding of Apple, so here are the basic facts: Apple was founded in 1976 by Steve Jobs and Steve Wozniak – who actually was an employee of HP. After going through a successful start-up phase and some turmoil, Steve Jobs made strategic design and human-minded innovation core elements of Apple's business model, and I was fortunate to be one of the drivers of that move.

After Apple ousted Steve, the company was able to do well for some time by capitalizing on his strategy and the stack of ideas and concepts he had created with the best people he could get. When that well ran dry, however, John Sculley and Jean-Louis Gassée started to believe that they could emulate Steve – with horrible results. The company suffered through a series of mediocre products and even some total flops, such as the Newton handheld computer. After the company dismissed John Sculley, Mike Spindler took over as Apple's CEO. Mike was a hardworking and brilliant marketing and sales executive, but the monumental task of managing Apple out of this crisis was over his head. One strange move he initiated, motivated by the Mac's shrinking market share of just 7%, was to license the Macintosh to low-cost manufacturers, such as Power Computing in Austin, Texas. The $50-per-machine or flat fees gave Apple a nice incremental income, but soon the clones were performing better than Apple's own Macs because the Mac had no added value such as design, usability, or quality. In effect, marketing had won over product, design, and innovation, and Apple had lost its soul. Apple's board also wasn't too competent, either, and when they promoted one of their own – Dr. Gil Amelio – to CEO in early 1996, the rain turned into a storm.

Amelio tried the usual turnaround tricks, slashing cost and laying off people, but Apple's losses accumulated to $1.6 billion during his seventeen month tenure. In a 1997 speech at the Commonwealth Club in San Francisco, Amelio defended his record (while also justifying his $7 million severance package), but in reality, Apple's position had grown worse. Sales of Macintosh computers and MacBooks fell to that of niche products, and there was no Apple winner in sight. Then, Amelio made his one good decision, and brought Steve Jobs back into Apple as an advisor and acquired NeXT, whose NeXT-Step OS would become the Mac OS. Apple's board finally fired Amelio just before Apple reported its sixth loss in seven quarters. Amelio, like many others in the organization, never understood that Apple had to be a creative product company, creating objects and processes people want to fall in love with.

When Apple named Steve interim CEO in 1997, I had the privilege of becoming one of his advisors. I recommended that Apple expand beyond personal computing into digital consumer-media technology, including entertainment content such as music and movies, a move that Sony had failed at due to internal disarray. I also advised Steve to once again place human-friendly, world-class design at the center of Apple's innovation and product development strategy. And, as I mentioned earlier in the book, I also thought it important to make peace with Microsoft – at least temporarily – and to regain control of the Mac OS by ending the licensing to low-cost manufacturers. Steve agreed that Apple should always be where convergent technology is most relevant and attractive for people, and he anticipated that intelligent technology would migrate into other products, such as phones and mobile computing.

Throughout the company, it was understood that any new technology had to be proven beyond any doubt before Apple would engage with it. Instead, they focused on new applications and combinations of technologies that could both make real sense for people and open a new area of business for Apple. Steve wasn't motivated by money, but by success. This may sound a bit strange, but his goal was always that millions of people would use and enjoy Apple's products. He put as much emphasis on the design of a smarter plug as he would on the development of a complex machine or software. What set him apart from the typical opportunistic executive was his fanatical pursuit of the complete experience that Apple's products had to provide for its customers. Of course, he could also be very Machiavellian in overcoming resistance. He wasn't willing to sell Apple customers a bad product simply because some "moron" got his way. Steve's unyielding determination was forged by his time at NeXt, so he had the tools to make people do their very best.

THE PROFIT EARNING POWER OF CREATIVE CAPITALISM

Apple has always had its fans, but it has become a huge success by being creativity driven. In 2011, it was the second most valuable company in the world, ranking only behind Exxon.[10] You can see hard evidence of its success in the fourth quarter of 2010's financial data I listed in Chapter 1 of this book, and in the charts below. This is the power of creative capitalism — success by focusing on strategic design and innovation, creating more value with less material, and delivering sustainable and positive experiences.

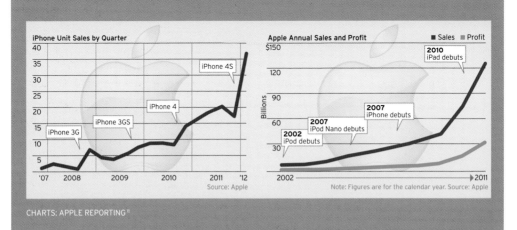

CHARTS: APPLE REPORTING[11]

Steve worked with a vengeance, focusing Apple's R&D efforts on convergent design and innovation in hardware, software, and content. He strengthened the Macintosh line through a speedy development of the iMac, the first masterpiece of Jonathan Ive and his design team. Steve convinced Bill Gates that Microsoft should invest in Apple – and, more importantly, that Microsoft should continue building applications for the Macintosh – and he also ended the licensing program, paying $100 million to Power Computing to end their business arrangement. After saving Apple from bankruptcy, Steve expanded into and invented new markets, such as digital consumer electronics (as in the iPod) and wireless mobility (as in the iPhone and iPad). Even though Apple outsources its hardware production, it has created a superior co-design and co-innovation business model with its ODM partners by paying for those functions rather than just buying whatever products and processes the ODMs have on their shelves. Apple's strategy under Steve Jobs caused a power shift from rational efficiency to innovative product design, from corporate behavior to finding and nurturing the best talent, and from cold logic to emotional creativity.

Today, many companies come to frog and say: "We want to be the Apple of our industry." And frog's response is: "First you must find yourself. Then you just must act and be as nimble and radical about excellence as Apple – adopting its framework of design as strategy, customer focus, innovation, processes with miracle-like prototyping, painstaking attention to detail, discipline, and real-money investment." Faced with this list, most walk off. Too many people still think they can mimic Apple's success without matching its courage to do the right thing, no matter how painful it may be. Most companies don't want to endure the effort of radical change and commit to the personal, emotional, and financial investments required to achieve excellence. Even though they see Apple's stellar success, the processes leading to it, and the personal passion shown by Apple's people, they still believe there must be a shortcut – something they might find in a book called something like *How Steve Jobs Does It, Etc.*

But the pathway Steve pioneered isn't for the meek. And that's part of the real challenge we all face today, as organizations – even governments – around the world try to find, mentor, and empower creative leaders with strong character on a bigger, even universal, scale. Steve Jobs's mantra lives on: Stay hungry, stay foolish. That's his advice for you. Now, here's my advice: Whoever you are and wherever you are, leap out of the hot water before it's too late and join the noble cause of creative life and work.

SIEMENS SCENIC MULTIMEDIA COMPUTER, 1996. PHOTO: DIETMAR HENNEKA

1   Walter Benjamin "Capitalism as Religion," unfinished fragment Nr. 74, 1913–1926.

2   "Apple Stimulates Brain's Religious Responses, Claims BBC," reported by Rich Trenholm, Cnet UK, May 18, 2011 crave.cnet.co.uk/gadgets/apple-stimulates-brains-religious-responses-claims-bbc-50003807/.

3   *The Value of Nothing: How to Reshape Market Society and Redefine Democracy*, by Raj Patel. Picador, an imprint of Pan Macmillan, 2010.

4   *Die Gemeinwohl-Ökonomie*, by Christian Felber. Deuticke, 2010.

5   *The HP Way: How Bill Hewlett and I Built Our Company*. Collins Business Essentials.

6   "Why Carly's Big Bet is Failing," by Carol J. Loomis, *Fortune* magazine, February 7, 2005.

7   Sources: *The Wall Street Journal*, dailyfinance.com.

8   Source: www.businessinsider.com.

9   "HP Reports First Quarter 2012 Results," *HP Financial News*, February 22, 2012.

10   Based on the average stock price at the end of 2010. In the meantime Apple has passed EXXON.

11   Source: www.brightsideofnews.com and *Silicon Alley Insider* 2/2011.

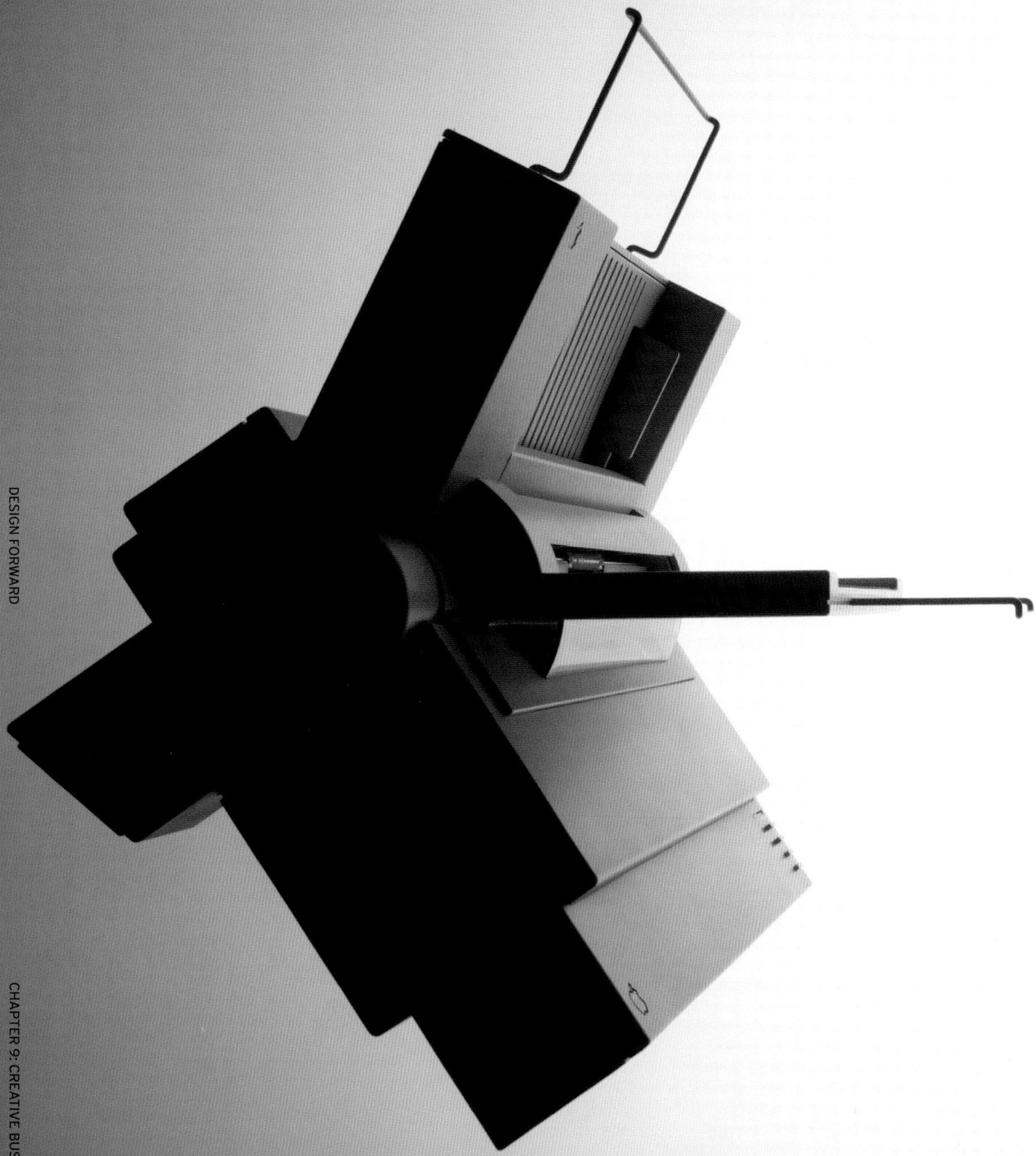

9 CREATIVE BUSINESS LEADERSHIP

BY JOHANNA SCHOENBERGER

In this chapter, another of my PhD students, Johanna Schoenberger, presents the findings of her research into the current state of the partnership between business and design. Johanna interviewed approximately one hundred business leaders from around the world, with the goal of finding out what roles creativity and design play in their organizations. Her findings reveal elements within the traditional corporate structure that actually inhibit the development of customer-focused innovations and design-fueled business strategies. Here, in addition to outlining her research and findings, Johanna reveals to us the indisputable benefits of bringing creative minds to every level of organizational leadership – including boards of directors – and offers some compelling ideas about how we might accomplish that kind of organizational transformation. H.E.

Designers design products, whether those are physical objects, user interfaces, or services. A critical part of the design process involves imagining how people will use the products, how they will handle them, and how the products should look, feel, and perform, all with the goal of creating a good experience that might lead to a genuine improvement in the user's life. In effect, designers are creating the connections that link companies to their customers. It would seem only logical, therefore, to consider design an essential component of an organization's strategic plan and to integrate it into every element of the business process. That way, companies would be able to meticulously shape the moments and relationships that connect them with their customers and, in the process, define their public image and establish their credibility in the marketplace.

      In speaking about design with designers, business leaders, and consultants, however, it becomes clear that the reality of the relationship between design and business strategy is very different. Most organizational leaders seem to lack even a rough idea of what design really is. Those who do think about design, tend to regard it as a kind of decorative

APPLE, IMAGEWRITER 1984. PHOTO: DIETMAR HENNEKA

flourish – a gift paper that wraps their product in a pretty package. To these executives, design remains largely an "add on" or an "added cost" and, therefore, not something they would think of or use as a key strategic element in their overall business process. In other words, there is a major discrepancy between the true nature and function of design and the way it is perceived within most organizations. I wanted to understand this discrepancy, and so I made it the subject of my doctoral dissertation, "Strategic Design," which I wrote from 2007 to 2011 under the tutelage of Professor Hartmut Esslinger.

My starting point was the question of why most organizational leaders have such a limited understanding of the strategic value of design. Next, I considered what would have to change for design to bring it squarely within this strategic parameter. Here, I offer a summary of what I believe to be the most elementary problems in the typical role of design within organizations, along with some approaches we might take to solve those problems. Although I am far from being able to claim that my work represents the full and definitive perspective into these issues, I hope that it offers a sound platform from which we can continue to study this critical issue.

Design's Three Critical Strengths for Business Strategy

While many business leaders have relegated design to the "gift-wrapping" department of their organizations, those few who understand the unique value of design and its potential as a key element of business strategy have a powerful competitive tool at their command. The discipline of design includes a broad spectrum of capabilities, but I believe that these three unique and valuable aspects of design encapsulate its essential value for business:

• Good design is based on design research and therefore reflects customer needs.

• Good design delivers "outside-of-the-box" ideas and innovation.

• Good design visualizes and concretizes.

Let's consider each of these strengths individually.

Good Design Reflects Customer Needs

As I said earlier, every company produces something and offers it to customers as an added value to their lives that they can buy. In designing products, the essential question is what this added value should be: how it should look, feel, and function in interaction with the user. Companies answer this question differently. Many copy what others have already made before them, possibly with minor improvements. These companies ultimately are satisfied with the manageable risk of introducing such a "me, too" product and the limited success they will achieve with that offering.

Then, there are the companies that constantly take over other firms in order to make their acquisitions' product portfolios their own. Still other companies repeatedly bring new versions of their initial products onto the market and in this way avoid the risk of innovation. And, finally, there are companies that embark on the great adventure of innovation and actually come up with new merchandise.

Regardless of the path that a company chooses, in the end it still has to produce something that satisfies the needs of people. Thus it would be good to know what these needs are. To learn more about human needs, however, it is not enough just to go up to people and ask, "What would you really like to have?" People adapt quickly to their personal circumstances and seldom maintain a constant and firm idea of their own needs. That means they are rarely able to give profound information about themselves and their needs in a spontaneous interview. So, companies must take another path to learn about the needs of their customers.

You might think that companies have well-established processes and entire departments just for this purpose, but that isn't always the case. Most organizations use marketing primarily to communicate information about their products and to place them on the market in the best possible light. To understand how their customers think and what might motivate them to buy the offered product, the typical marketing effort undertakes qualitative as well as quantitative market research. Customers are asked to appraise existing products, and the resulting data more often leads to benchmarking and following trends rather than innovating. Marketing departments query existing knowledge in order to shape product portfolios and develop marketing campaigns on that basis.

Marketing does not, however, observe people in the context of their lives with a view to describing, in depth, their actual needs. Many development cycles last years, from the product's launch date and on through its subsequent years of successful sales. From the moment a product is launched, therefore, its information becomes historical data. For planning and producing products that will be relevant in the future, knowledge about existing products is of little help. To develop products targeted toward the actual needs of people and customers, we need a method set that is capable of fundamentally recognizing those needs, and collecting and translating them into relevant product concepts. This method set is precisely that of design research, which represents the first phase of the design process.

After interdisciplinary design teams have used various methods to appraise which target groups might offer relevant, informative insights for the subsequent product development, they try to immerse themselves in the world of these target groups. If possible, they accompany people for hours, days, or sometimes even weeks of their life. They observe, listen, and search for a deep understanding of their research subjects' problems, desires, and hopes. At the end of this phase, the researchers collect their information, then compile and process it in order to crystallize a set of relevant core themes and problems, which the designed product should solve. At this stage of the design process, designers must carefully consider the context and the system surrounding the question under consideration, otherwise they may find themselves improving a situation rather than solving a problem. The more fundamentally a merchandise line embraces and answers a substantial problem, the longer it will remain successful in the marketplace.

Using this design research process, product development teams are able to develop a clearly defined orientation toward the customer and a clear objective in what then becomes a much more strategic development process. Through design research, therefore, design can help companies define the basis for a sustainable product strategy – a strategic tool that too few companies know how to use. Those who know how to leverage design and the product strategies that design research can produce have a decided competitive edge in any marketplace.

Good Design Delivers "Outside the Box" Ideas and Innovation

After collaborating with other areas of the organization to formulate a customer-oriented starting point for a product's development, designers can use their unique skills and perspective to help find innovative answers and approaches to problem solving throughout the development process. Whereas other professional classes often concentrate on applying their experience and learned best practices to problem solving, professional designers seem to have an innate drive to break away from habitual thought patterns, to question implicitly accepted rules, and to push past perceived boundaries of what is feasible. If you tell a designer to develop a concept for a new product that is to be red and mounted on a shaft, you can almost bet that the designer will immediately discuss whether the product really has to be mounted on a shaft and be red. In the United States, there is a joke about designers that begins: "How many designers does it take to change a light bulb?" The answer: "Does it have to be a light bulb?"

Designers' fearlessness in regard to embarking on new, unknown approaches to solutions is one of their most important benefits for business. As one of the interviewees in my research Mathew Locsin noted, "The [...] thing that designers are really good at – and it's part of their discipline – is this attitude of 'Well, I don't know, but let's make it and see what happens. Let's prototype. Let's learn. Let's adapt and let's be iterative about it.' [...] There's nothing [...] that can't be addressed or attempted to be addressed with design discipline."

Since designers are willing to attack problems from new directions and through innovative means, they can help to ensure throughout the product development processes that product concepts grow beyond the bounds of what was previously thought possible. In so doing, designers help to ensure that the development process results in truly innovative, people-oriented products.

PACKARD BELL MAILBOX PC, 1995. PHOTO: DIETMAR HENNEKA

273

Good Design Visualizes and Concretizes

After the development process, a third unique strength of design remains in play – its ability to visualize and give concrete form to suggestions. Even in the very early stages of product development, design can make ideas comprehensible through drawings or prototypes. These early works don't have to be particularly pretty, precise, or detailed to transform an abstract concept into a comprehensible design that gives everyone involved a shared launching point for further development. This visualization promotes cross-disciplinary collaboration and enables, for example, more productive discussions between various business units or with outside partners and suppliers.

By giving form to abstract concepts, designers facilitate discussion and help all participants contribute to the development process. Design mock-ups can be tested by volunteers, enabling concepts to pass through numerous evolutionary stages on their way to completion. This process of refinement avoids the expense of launching an untested product into the marketplace and letting customers be the beta testers. Bad experiences can permanently drive customers away, so the pre-market testing developers can conduct through designer drawings, and prototypes can save businesses money and help to preserve customer goodwill. Once the product concept is ripe for realization, designers then translate all requirements imposed on the product into a concrete, final form.

Why Organizations Fail to Capitalize on Design

We have seen how design can help companies orient themselves toward customer needs, develop innovative product concepts, and translate them into tangible experiences, products, and services. As a strategic orienting parameter, design helps organizations translate their defined strategy into comprehensible, relevant merchandise in a collaborative, project-related way. So why is it that, in spite of design's broad spectrum of capabilities and the increasing competitive pressure on companies to differentiate themselves in the marketplace, only a few organizations are consistently using design to bring innovative, brand-related, customer-oriented products to market? To answer this question, I think we have to consider three options.

The first reason for this oversight may be that design thinks and functions in ways that are completely different from other areas of the company. Where, for example, production, sales, or service departments typically are oriented toward efficiency and effectiveness, design is focused on new development. It requires creativity and innovation. These skills demand completely different forms of implementation and evaluation in order to achieve success. The design process requires time for open-minded fundamental research, pure development of inspiration, formation of initial ideas, and additional phases for developing and refining final concepts that are technically and financially feasible.

A second reason that organizations fail to leverage the potential of design may be that leaders need specific skills in creative management in order to plan and conduct creative processes. The more complex a merchandise line or product, the more management knowledge must be available to integrate its creative processes at the right time, and with the appropriate budget, within the overall context of the company. This kind of creative knowledge and understanding is essential in order to anchor design in the company in a way that enables it to exert a long-term, profound influence on business strategy and product development. Since most managers have a background in business economics or technology, however, with no creative background, they often lack the necessary know-how for dealing with design. As a result, leadership often prevents design from being integrated effectively in the company.

A third reason for the chasm that separates design from business strategy in most organizations may rest with the designers themselves. Most designers have relevant specialized knowledge and method sets (from the company strategy perspective), which they continue to sharpen and deepen in the course of their careers. In their hearts, however, many designers are still more comfortable with art than with economics. This attitude is greatly encouraged by many design education institutions, especially in Europe. Many curricula are oriented purely toward teaching the esthetic understanding and artisan skill of designers, without giving them any insight into the context – the economic-social system – in which their future professional activity will play out. A design student at these institutions can search in vain for curriculum topics such as organizational leadership and product strategy.

As a result, designers often lack any interest in the basic economic conditions of their profession. They make no effort to understand organizational structure, finance, or the factors that often dictate decisions that strongly conflict with a holistic, customer-oriented company direction. Thus, instead of recognizing the levers that designers could push to guide companies in a customer-oriented and design-competent direction, designers over and over again regard their grievous destiny with humiliation as that of "the creative victim in a profit-hungry economic world."

To avoid fighting what they see as a losing battle for the rest of their professional life, designers often withdraw into internal exile. While the lack of economic understanding is not always a problem for the actual design activity, the long-term occupational positioning in the company greatly exacerbates this reluctant attitude toward economic contents and relationships. Due to their separation from the organization's economic drivers and parameters, many designers are incapable of making a compelling case for the value of design within their company. Instead, they argue vehemently with artistic, esthetic positions that may persuade other designers but are unlikely to resonate with a manager whose thoughts are oriented toward numbers, measurability, and risk minimization. This in turn means that designers and managers talk at cross-purposes in numerous debates, and so their companies will never understand the true value of design.

SONY WEGA AUDIO EDITION FIREBALL, 1976. PHOTO: DIETMAR HENNEKA

The Costs of "Old School" Rules

The traditional value-creation process of a company passes through several phases: It begins with development of the strategy and identification of customer needs, takes shape within the innovation process, is realized through the operative process of production, and is supported in the service process. When customer needs are satisfied, the value-creation cycle can begin anew. Since many companies fail to recognize and leverage the full spectrum of design capabilities, however – including design research – they often lack any method for understanding the real needs of their customers. On one hand, these companies tend to lack the holistic company presence consistent with a brand; on the other, they often develop products without regard for the customer.

Companies that do utilize design may have internal design departments and/or contracts with external design consultants. In the external model, companies commission design agencies on a project basis. In the internal model, companies have their own design department and use the services of external design agencies additionally as needed. In both models, some organizations can make fundamental errors in the design process.

Where companies exclusively use the services of external design agencies, different company departments may commission different agencies for different problems. Rarely is there an internal leader with responsibility for directing all hiring of creative consultants. As a result, initiatives are not often matched to one another, sometimes proceed in parallel, and are not integrated in the roadmap-planning portfolio. While these projects might involve a great deal of expense, the overall result is uncoordinated and therefore cannot be a persuasive strategy for the company – even if each project alone may seem very promising. Without a single, well-coordinated vision of creative direction and implementation, companies can't follow a targeted approach to customer-focused design and brand-building. If design is to operate as a strategic parameter, it must be seen as a bright, strong thread running through the company and a basic part of the company's strategy and planning.

Companies with internal design departments can suffer from a different type of problem. Since too few managers bring along too little knowledge about the working principles and value of design, it is obviously rarely in their interest to give design a prominent position in the organization from which designers could have a decisive influence on the company's alignment and product development process. Instead, design – often positioned at the bottom of corporate hierarchy – is brought into the development process only at the very end. Designers in these organizations typically receive product concepts with established content; their task, then, is to wrap everything up quickly in a pretty package so the company can get the product out the door.

These designers are sometimes confronted with technically overloaded feature sets from which they are supposed to conjure up a customer-oriented product experience in a very short time. In this late phase of the process, the contracts with manufacturers and suppliers have often already been sealed and numerous production steps have already begun, and so any concept change proposed at this point has far-reaching financial consequences. When designers are able, by means of airtight, customer-oriented arguments, to successfully argue for a change of concept, the aftertaste throughout the organization can be bitter, as participants in the project agree that design was responsible for a massive increase of the manufacturing cost. This is one of the reasons that design departments have to struggle with persistent burn-out symptoms among employees, since fundamental procedural problems (such as too late involvement in the product development) recur over and over again from one project to another, leaving the impression of fighting a battle for lost causes.

The Wrong Direction of "Bottom Up" Design

As we have seen, design cannot function from the bottom up if it is to be a strategic parameter. If design is to be able to achieve comprehensive orientation of the company toward the customer accompanied at the same time by increased brand recognition, it cannot be relegated to the end of the decision chain. Organizations will only be able to use the full spectrum of design's capabilities by placing the fundamental questions of customer orientation at the beginning of the product planning phase. This is where design can derive holistic concepts from customer needs, accommodate the artistic as well as content-related criteria imposed by the brand, and — in collaboration with other product-design participants — incorporate all of these elements into harmonious complete packages.

But if design is anchored lower in the company structure, designers will complain anew in every project that they were brought in too late, that there are too many stakeholders with decision-making authority pulling in different directions, that design's budget is inadequate, and that they cannot achieve the results requested of them with the allocated resources. This no-win situation frustrates even halfway ambitious designers to the point that they will leave the company after a certain respite. Companies consequently have difficulties in achieving and sustaining the high potential of creative input. But even more damaging is the fact that such companies are unable to utilize the strategic customer-oriented potential of design, with the result that points of friction, which do not make sense in terms of people, money, or time, are created in the product development process.

Building a Structure that Works: Design from the Top Down

As my research has shown, if companies want to derive the full benefit of design and orient their organizational brand and product development processes toward their customers, they must make meet two criteria:

• They must learn to understand the full value of design and its essential prerequisites and then implement design commensurately in the company.

• Design must serve as a core element within the organization and form a continuous thread throughout company processes from the very beginning under the leadership of a responsible person with clear vision.

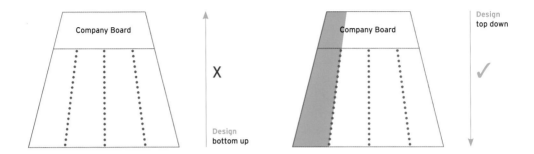

At the beginning of product and portfolio planning, therefore, design research should determine the customer needs. Design, together with company management and the other relevant company departments, such as development and marketing, should define the target direction for new products on the basis of the customer needs and manage the respective individual projects with the same target direction. In this way the use of external design agencies can be managed by the internal design team across all company departments and aligned with the defined target direction.

The correct customer orientation and a consistent company presence represent such a far-reaching strategic fundamental decision within organizations that it can be made and implemented only at the highest hierarchical level. If companies want to orient themselves toward the customer and achieve a harmonious company presence by means of design, they must broaden the content of their fundamental strategic discourse through a customer-focused orientation.

Since both the executive board and board of directors shape the strategic pattern of a company, both boards are capable in themselves of anchoring creative thinking at the strategic level. In the American board model, both the tasks of management and supervision are incumbent upon the board, and so the distinction between executive board and board of directors is superfluous. In the German dual control system, however, both boards are capable in themselves of anchoring creative thinking and knowledge at the strategic level. Since the supervisory board appoints the board of management, however, and therefore lays the foundation stone of any further company alignment, I would first like to discuss anchoring of creative thinking in the supervisory board.

Forging Connections between Design and the Executive Suite

One of my interviewees (whose name will remain confidential) is a partner in an internationally active design agency and a board member of an American firm. He told me: "There are plenty of marketing people on boards, but most CMOs and senior marketing staff are business people, not creative people. There are very, very few designers on boards, and it has become really interesting to be on this board where everybody else is male, mid-50s, and from one specific area within the United States."

If people do not have their opinions challenged by dissidents, are not tempted out of their comfort zone, and are not exposed to alternative thinking approaches, the capacity of their judgment can become limited over the long term. So writes Daniel Rettig and Liane Borghardt in Wirtschaftswoche [German Business Week]: "Experts such as Daniel Kahneman are convinced: It is precisely the isolation on the executive floor that forms a fertile feeding ground for an overinflated ego. The managers of today's generation initiate projects without having appraised their prospects of success with a sufficient self-critical viewpoint beforehand – often because of pure egotism. Wherever narcissism has settled, self-overestimation is not far behind."[1] In order to put a stop to self-overestimation, to do justice to the increasing demands of ever more complex markets and competitive situations, and to achieve the alignment of companies in a sustainable, creative direction, today's executive boards should be diverse – made up of both male and female members, multiple ethnicities, multiple age groups, and diverse backgrounds and professional orientation and skill sets.

One of the greatest strengths of creative minds is their empathy. Because of their daily work and the design processes they use, designers are trained to get a feel for people and to search for motivations for their actions. These soft skills can be helpful in many respects for the activity of a supervisory board. Whereas the traditional analytically oriented supervisory-board members concentrate on establishing performance figures such as the EBITDA (Earnings Before Interest, Taxes, Depreciation, and Amortization), or how the profitability of the company has evolved since the last meeting, a designer inquires about the human causes of this evolution. As my interviewee noted:

"So, whenever you go to a board meeting it's so funny because you get the board book, and everybody's looking for this one number, EBITDA [...]. It's the number that wraps up all your assets, all of your debt, all your amortization into one number. So, you look at that number and you judge that number on where the number was last time, and it tells you from a financial business perspective how you're doing, but there's no "but this or then that." So everyone jumps at that number, and then the conversation is around "but we've got $1.2 million worth of letter stock" and everyone goes "okay, well," and then everyone in their own brain decides what that actually means, and we've got this stock in this warehouse, and we have this equity over here, and we have this building here. The conversation is very much like that. I'm in a room of

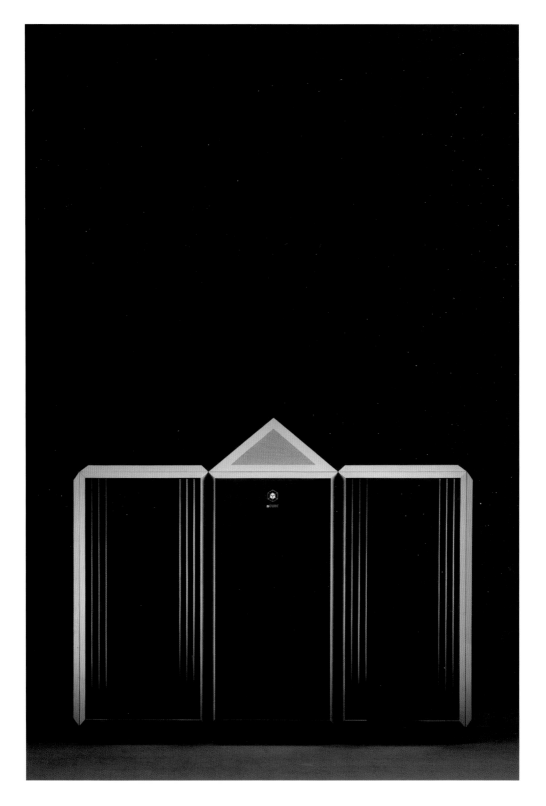

ORACLE NCUBE, SUPER COMPUTER 1992. PHOTO: DIETMAR HENNEKA

HEAD, CARBON TENNIS RACKET, 1988. PHOTO: DIETMAR HENNEKA

nine people, and I'm the only person that doesn't look at that number first. I think for a consumer company, that's just really important, because even if that number is a great representation of how the company's doing, it's only one. It's only one representation. It's very powerful, but if this company wants to change, having somebody at the board level who has an informed, powerful voice to help make decisions I think is really important.

Thus, whereas the economically oriented supervisory-board members control the payment and operational capability of a company, designers can check the relationship of the company to its stakeholders. Thus they ask questions such as "Have we actually recognized the fundamental problems of our customers?", "Are we responding to the needs of our customers with the right product or perhaps can we find a better answer?", or "How is our product changing the life of our customers, and how can the positive change be further enhanced?" Creative minds always try first to find specific motivations for human behavior so they can paint a general picture of a phenomenon and then be able (in principle) to solve it. With this qualitative thinking, designers ensure in the supervisory board that companies remain close to the reality of their customers, employers, and owners. As long as the organization retains that closeness, the danger that a development will disregard the needs of the customer becomes progressively less.

Creative minds also help to improve the discussion and working culture of supervisory boards, thanks to their orientation toward people and by virtue of their love of asking questions. Supervisory boards – directors are often chosen by the chief executive officer – are always in jeopardy of becoming panels of "yes-men," whereas a creative mind in the team will consistently reject complacency. Few things stimulate creative minds more than asking questions and triggering discussions about absolutely held beliefs and complacent assumptions. The qualitative thinking approaches of a creative supervisory-board member have the power to challenge the board to partake in genuine discourse. In this way, by virtue of creative participation, companies can also develop fundamentally innovative and sustainable long-term strategies. In other words, where analytical supervisory-board members work toward good quarterly results, creative minds remain focused on maintaining a high-quality, innovative, people-oriented company profile.

Companies that unite creative and analytical minds within their supervisory boards enjoy the greatest success, although many organizations tend to focus on a "quarterly figures" orientation just at the time they most need to muster their creativity. Radical cost cutting often seems the fastest possible way for a company to recover in terms of numbers, and the board of management is faced with the question of choosing in which department to make the cuts – in the innovative or operative business unit? Since operative business units can be calculated down to the minutest detail, cost-cutting effects are painfully obvious within a short time. Any savings lead to direct consequences.

The case is entirely different for innovation initiatives. Their success generally cannot be guaranteed, and even in economically good times they always represent an investment fraught with future risks. If innovation initiatives are erased, no one will be able to prove how much profit or growth the company will forgo as a result. And if a company succeeds in implementing an innovation project, the success is usually credited to the next generation of managers. For analytically oriented managers, therefore, it is an obvious first step to cut out innovation initiatives. But companies that stop their innovation processes in times of crisis not only wipe out some individual projects and the capital already invested in innovation, they also destroy hard-earned innovation momentum. In doing so, they excise all development offshoots that could have helped the company achieve long-term growth.

When designers hold seats on supervisory boards, they give companies the opportunity to deal more effectively with times of economic crisis. Through their creative thinking ability, creative board members keep aspects such as innovation and product improvement in their sights despite economic difficulties. Instead of doing what most non-creatively managed companies do, such as panicking, hoarding cash reserves, laying off employees, and postponing or even eliminating innovative initiates, creative supervisory-board members are able to instill the mantra of "crisis as opportunity" in the company. If companies continue or even increase their innovation initiatives, they can establish a sustainable jump on competitors who are hunkered down in survival mode. One interviewee told me about his posture during crisis times: "I was saying, 'When people start buying our stuff again, we have to have the best stuff in the world to sell. So, all this stuff we all said is good for a long time – it's shit. Get rid of it!' We've made some really good stuff in the meantime. So, we've come back up again. We've had the two or three best months that we've had in four years. It's amazing. [...] Maybe if I hadn't been at the table people would have been saying things like, 'We can't invest in that now. We can't spend that $200,000 on bringing this other person on board to design these things for us,' or whatever. I think that didn't happen. I was at the table, and it was a good conversation."

Thus, if the board of management is encouraged by the supervisory board to support the preservation of innovative initiatives and product improvements, the company has the opportunity to advance the orientation and quality of its products, to constantly add depth to its company culture and brand communication, and to lay the foundation stone for a prosperous future. Board members from creative professions are essential for considering the entire bandwidth of strategic options, ensuring diversity of thinking and attitudes, keeping companies close to the needs of their customers, defending innovation projects against premature cost cutting even in crisis times, and maximizing the strategic strength of the organization (especially in times of increasing globalization). Specifically, companies should fill at least one post within their board of directors with a creative professional – not to fill some quota, but rather with the clear intention of utilizing qualitative, creative thinking. In that way, the organization can remain awake and agile in establishing and maintaining a holistic company strategy. As my interviewee noted, "I think a lot of the companies that we work for would get even more value out of us by having people like me on the board, senior people who've been through a lot in the design industry. But bring them on the board as business people as opposed to, 'We've got a designer on our board, isn't that kooky?'"

Incorporating Creativity in Active Business Management

Even in the active executive boards of companies, qualitative creative thinking is vital for survival. Since top management, together with the board of directors, is responsible for formulating the company strategy and then implementing it under its own responsibility, the supervisory board as well as top managers must be capable of utilizing the entire spectrum of strategic options for long-range strategic planning. Organizational structures and processes must deploy and use creativity in accordance with its potential. Companies must understand and respect creativity in order to provide creative minds with suitable working conditions. Creative minds need suitable working conditions in order to exploit all of their capabilities. And only when creative minds are able to fully exploit their creative capabilities does cooperation between companies and designers lead to success.

My research also tells me that companies need a new generation of top executives who are capable of considering analytical and creative thinking equally and of deploying the design phase appropriately in the product development process. Certainly, every company and industry will have its own management structure, but in a sustainable, customer-focused, and well-organized business, at least one position on the board of directors and at least one position of the active business management should be occupied by a creative professional. Neither of the two orientations – rational numbers and visceral creativity – can replace the other; their basic thought patterns are too different. Instead of negating each other, it is important for both sides to demonstrate the highest degree of professionalism and communication strengths. It is only by the combination of analytical and creative thinking that organizations remain oriented toward qualitatively sustainable and meaningful goals and values that will be successful over the long term.

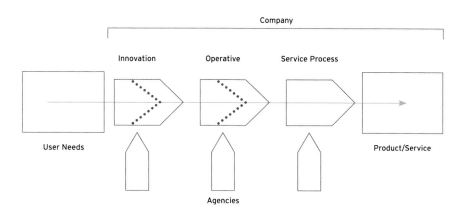

Leadership by Design

As we have seen, design offers companies a far-reaching spectrum of capabilities. Through design research, organizations can build customer-oriented product portfolios and a sustainable company presence. Design thinks outside the box and thus permits innovative approaches to solutions. And design visualizes – it gives concrete form to ideas. In this way it helps to maintain efficient communication with all project participants during the product development phase and to obtain the first feedback from later customers. In the realization phase, designing transforms all defined product requirements into a comprehensible merchandise line, which later delivers a satisfying product experience to the customer.

If companies wish to utilize these strengths of design, they must learn to understand its full value and prerequisites and then implement their design program accordingly. This means that organizations must involve design in their strategies and throughout the product development process from the beginning to the end. As regards hierarchy, design efforts must be directed from the highest strategic level by a person with general responsibility. In this way companies will be in position to convert their alignment from a temporarily strong focus on efficiency, effectiveness, and profit to an orientation toward customers and people, thus assuring them of long-term growth on the basis of holistic innovation.

1   Daniel Rettig and Liane Borghardt, "The Ego Cases," in: *Wirtschaftswoche*, August 23, 2010, p. 80.

KOENIG + NEURATH, KING ZETA, 1982. PHOTO: DIETMAR HENNEKA

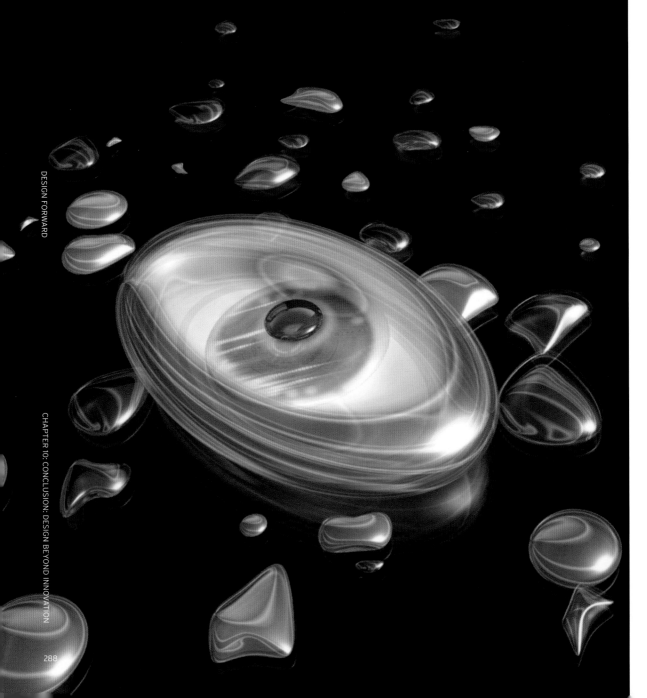

10 CONCLUSION: DESIGN BEYOND INNOVATION

"Culture: the cry of men in face of their destiny." ALBERT CAMUS

I called this book Design Forward with a specific meaning in mind – that of using design to improve the world for all of us by providing a humanistic future our children, our grandchildren, and our great-grandchildren. With far too many developments going totally wrong today, I think it has become clear that we have to change the way we think and act. Change isn't easy, but it is inevitable and essential; the only other option is economic, ecological, and human catastrophe. The Earth's population is growing at a stunning pace; from 1950 when it was 2.5 billion, it has expanded by nearly threefold to 7 billion today, and is on track to reach 10 billion by 2050.[1] To make the challenges of this population expansion even more daunting, the areas of largest growth are occurring in the poorest countries, some of them already hit by famine and epidemics. Medieval fundamentalism and zealotry within all global religions, political-fundamentalist movements, and the state-sponsored suppression of women and children in many of these countries accelerates the crisis. And this list of issues doesn't include the ongoing plague of wars everywhere, which are punishing humanity. We not only need to change for economic success, we need to change for a better life. Here are the five keystones of change that I believe we need:

• To establish Creative Science educational programs, so we can find and mentor all creative talent early.

• To replace wasteful consumption with meaningful usage and long-term enjoyment.

• To develop a new economic model – what we might call humanistic capitalism.

• To create human-centric and sustainable businesses and experiences for all people.

• To replace complacent conservatism with progressive and inspired action.

I hope I have laid out my hopes and ideas for these changes throughout this book in a compelling and thoughtful way. Now, I want to finish with a discussion of what I understand best: the power of Strategic Design, and how to make it work for people, for companies, and for the marketplace.

A Recipe for Change

My goal for implementing the principles of Strategic Design isn't to destroy the current system or throw it into chaos but rather to humanize and improve the system, so that amoral greed and professional incompetence will no longer have a chance to thrive within it. All this may sound very utopian, but it isn't. In fact, I can offer some specific ways we can all join the drive for change.

We can begin by changing the way we think about innovation. After years in which "innovation" has been the buzzword of business and industry, we are beginning to see the limits of its human, social, and ecological dimensions. To break through these limitations, we need to move beyond the current innovation-driven business model, and Strategic Design will be an important driver toward this new direction. We also need to change the way we think about design. As a young and very dynamic profession, design has come a long way from its "artsy" roots to become a problem-solving discipline requiring conceptual vision and competent implementation. This transformation hasn't been easy, but it has resulted in a rapidly growing recognition of the true power of the business-design alliance and the need for cultivating it. At the heart of this alliance is a firm understanding of the vital role of design in shaping a new type of innovation-driven business model that

• Views consumers both as individuals with a complex set of needs that consumption of products only partially satisfies.

• As members of a larger community with complex interdependencies concerns itself with today's underrepresented communities.

• Acts with a focus on tomorrow's communities and the generations of individuals that will follow our own, all of which depend critically on our current decisions and behaviors.

Throughout this book, we have seen numerous examples of the essential role of designers in shaping business strategy and the evolving model that businesses are developing to leverage the benefits of Strategic Design. But, it's also important to consider the business-design alliance and the sustainability-driven business model it promotes from a broad, cultural perspective – a "big picture" view that can clearly reveal new emphases in business strategy that I believe designers are especially well suited to develop and apply.

Next, we have to change the way we think about consumers – about ourselves as consumers. In the larger context of creativity, design is the living link between our human goals and needs and the material culture that helps to fulfill them. Our material culture is man-made – every component of it is manufactured, sold, used, discarded, recycled, and (hopefully) reused. Every individual element of it has passed through a process in which human ideas are shaped into designs, and designs are manufactured into physical and virtual matter. Designers and their business partners, therefore, have an almost unparalleled opportunity to build an environment that's not only livable and sustainable but also fun and culturally inspiring. To do so, however, we have to remain ever alert to the opportunities – and sometimes dangerous temptations – of our business models, our strategies, our tools, our processes, and our factories.

With increased communication technologies and market globalization, consumers have become members of larger, interdependent communities and, as such, have much more complex needs than in the past. The holistic challenge for design is to create physical and virtual objects that are useful art, that inspire spiritual values, and that use as few atoms and bits as possible to meet these more complex consumer needs. In my view, design is our modern-day continuation of "technical" functionality converted into human-historic and metaphysical symbolism. When designers create a new and better object, a more useful software application, or a more inspiring, human-centric experience, they are creating a branding symbol that stands for meaningful innovation, good quality, and ethical behavior. People recognize the resulting visual symbols of that brand as a cultural expression of humanized technology and not just a fashion statement. Such strategic designs advance our industrial culture by providing sustainable innovation, cultural identity, and consistency, and, as such, they contribute to consumers' sense of emotional and social belonging. Designers have a responsibility to connect human aspirations with new opportunities in science, technology, and business. Only then will the products they design be culturally relevant, economically productive, politically beneficial, and ecologically sustainable.

Finally, we have to change the way we think about "business as usual" and its impact. The acceleration of globalization – including the current crisis caused by financial excesses and cultural colonialism – poses huge challenges for designers, even as it offers them new opportunities. It requires designers that are both talented and competent to influence and define new trends, such as mastering the problems of outsourcing to "lower cost" economies and reversing the current excesses of overproducing generic and hard-to-use products. Designers also need to participate in developing new concepts for "home sourcing," by helping local and tribal cultures develop new and better approaches to producing goods.

As I mentioned early in this book, to succeed as competent and respected "executive partners" in the rational world of business, designers must themselves become creative entrepreneurs and executives. Ultimately, designers must raise their profession above its commercial-functional benchmarks and aspire to near-eternal cultural relevance. These are very achievable goals. While, in my view, most products advertised and sold by the Design Shop of the MoMA New York are "designer trash" – that is, imposters – Arne Jacobsen and Fritz Hansen's Series 7™ chair or Herman Miller's Aeron chair offer proof that great design succeeds.

As a creative strategist and entrepreneur, I am optimistic that the currently evolving design-business paradigm will promote livelier, lovelier, and more emotionally fulfilling products and that a more appealing product culture will actually be part of a winning green strategy. And this will be true for all countries and cultures on Earth. Humanizing our industries in Europe, the United States, and Far East/Asia involves developing and implementing a smarter ecological and economical model – one that will enable us to industrialize poorer countries without destroying their identity and culture.

Let's take smartphones, for example, which today are typically designed in the United States, Japan, or Korea, then engineered and manufactured in China, and – in most cases – poorly recycled. A better model for this process would be to conceptualize and design future smartphones within the communities and cultures where they will be marketed and used. These smartphones could be engineered in a modular way, so the components could be produced where it makes most sense. Final assembly would then take place within the "home" country, market, and culture. Such a modular production model would be ideal for many countries, including those in Central Africa, the Baltics, Eastern Europe, or in Brazil, and it would enable more of us to buy locally and therefore be more closely engaged in the full life cycle, the profits, and costs of our consumable goods.

Design, like marketing, is mostly about driving mass consumption, and anything produced on a mass scale contributes to pollution and global warming. That makes designers and their business clients systemic players in an economic model that has a profound effect on the environment – with significant implications for tomorrow's communities. The more items we send flying off the production line, according to traditional business reasoning, the better our chances for economic success. But now we've realized that the traditional indicators of economic success might not have been giving us the whole story. We've seen the powerful influence of design on the business model, and how strong leadership shapes and implements creative, innovation-driven strategies to achieve more sustainable profitability. We also have to understand that design's role in building sustainability extends well beyond the profits of individual enterprises.

All of those "cheap" goods that have been churned out have proven themselves to be much too expensive culturally, socially, and environmentally – in fact, they're killing us – and "green thinking" has finally taken hold as a mainstream political and economic issue. Today, governments around the world are joining forces, admitting that our thoughtless destruction of the Earth's environment has created an immense, man-made problem. We can only hope that

FORESTER RESEARCH, 2005. TOP: SYMBOTS. BOTTOM: TRIBONS

our human intellect and ingenuity will be up to the task of solving that problem and saving the planet. The growing movement toward eco-capitalism isn't an exercise in "do-goodism." It's driven by self-preservation, and it demands a rapid change of course in our approach to production and consumption.

We need to envision and design a more intelligent and ecologically responsible industrial model of production, product support, and recycling. And our solutions can't stop with good product designs. Outsourcing our designs to be produced elsewhere doesn't eliminate our responsibility for the pollution and other negative outcomes of that production, just as we can't take care of our own trash problem by tossing it into our neighbor's yard. The "out of sight, out of mind" paradigm must shift if we want to be responsible industrial citizens. I believe we have a philosophical obligation to strive for a better world. We have to create a more human-centric conscience in science and business by rethinking our objectives and processes. The results of our business efforts need to look good to our financial analysts, but they also need to look good to our families and friends, our neighbors and communities, and to people all over the world.

Essential and quite challenging objectives, such as social accountability and conservation, will help to reverse the destruction of the planet. If we create strong, responsible business and production models, the money will follow; even The Wall Street Journal has recognized that sustainable "green" products are growing in popularity and outperforming traditional products. Designers – like all leaders of business, politics, education, and industry – have an important role to play in creating a vibrant and viable future for all of our planet's inhabitants.

Designing Our Future

Traditionally, ecology hasn't rated high in the value perception of many. That's changing, of course, for many of the reasons I've written about here and in a fine line. Biofuels are beginning to liberate us from "big oil," and solar and wind energy technologies are making inroads into the traditional coal-fired energy sector. The Internet is unraveling the old telecommunication companies' hold on customers. And, as we've learned, more companies are adopting sustainable strategic goals and building business models based on long-term vision and ongoing innovation. In short, the old-fashioned monopolies are falling, and creative endeavors are rising.

One of our most powerful methods for promoting that shift is to reshape the industrial process. Designers and their business partners have a strategic opportunity to affect the early stage of the product life-cycle management system. In fact, we must define the strategy in that early stage if we want it to be effective. By changing the industrial process model from one designed to support mass efficiency to one designed to promote socially and environmentally responsive innovation – for example, by incorporating ecological competence and waste reduction or elimination into our process model – we can both increase the value of a company and improve its sales.

This shift in industrial processes requires a change in the way companies work and in the way they interact and collaborate with their customers. We have to create new business models that place customers on an equal footing with executives, employees, and owners/shareholders as competent "caretakers" of businesses and the world they serve. Designers, whose work forms the interface between humans and science, technology and business, have the obligation and opportunity to shape the drivers of the new "green" economy and to be on the front lines of that effort. Given the size of the challenges, no single discipline – even design – can single-handedly take on the task of "greening" industry and business.

Alix Rule, a student of politics at Oxford, underscored this point in her January 2011 *In These Times* blog entry titled "The Revolution Will Not be Designed." [2] Rule noted that, in spite of the optimism expressed by designers, we need more than a "can-do attitude" to address "the nastier socioeconomic and environmental corollaries of growth." The industrial system is too complex, with too many different players. The cycle of production, usage, and recycling is finite; nothing will just disappear, and we can't just discard established systems, such as our electric grid or transportation networks. Instead, we have to transform them organically, in stages. And, in spite of the many obstacles we all face in bringing about that transformation, I believe that designers have a unique opportunity to drive the development of sustainable products by virtue of our role in the early stages of the product life-cycle process.

Putting Principles into Practice

A couple of years ago, Patricia Roller – my business partner and wife for life – and I were explaining the "inner makings" of Strategic Design at frog design to Michael Marks, who was then the CEO of frog's majority shareholder, Flextronics International. In the course of our conversation, Michael wondered out loud, "Why isn't everybody hiring you guys?" Then, Michael went on to answer his own question. He told us that just showing off great client work and easy-to-digest processes isn't enough. Together, we discussed how frog had to adapt its typical form of communication in order to connect positively with rational people. Michael was right; both rational-minded business leaders and right-brained design professionals must share and discuss the deep and true stories – success and failures alike – of their experiences with Strategic Design so they can apply it at its highest professional level. And managing a large, global design agency also involves the challenge of managing creativity "at home."

At frog, we always tried to find and attract the most talented partners, employees, and clients, with the expectation that they would make the very best of their gifts and embrace the principles of ethics, discipline, process orientation, and professional growth. I am blessed with some talent, but I couldn't have achieved my current level of success without the deep belief that working with others and helping them to be their best is a far superior method of gaining professional recognition than any individual effort, no matter how talented or competent the

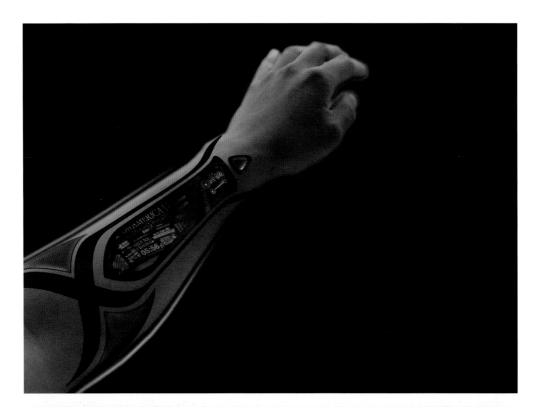

FORESTER RESEARCH, 2005. TOP: DATTOOS. BOTTOM: TRIBONS

individual may be. One of the most rewarding aspects of my work is to attract, find, inspire, mentor, and encourage creative people to embrace their talent as a gift and then live up to it – through discipline, diligence, an ethical character, and a rejection of the poisonous influences of envy, greed, and fear.

The good news is that more and more young entrepreneurs and business leaders are looking for creative partners in designing a more productive, profitable, and sustainable future. They are frustrated by the status quo in politics and disgusted with the business world's addiction to mediocrity and its associated lack of vision, trust, and joy with life. They also know that the old way of doing business is neither desirable nor sustainable. They understand that the widespread lack of vision and courage in business is a direct result of weak leadership by "maintenance CEOs" and compromised "old-boys'-network" boards that suck up to Wall Street, eliminate the research and talent that drive success, and award ever bigger bonuses to the very "leaders" who destroy the company by cutting cost instead of creating value. The new breed of business leadership is quick to say: "We know that the world is in trouble and we have courage and vision – but we need creative oxygen." In other words, today's true business leaders know the "why" of Strategic Design alliances – and they also want to know the "how."

Strategy in itself is a universal issue for any organization's competitiveness and culture: along with human resources, technology, marketing, and finance, strategic design just is one part of an overall business model. However, creative imagination is an essential element in identifying new opportunities and understanding what they could mean for a company or brand. In keeping with the Japanese value "Simple is Best," strategic entrepreneurs and executives also have to look beyond design and force their designers to do the same. Just as consumer-focused technology and marketing were the drivers of the "golden age of industrial design" during the 1970s and 1980s, the creative economy – fueled by the openness of the Internet and social media – is driving a "new age of strategic design." In this era, many products are replaced by inspiring human experiences, a development made possible by combining convergent technologies with new thinking in regard to social progress and economic and environmental sustainability.

Building a Platform for Creative Advancement and Achievement

Today, one of the questions asked most frequently of professionals and students alike is about what it takes to devise creative strategies and apply strategic design. Well, nobody can do it alone. We humans have different talents, which we need to combine in cross-disciplinary collaboration – which includes design. Designers who want to become competent in strategy need to take a more universal approach to their profession and remain interested and competent in all areas of business operations. I also believe that being "strategic" requires a broader mind-set, a respect for different cultures, a willingness to fight for sustainability, and an understanding of "brand" as something more than just a driver of market share, sales, and profitability. Ultimately, design involves using artistic expression for a higher purpose – that of humanizing industry. And that understanding takes us closer to the bigger challenge of design-minded strategies for entrepreneurs and executives.

We hear a lot today about rapid change driven by the speed of innovation in technology. But our world also undergoes constant slow change, which happens at what I like to call human speed and is deeply rooted in history, behaviors, and cultural traditions. This dual-paced march toward the future makes the task of innovation daunting. On one side, our progress is slowed by the unique challenge of declining economies, dragged down by the ongoing financial "acrobatics" of wealth redistribution that depends upon enigmatic speculation rather than the creation of any new value. On the other side, we must move quickly to master the growing opportunities of accelerating technological advancements, which will enable us to create a more socially benign product culture and a more humanized industry.

The key challenge I see for those of us engaged in the work of designing new products and the resulting systems is to take a thoughtful look at the history of current products and systems and then imagine a future in which we keep the vital values (especially in usability and semantics) and throw out the "trash." In keeping with this task, designers must project and create future products based upon paths of developing technologies before these technologies result in cultural, economic, and ecological atrocities. Throughout the course of my career, I have seen many such technologies come and go. Some have been evolutionary, such as household goods; others have become (or are becoming) obsolete, such as typewriters, VCRs, CRTs, and desktop computers.

What remains as a "human speed constant" of these developments, however, is our attachment to some of the smarter usability standards, and some of the "not-so-smart" ones as well – here, think of the clumsy QWERTY keyboard, work-oriented operating systems, and user-interfaces that force humans into "digital" interactions. And, of course, our culture remains engaged with century-old habits, such as writing with a pen or a brush, and the ancient symbolic shapes of some modern-day industrial products, such as the slate-like surface of a tablet computer or the pebble-like curves of a cell phone. It falls to Strategic Design to make all players in the business-design alliance aware of the new opportunities before them as well as the pitfalls of decision-making based on meek or arrogant conservatism.

All of these ideas, dreams, and imperatives are especially critical now, at a time when so many "old-school" designers and business leaders are immersed in a losing battle to maintain the status quo (which means market share and profits) – and that brings us back to the urgent need for a new educational approach. As said before, we need to replace – not reform – a wicked system that rejects creativity. I am setting great hopes on a new initiative in creative education by avoiding the institutional complacency and arrogance of the traditional model. We must build curricula that emphasize cross-disciplinary collaboration and integration.

This emphasis will enable us to introduce "creative education" into the related educational fields of economics, business management, science and engineering, ecology, and life sciences.

Strengthening the Alliances That Will Shape Our Future

The belief that design alone can save the world without a coherent set of ideas and operational methods represents a type of progressivism that is naïve, at best. That's why designers rely on strong alliances with marketing leaders to devise sustainable strategies that will succeed in the world as it is while helping to shape the world as we want it to be. For this reason, evolving our industrial processes is going to require a much deeper understanding of our potential.

In this book, we have explored numerous opportunities for applying technologies, products, and practices that are either currently available or easily adaptable from existing models. Realizing those opportunities will involve innovating new design methods and creating new business models and processes. Naturally, this transformation will result in some radical change and require a lot of work. New ideas for greening and humanizing our industrial-business model will become critical elements in the development of sustainable strategies for a better and more viable future. Together, we can build that future, confident in the understanding that environmental conservation and social balance, like Strategic Design, are just good business.

As I said earlier in the book, I believe that all people can be creative in the way they employ their own specific talents, and that we can unleash that often dormant creative potential. To do that, we must mentor and reward creativity in all its forms and demand it in our professional and political leadership. But, most importantly, we must use creative education to create a new pattern of connections – between minds and money, culture and science, sustainability and economics. This creativity cross-pollination will help put an end to the dogmatic classifications that separate "incompatible" left-brained and right-brained people. But, it will require new faculties and universities that breed creative thought in the same way our current elite universities run as fertile grounds for innovation and scientific progress. By combining the best creative teachers and researchers with the most talented students and the most advanced processes, we can become trailblazers in the grand mission of promoting human-industrial progress and sustainable development.

1   Source: www.npr.org

2   Alix Rule, "The Revolution will not be Designed," in: In *These Times*, January 11, 2008. Available online at: www.inthesetimes.com/article/3464/the_revolution_will_not_be_designed/

FISSLER MAGIC LINE COOKWARE, 1986. PHOTO: CONNY WINTER